A PEDAGOGY OF
ANTICAPITALIST ANTIRACISM

A PEDAGOGY OF ANTICAPITALIST ANTIRACISM

Whiteness, Neoliberalism, and Resistance in Education

ZACHARY A. CASEY

SUNY
PRESS

Published by State University of New York Press, Albany

For information, contact State University of New York Press, Albany, NY
www.sunypress.edu

Production, Jenn Bennett
Marketing, Michael Campochiaro

Library of Congress Cataloging-in-Publication Data

Names: Casey, Zachary A., 1985- author.
Title: A pedagogy of anticapitalist antiracism : whiteness, neoliberalism,
    and resistance in education / Zachary A. Casey.
Description: Albany : State University of New York Press, 2016. | Includes
    bibliographical references and index.
Identifiers: LCCN 2016007694 (print) | LCCN 2016020254 (ebook) | ISBN
    9781438463056 (hardcover : alk. paper) | ISBN: 978-1-4384-6306-3 (pbk. : alk
    paper) | ISBN 9781438463070 (e-book)
Subjects: LCSH: Public schools—United States—Finance. | Discrimination in
    education—United States. | Capitalism and education—United States. |
    Privatization in education—United States. | Teachers—Training of—United
    States. | Whites—United States—Race identity.
Classification: LCC LB2825 .C327 2016 (print) | LCC LB2825 (ebook) | DDC
    370.11/5—dc23
LC record available at https://lccn.loc.gov/2016007694

10 9 8 7 6 5 4 3 2 1

For my teacher-students, and student-teachers

Contents

Prologue

"What are you?" she asked.

It was the first week of class, in the first semester of my PhD program at the University of Minnesota. We were sitting in a circle at the Kitty Cat Klub, a local bar, just after a public talk called Policy and a Pint. The event featured a representative from Teach For America and the TFA alum who had just won Teacher of the Year for the state of Minnesota. We were all in the same program, at the same university, and we were all white. We then had a conversation that I have engaged in many times with people of many different races, but particularly with white people. For some reason, it seems to me that these conversations happen more often with white people who have an aversion to alienating racial others, or more bluntly, to sounding racist. "What are you?" in these moments most often asks the questioned party to list one or more (for white folks, European) countries they are descended from, and thus "are."

When prompted I usually answer, "I'm white, and from the U.S." Which of course does not answer the question in the way it was intended, and so I shift to saying, "I'm mostly Irish, Swedish, French, and Ukrainian." I am sure there are many countries missing from this list, but of course, any list of this kind is absurd. I'm from the United States, and having had the unique privilege to visit the countries I am "from" in this context, I can assure the reader that I am not from any country in Europe, and thus a term such as European American lacks any relevance for someone like me, whose ancestors have been in the United States for many generations, and who have been white so long that any other identity would simply not do us justice.

Answering the question "What are you?" represents a form of hailing[1] that places the respondent in a series of codes of conduct, which I will refer to moving forward in this work as ideology.[2] And this very move may well turn off some readers—because it brings us back to the problem of "What are you?" This is a work that makes explicitly materialist, structuralist, and Marxist arguments (among many influences) to better understand our present realities of white supremacy, white racial identity, antiracist pedagogy, and teacher education. But it is not a text that is only for those who would answer the question "What are you?" by stating, "I'm a Marxist." This kind of attitude is rife in the academy, and can be seen in an array of books, articles, and lectures with titles like "Marxism against Postmodernism in Educational Theory"[3] and "Post-Ality: Marxism and Postmodernism."[4] These works seek to defend the insights of critical theory in the Marxist tradition against the influx of critical work that characterizes itself as poststructural, postmodern, and the myriad other "posts" we could list here. It is not my aim to make such arguments here—in other words; this is not a text that is written solely for Marxists, or a text that attempts to dissuade people from mobilizing poststructural insights or theories. I have made every effort, in fact, to present the theories and histories I detail in such a way that many different practitioners and thinkers can appropriate for themselves what they deem to be the worthy elements and arguments of this work. For me, this brings to mind one of my favorite quotes from bell hooks (1994), who in her discussion of Paulo Freire's work that includes sexist and patriarchal language writes, "Think of [his] work as water that contains some dirt. Because you are thirsty you are not too proud to extract the dirt and be nourished by the water" (p. 50).

Thus, I ask the reader to not get stuck at the level of "What are you?" and rather to approach this work critically with an aim to extract whatever "water" might exist in it for you, and to spit the "dirt" as it may feel to you, in an effort to appropriate for yourself what this text can help us with. Specifically, this work is imagined for teacher educators and antiracist practitioners in a variety of pedagogical settings. This work offers historical accounts, theoretical critiques, and details of anticapitalist antiracist pedagogy broadly imagined.

As will become clear in the chapters that follow, there is much work to be done to mobilize white people, and white teachers in particular, for antiracist action. We should take seriously the finding that white privilege as a concept and as the primary means of engaging white people in antiracist struggle has not been able to capture the hearts and minds of all of those for whom it was intended. We should also take just as seriously that the "professionalization" of the teaching force has not brought with it the longed-for outcome of a more critical, respected, and better prepared mass of teachers. There is more work to be done, that must be done, and there is a need for new theories, arguments, and discourses to aid us in this work. My aim here is to move antiracist pedagogies toward a position of radical solidarity—a comprehensive attitudinal paradigm that creates spaces for all those engaged in anti-oppressive struggle to approach their work with new insights, aims, and questions.

And thus, with these caveats and frames in mind, I begin.

Acknowledgments

I am grateful for the support on this project from Elyse M. Wigen, Timothy J. Lensmire, The Midwest Critical Whiteness Collective, Shannon K. McManimon, and Brian D. Lozenski. This text would not have been possible were it not for the countless hours spent discussing, reading, and learning together.

Portions of chapter 6 are adapted from Casey, Z. A. (in press), Whiteness, Nationalism, and Neoliberalism: What Pat Buchanan and the Right Can Teach Us about Resisting Neoliberalism in Schools. In M. Abendroth & B. J. Porfilio (Eds.), *School against Neoliberal Rule*. Information Age Publishing.

Portions of chapter 7 are adapted from Casey, Z. A. (2013). Toward an Anticapitalist Teacher Education. *Journal Of Educational Thought, 46*(2), 123–143.

ONE

How My Family and I Became White

Introducing the Task at Hand

> Therefore this presupposition by no means arises either out of the individual's will or out of the immediate nature of the individual, but that it is rather *historical,* and posits the individual as already *determined* by society.
>
> —*Grundrisse*

> The philosophers have only *interpreted* the world, in various ways. The point, however, is to *change* it.
>
> —*Theses on Feuerbach*

Introduction

I have spent virtually the whole of my teaching life feeling too young to be doing what I do. The result is that very few people actually know how old I am, and I like it that way. Now, in my work to understand the history of white supremacy and the ways in which my own experiences and history have been shaped by its ongoing legacy, it feels important to locate myself and when I was born—because I was born white, and being born white is a relatively new phenomenon.

Amanda Lewis (2003) reminds us that we are marked with racial, gender, and national identities the moment we enter the world in the United States (U.S.): in the form of birth certificates.

I was born white, male, and a U.S. citizen in the 1980s—after civil rights, after May '68,[1] at the beginning of the end of "really existing socialism" (Žižek, 2009). And I believe that it is from this starting point that we can better understand the critique of capitalism put forward in the pages that follow, and its interconnection and intersection with white supremacy and the work of teaching and learning in public schools and in teacher education. This is thus not a dated polemic from a "more Marxist time"—this is critical engaged scholarship from the standpoint of someone who missed the "cultural turn,"[2] the "discoursal turn,"[3] and now finds himself caught in the midst of what seems to be the complete neoliberalization[4] of public education (one could essentially think of neoliberalism as "market fundamentalism," applying the logics of the "free market" to all social spaces and goods, especially those historically considered "public" and distorting them into functioning with "private" aims for efficiency, see Casey, 2011, 2013; Harvey, 2005). I begin in this way to remind the reader that this work does not stem from someone attempting to recuperate past scholarly trends and fads. Rather, it is from someone young enough to have only known permanent war, neoliberalism, and mass incarceration as the benchmarks of our national political order. It is also written by someone whose hope has not yet run out, and the need for hope in teaching and teacher education will be a serious focus of this work in later chapters.

My work and interest in critical whiteness studies came out of my experiences working as the campaign manager for Corey Woods, the first-ever elected African American to Tempe City Council, the city in which I lived and completed both my bachelors and masters degrees. I was struck by the moments when I would be standing on a doorstep, in my blue polo shirt with matching campaign literature under my arm, and a white person would first greet me kindly and then become increasingly uncomfortable once they saw the face on the campaign flyer. The three white people I most vividly remember who reacted to seeing Corey's face with a kind of alarm or disgust all trouble me deeply, not only because of their apparent racial bias that made them uninterested in even learning about an African American candidate (let alone voting for one), but also because they all seemed willing to speak with me until they saw a picture of the candidate I was supporting. My whiteness was hypervisible to me in those moments, and my inquiry into the history of white supremacy, theorizations of white racial identity, and critical work to connect these insights to antiracist praxis (action and reflection in equal measure on the world in order to change it, see Freire [2000]) are all informed by those deeply troubling and uncomfortable moments on the doorsteps of other white people.

While I had heard at various conferences that a potentially powerful practice for white people committed to better understanding their own relative racial privilege would be to examine the history of their family's immigration to the United States, I never actively sought to learn this history. Instead, in a rather serendipitous moment when I was helping my parents and Grandpa organize my grandparents' house after my grandmother passed away, I found the obituary for my great-great-grandfather, Frank Casey. I provide the full text here of that obituary, written in 1950, in the hopes that the reader will better understand why this "discovery" of mine has led me to believe that examining one's own family history of whiteness can be a powerful force in mobilizing white people for antiracist praxis. Or, at least, serve as an example of the ways in which every white person's family, to varying degrees, engaged in the creation or maintenance of what George Lipsitz (2006) has termed the "possessive investment in whiteness."

> Indian Fighter, 92, Dies in Wyoming; Funeral Here
> Frank Casey, 92, one of the last of a vanishing group of Americans—the army Indian fighters—will be buried here Tuesday with the military honors he earned more than 70 years ago.
> Casey, who served with the famed fifth infantry, better known in 1879 as Custer's Avengers, will be buried in Mount Olivet cemetery. Military honors will be bestowed by the Veterans' council. Funeral services will be Tuesday morning at 9 from O'Connor's chapel and at 9:15 at St. Ann' cathedral when requiem mass will be offered.
> Casey died Wednesday morning in Sheridan, Wyo., after a long illness. He spent 73 colorful years in the west, years which were highlighted by his army service, work on a Missouri river steamer, and law enforcement as an early day constable in Miles City, then a turbulent cattle center. Casey was a witness at the hanging of Jack McCall, the last

act in one of the west's most famous dramas—the murder of Wild Bill Hickok.

Casey, who "came west from Boston to fight Indians" was born in Salem, Mass., March 17, 1858. As a boy he read avidly of the great west and his one ambition was to travel west and fight Indians. In 1877 he arrived in Sioux City just in time to sign on as a crew member of the steamer Butte. The Butte had come up from St. Louis and had stopped at Sioux City to pick up a load of freight before going on upstream to Fort Benton.

"Fort Benton and the wild country along the upper river was different from anything I had ever seen," he later related. "I got quite a kick out of it."

Casey made the downstream trip only as far as Yankton, S.D. He left the steamer there just in time to see McCall's hanging. McCall had been convicted in a Yankton court of shooting Hickok in the back in a Deadwood, S.D. saloon in August 1876. He was sentenced to death. Casey arrived on the scene just in time to hear McCall tell his executioners that he had no last statements to make.

"And I saw them hang him," Casey said in later years.

Two years later in 1879 Casey showed up at an army recruiting station in Chicago. He was assigned to the Fifth infantry and sent to Fort Keogh to serve under Gen. Nelson A. Miles. The outfit was known as "Custer's Avengers" since the Indian campaigns following the Custer massacre were still the principal business of soldiers on the Yellowstone.

After five years at Fort Keogh, he was sent to El Paso, Tex. for service. In 1890 Casey left the army and drifted northward finally locating at Miles City. He served several terms as constable there.

Casey is survived by two sons, John H. Casey Great Falls, and Frank Casey, Miles City, and a daughter, Mrs. R.W. Wilson, Vancouver B.C.

The story of how people of European descent became white in the United States is well researched, and will be the focus of a later chapter in this work. The story of how my patrilineal family the Caseys became white, however, is something that I do not believe any of us have ever written about, nor even given much thought to. There are perhaps several questions that then must be answered: Why write about this now? What difference does it make how one's family came to live in the West? What connection do I have to someone who lived in the nineteenth century? So what if we have the same last name? As a way of introducing my larger project, I will seek to answer these questions, both in terms of my own reasons for why I think it is important to know one's family (and thus often one's racial) history, and in terms of the broader antiracist struggle, to seek an end to white supremacy. In sum, the question I hope to answer is: What does it mean for a self-proclaimed antiracist to have come from "Indian Fighters"?

My Own Whiteness

While I knew all my life that the Caseys came from Montana, I did not know how they came to be in Montana until finding this obituary. I did not know that my family came from Boston. I did not know that the reason I grew up on the West Coast was because my great-great-grandfather wanted to move west to kill Native Americans. While I have long known of the genocide committed by Europeans in the Western hemisphere of indigenous people, I never knew someone with my last name, someone whom my Grandpa called Grandpa, participated in the removal and extermination of Native peoples. When I read the article it was heartbreaking and dehumanizing. I held in my hands the white supremacist way that my family became white.

While I know that not all white people in the United States have an equivalent story of how their family participated in racist and hateful acts of genocide, I think this story is one that can help us better understand what it means to be white. Or at least, can help me better understand who I am as a white man living today in the United States, and can further help readers better understand the complexity of white racial identity and theories of pedagogy and praxis that make up the remainder of this work.

As my family immigrated to the United States from Ireland, and as being Irish was not synonymous with being white for nearly all of the nineteenth century (Jacobson, 1999), it is possible to ask the question of when my family became white.[5] On the East Coast, my great-great-grandfather was not considered white. In moving West away from an East Coast context where European ethnic groups were struggling to carve out their own niche in the United States, my great-great-grandfather was white on arrival in South Dakota. There, distinctions among various European ethnicities mattered far less than the simple racial binary of white settler and Native Indian. If it was the desire of the federal government to eradicate Native Americans based on the notion of Manifest Destiny and white supremacy over indigenous people, the extent to which my great-great-grandfather bought into this ideology and could "pass" as someone who would benefit from it is a way to understand his whiteness. That is, if he looked white, and was acting in solidarity with other whites for white aims, he must be white. Mathew Frye Jacobson (1999) made precisely this point in reference to the co-construction of "white" and "citizen" in the United States, as he writes, "Because what a citizen [of the U.S.] was, at bottom, was someone who could help put down a slave rebellion or participate in Indian wars" (p. 25).

My great-great-grandfather's children, and every subsequent generation of Caseys with white parents, never had to question their whiteness. Remaining in the Mountain West where the presence of Native Americans, even in very small numbers, served as a constant check against whiteness meant that the Caseys no longer had to think about themselves as anything other than white. While they maintained claims to an Irish ethnicity, that cultural background was reduced to foods and religious practices, eventually becoming more of an answer to the question, "What are you?" ("We're Irish") than a source of cultural identity.

Being born in the 1980s in Billings, Montana, and moving before I was a year old to a suburb of Seattle, Washington, I grew up seemingly far removed from my cavalier great-great-grandfather, the "army Indian fighter." Yet when I read the obituary it made me feel uneasy. My stomach reacted physically to the news that I was a direct descendent of someone who had joined the army and moved west to kill Native Americans. No longer were the Plains Wars an ugly piece of U.S. history; they were now my history. As someone who is proud of his work in education and local government to combat racism and white supremacy, I worried that I was somehow no longer fit to do the work. How could the descendant of someone who wanted to eradicate an entire people ever hope to help those same people?

But then I have to stop. Am I really trying to help Native American people? While I certainly do not wish to harm native peoples, I am at this very moment writing this in my apartment that was built on land that was at one point stolen from the indigenous people who lived here before contact with white colonizers. Am I harming native peoples just by being here? Is there any way to be anywhere in the United States as a white person and not be on stolen land? What would be the most anti-oppressive thing I could do, leave the country?

It seems that I have in fact inherited my great-great-grandfather's legacy. Many people were killed so that I could live in this part of the world. Many people are killed today to support the ways we live in this part of the world. While I am not directly doing the killing, I buy things from companies that I know are exploiting their laborers. In that way, I'm helping to pay for the continued marginalization of millions if not billions of people around the world. While this can seem and feel overwhelming, it is the true link between my great-great-grandfather and me. I am not here, in the United States as a white man, by chance or accident. People killed other people so that I could live here. While I did not author this plan, I am here because of it. And while my great-great-grandfather was certainly not a high-ranking official who devised plans of killing an entire race of people so that white people could move on to their land, he contributed to it just as I contribute today to oppressing people of color the world over in the system of global exploitation known as capitalism.

And so, when I think about the question, "How did I become white?" I am left with at least one potential answer: I was born white, the inheritor of the privileges accrued by my white ancestors as they oppressed, stole from, and killed people of color. But this is too simple a story, and is far too close to some kind of woe-is-me white male rant about how hard it is to live in a white supremacist society when one is white. Yet time and again, white scholars of whiteness seem to offer little else to their white readers than an endless stream of accounts of white racism. The research literature has documented the continuing racism of white people, yet we find almost no mention of white people who are motivated by the realities of white supremacy and structural oppression and wish to work in their own lives and contexts to dismantle exploitative, dehumanizing systems. These critiques will be mobilized in significantly greater detail later, and will be at the center of my calls for a critical whiteness studies that re-centers oppression, rather than privilege, as that which we must better understand in order to work for justice.

On Pedagogy

This work is also deeply pedagogical and stems from my commitments to teaching and learning in ways that seek to empower both teachers and learners in their struggles for humanization and self-actualization (Freire, 2000; 2006; hooks, 1994; 2003). It is worth defining pedagogy in clear terms here, as I am often reminded that my regular use of the term and its political meaning can be lost on readers who do not often encounter it. Pedagogy, in its simplest form, is the art of teaching. But pedagogy is more complex than that. All teaching and learning is inherently political, beset with competing claims of right and wrong, justice and injustice, and these claims are often masked and depoliticized. To approach a problem or theory pedagogically is to privilege the learner and ask the critical question "What is this teaching?" But there are, of course, myriad pedagogies and thus an infinite number of ways to approach something pedagogically. It becomes imperative, then, to be clear from the beginning what is entailed in my own pedagogy and approach to teaching and learning and how these commitments manifest in my work here.

On Oppression

Critical black feminist scholar Patricia Hill Collins (2000) defines oppression as "any unjust situation where, systematically and over a long period of time, one group denies another group access to the resources of society" (p. 6). I am calling my pedagogy anticapitalist antiracism in order to make clear what I believe to be the two greatest systems of inequity preventing the realization of a more fully human society in the United States and in the world more broadly. While these two systems of oppression do not encompass the whole of human cruelty, their abolition would usher forth a reality we as yet lack the language to articulate. Any focus on one, or even two, systems of oppression leaves out other systems of oppression in problematic ways that can undermine the critical work that is necessary to re-theorize our efforts for justice (Kumashiro, 2009). The abolition of capitalism and of racial hierarchy will not automatically nor completely end gender exploitation, heterosexism, and other forms of oppression we could list here; but it would fundamentally alter the way those other systems of oppression are understood and experienced.

For example, when discussing the present reality of patriarchy and gender exploitation one almost always hears reference to the difference in pay between men and women with the same job and/ or credentials. As of 2010, women make approximately seventy-seven cents for every dollar made by men in the United States (National Committee on Pay Equity). Similar arguments are leveled to understand heterosexism and racism as well, by comparing income and other economic factors against heterosexual white men. Returning to Collins's (2000) conception of oppression, the central role of patriarchy in the United States political economy practiced in slavery continues to function in wildly dehumanizing ways, particularly in the case of black and other women of color. My point here, however, is not to play the "Oppression Olympics," or to insist on a hierarchy of exploitation based on various subject positions. The "vulgar Marxist" insistence that all forms of oppression pale in comparison to capitalist exploitation is simply not helpful, and it is certainly not my aim to make such a case here. Rather, we must remember Kevin Kumashiro's (2009) insight that "no practice is always anti-oppressive" and that as we seek to combat forms of oppression, we might well be supporting other forms of oppression at the very same time (p. 3).

An example of this process is helpful. We can imagine men who with all sincerity seek to support and involve themselves in women's movement, and yet they still hold biased and bigoted beliefs about "effeminate Asian men" or use terms like "guys" to refer to multigendered groups. The point is this: any time we select a specific form of oppression to focus on, we are at the same time downplaying other forms of oppression. While this is an inevitability, this work is careful to always locate systems of oppression intersectionally, meaning that no system of oppression operates in a vacuum and that each of the various forms of oppression informs other forms of oppression and other oppressive systems (Casey, 2011; Crenshaw, 1992).

This is why the title of this work uses the discourse of anticapitalist antiracism, a form of antiracism that locates capitalist exploitation at the center of white supremacy and sees the two systems of exploitation operating under the same perverse logics of greed, nationalism, and exceptionalism. It is my aim in this work to demonstrate the present pitfalls of how we have imagined both antiracist struggle on the part of white people, as well as teacher education for social justice, to show how capitalist logics such as neoliberalism have pervaded both spaces and closed off opportunities for social transformation. We cannot simply be antiracist if the system of exploitation enforcing racism is also enforcing other oppressive systems.

In the remainder of this chapter, I briefly sketch the direction of this work and the contents of the various chapters that follow this one. These descriptions are not exhaustive, but will provide the reader with a guide as to what to expect in the arguments that follow. A few more words about the nature of this project are in order, however, before beginning this sketching.

On Theory and Teacher Education

For the past ten years I have been working and learning with both teacher candidates[6] and practicing teachers in the college and university courses I have taught. My belief in the transformative power of classrooms and the joy I have experienced in learning and growing with my students is at the center of this work. I write this now because the arguments that follow, and perhaps those that have already been presented, will at times likely strike the reader as significantly removed from the context of teaching and learning in teacher education. But this feeling should be resisted, if at all possible. The role of theory and conceptual arguments in teacher education is under attack from the highest educational office in the United States: Secretary of Education Arne Duncan. Henry Giroux (2010) characterizes Duncan's policies and attitudes this way:

> Emphasizing the practical and experiential, he seeks to gut the critical nature of theory, pedagogy and knowledge taught in colleges of education. . . . According to Duncan, the great sin these colleges have committed in the past few decades is that they have focused too much on theory and not enough on clinical practice; and by theory he means critical pedagogy. (p. 2)

The result is that we are increasingly seeing foundations of education courses, which focus on theory but include the disciplines of philosophy, history, sociology, and anthropology in education, reduced or outright eliminated from teacher education course work (Hartlep & Porfilio, in press; Kerr, Mandzek, & Raptis, 2011).

We must challenge the reduction of teaching to technique, and thus challenge the dominant logics that enable the elimination of educational and societal theories from teacher education course work. Part of what this entails, however, is that teacher education look outside its own parameters to uncover new insights and directions. Teacher education, under attack as it is (Casey, 2013; Kumashiro, 2009; 2012), must re-center theory if it has any chance of surviving the neoliberal onslaught that is seeking to privatize every element of public education. The famed line from Lenin (1901/1960) comes to mind: "Without a revolutionary theory there can be no revolutionary movement." But we in education should also remember the Freirean (2000) conception of praxis: action and reflection in equal measure on the world in order to change it. If we eliminate reflection, akin to theory in this formulation, we are left with what Freire called "activism" defined as "action for action's sake" unmediated by critical reflection. For Freire, such a formulation makes dialogue impossible.

I argue that what Duncan and others such as Joel Klein are advocating in their attack on educational theory constitutes precisely Freire's fear. They advocate teaching (action) for teaching's sake rather than placing the authentic needs of learners and the goals of a more fully human experience as the fundamental justification for the work of teachers. Instead they advocate for a narrow, more teacher-proofed curriculum (Crocco & Costigan, 2007) that comes with the descriptor of "standardized" and is seen as evidence of "raising standards" and neoliberal "accountability." Teachers as unthinking machines seem to be the end goal of such measures, or if not, teachers who only think about their classrooms in isolated individuated moments where the need to "adapt" their lesson or instruction comes about.

The link between the realities of the classroom and the world that surrounds and informs those within it must be a central part of teacher education for the simple reason that no matter how expertly adaptive a teacher is within her classroom, there will always be societal and systemic forces that impose on classroom practice. Teachers and teacher educators both have become too complacent in our celebration of best practices and value-added models, respectively, to remember that the complexities of the entire social strata manifest in classrooms and must be acted upon by teachers and students. Denying teacher candidates course work on the nature of oppression in our oppressive society, denying teacher educators from engaging in critical conceptual research: the same ideology is at work in both realities. What I offer here is an intervention in this onslaught of anti-intellectual neoliberal privatization, from the perspective of a teacher educator.

Overview of Subsequent Chapters

Chapter 2 focuses on my method in this work, a method I am calling Freirean Critical Study. Paulo Freire's (2000; 2006) insights into critical pedagogy, into reading the word in order to read the world, and the political act of teaching in ways intended to enable both teachers and students to *practice* critical consciousness (*conscientização*, to use Freire's term) must inform not only our critical teaching and learning, but also our inquiries into those political acts and the "limit conditions" of the contexts in which teaching and learning take place (our *theory*, to be coupled with *practice*, in order to live out *praxis*). The central aim in this chapter is to elaborate a way of reading the word and the world of teaching and learning in a way that Freire (2006) elaborated in the first of his *Letters* to *Those Who Dare Teach*, of "critical study" and its necessity to be practiced by teachers. He wrote, "*Critical study* correlates with *teaching* that is equally critical, which necessarily demands a critical way of comprehending and of realizing the reading of the word and that of the world, the reading of text and of context" (p. 40; my emphasis). This chapter focuses on what it means to engage theory pedagogically, to *be* in theory as a teacher educator with political commitments to affecting a more just reality.

Chapter 3 is an overview of Marxism in which I work to detail various key insights from Marx that I use in subsequent chapters. First I work to explain Marx's theories of class and the historical classes of proletariat and bourgeoisie, his theories of alienation and surplus labor as the source of wealth in capitalism, as well as his theories of exploitation, use value, and exchange value. Next, I work to show the ways in which Marx's theory of production offers us new insights into demystifying the abstract notion of alienation into a concrete conception of dehumanization as a result of capitalist exploitation and the warping of what it means to be human. After reviewing several other key components of Marxism, I work to respond briefly to some common criticisms of Marx and provide an account of why Marx's work remains useful to us now in our present historical era.

Chapters 4 and 5 represent a critical reading of whiteness studies literature. I first survey the field with a focus on the history of whiteness, white racial identity, and white supremacy. I focus especially on the work of the Reverend Thandeka, David Roediger, Mathew Frye Jacobson, and Jonathan Jansen to demonstrate the various ways in which whiteness has been approached historically and sociologically in the research literature.[7] The reader will gain a sense in chapter 4 of the linkages between white supremacy and capitalism from the very early days of the Virginia Colony to our present neoliberal reality.

Chapter 5 follows this with a critique of two dominant bodies of literature in the field of whiteness studies: white privilege and race treason. Both overemphasize whiteness and white privilege as a cause of structural oppression, rather than as an effect of systemic and intentional exploitation. After reviewing both schools of thought, I analyze the underlying assumptions and ideological underpinnings of each before finally elaborating what I am calling a more generous account of white racial identity. This conception of white racial identity is based on the work of the Rev. Thandeka, South African scholar Jonathan Jansen, as well as Freire and other whiteness scholars who resist both the White Privilege and Race Traitor approaches to antiracist work with white people.

Chapter 6 explores the connections of white supremacy, neo-liberalism, and nationalism in the context of the United States. Here I work to show, through the examples of the Tea Party and the presidential candidacy of Mitt Romney, how whiteness, capital-ism, and nationalism become so entangled that we cannot address one without addressing the others. I work to develop a theory of nationalism that functions alongside a theory of racial identity formation in a capitalist order of creating and maintaining "others" against whom we construct our identities.

Chapter 7 focuses on the impacts of neoliberalism on educa-tion, and teacher education in particular. I work to show how the movement to professionalize teaching has served to undermine justice efforts on the part of teacher educators and has accelerated the pace of neoliberal efforts in education. After exploring teacher professionalization I examine Milton Friedman's efforts to create a national school voucher system with the explicit intention of abolishing public education as a precursor to our present neoliberal reality. Finally, I examine the ways in which teacher education has been culpable in supporting neoliberalism and utilizing market-based logics with which to understand itself and its efficacy.

Chapters 8 and 9 use the ideas detailed in previous chapters to elaborate an anticapitalist antiracist pedagogy, first in classrooms, and second at the programmatic level for teacher education. Focus-ing on contemporary insights from critical pedagogy, culturally relevant pedagogy, and multicultural education, I show the ways in which such calls as that of Gloria Ladson-Billings (2006a) that culturally relevant pedagogy entail "socio-political consciousness raising" be actualized in the anticapitalist antiracist classroom. Next, I elaborate how such a pedagogical stance and approach can be mobilized across a teacher education program and discuss rec-ommendations for course work and school-based activities that are consistent with an anticapitalist antiracist approach to teaching and learning. While these chapters rely on conceptual formulations and are not specific to any one college or university teacher education program, they still can function as a guide and outline of what such a program of teacher education could look like, and what is necessary in order to realize these commitments.

Conclusion

And so, with the outline above of what is to come in the pages that follow, I ask the reader one more favor as you engage this text, especially if you are not someone who would readily proclaim their solidarity with Marxist political theory and action, or are resistant to the notion of "anticapitalism." Our present strategies for combatting racism have not abolished racism, and have perhaps even made antiracist struggle more impossible now with the conception of white privilege put forward as the primary and most important way for white people to learn about and combat racism. The color-blind Obamania of this decade is not only a result of conservative efforts to abolish affirmative action and other policies intended to redress the violence done to historically marginalized people. Rather, it is also a result of the failure of those on the Left to elaborate a vision of antiracism that transcends individual acts of language policing and the emotional solidarity with people of color that too often passes for antiracism. Talking about antiracism, especially in a group of white people, is only antiracist if it leads to material actions to address racism. And presently, we seem to be lacking in such actions.

Thus, even if anticapitalism strikes you as too radical, too impossible a way to combat racism, I ask that the reader take seriously the insights and arguments mobilized here to defend anticapitalist antiracism as a pedagogical theory of action. If our present theories of racism and whiteness hinder more than help the cause of racial justice, surely there must be room for new theories of what is possible, of what could be. And so I conclude this introduction with this final request: read this text generously and then decide for yourself what must be done.

TWO

Freirean Critical Study

Population is an abstraction, if we leave out, e.g., the classes of which it consists. These classes, again, are but an empty word, unless we know what are the elements on which they are based, such as wage labor, capital, etc.

—*The German Ideology*

Private property alienates the individuality not only of people but also of things. Land has nothing to do with rent of land; the machine has nothing to do with profit.

—*The German Ideology*

In education we tend to focus[1] on methods, and in educational research on methodology. Methodology, in this sense, takes on different meanings depending on one's context, and if one is referring more to research or to classroom practice.[2] In the realm of educational research, methodology refers to how one gathers, analyzes, and comments on research findings—the methodology of the research, how did one *do* the research? For classroom teachers the term *methodology* is actually far closer to what in the theoretical language of education we would call pedagogy. That is, methodology for many teachers means the things one does as a teacher in the act of teaching. Yet, perhaps more than any other term, I am continually struck in my own classrooms of how uncertain both practicing teachers and teacher candidates are of what is entailed in the concept of *pedagogy*. A simple dictionary definition of the

17

term would read "the art or science of teaching," but as is so often the case, this concept of pedagogy does not carry with it the weight so many of us engaged in critical educational work invest in the concept of pedagogy. And so it has become a part of my first-day-of-class discussion with my students to define what I mean by pedagogy, and what I mean by pedagogical.

No thinker has informed my work in education more, either in the classroom or in my scholarship, than the late Brazilian critical educator Paulo Freire. While his life story is amazing—being thrown out of his own country, and later others, after his adult literacy program was so radically successful that it resulted in a whole new section of the electorate being able to pass the voting literacy test and thus to participate in elections,[3] to name only one example—I have always been far more captivated by Freire's attitude about his work. Freire believed that, rather than employing his method, educators needed to reinvent it for their own context. He said to Donaldo Macedo, who translated Freire's work into English and maintained a decades-long friendship and intellectual partnership with him, "I don't want to be imported or exported. It is impossible to export pedagogical practices without reinventing them. Please tell your fellow American educators not to import me. Ask them to re-create and rewrite my ideas" (Macedo and Freire, 2005, p. x). This attitudinal gesture is at the heart of Freire's pedagogy, and when I first talk about Freire in the first class meeting, I tell my students that for Freire all teaching and learning is political, and that as such, pedagogy means intentional political teaching. I then tell them I will be using the term *pedagogical* regularly in class, and that when I do I mean it in such a way that the political nature and intentionality of the teaching moment is explicit. When we are being pedagogical with one another, we are approaching the other with an attitude of inquiry that seeks to foster the other's self-appropriation of meaning; their reading of the world. In other words, being pedagogical means acting in such a way as to foster (political, partial, and humanizing) learning, in ways that acknowledge the political nature of all human interaction and the various context(s) in which we live.

Freire's (2000; 2005) insights into what has come to be called critical pedagogy, into reading the word in order to read the world, and the political act of teaching in ways intended to enable both teachers and students to practice critical consciousness (*conscientização,* to use Freire's term) must inform not only our critical teaching and learning, but also our inquiries into those political acts. It is not enough to act in pedagogical ways when we are in the classroom and then to switch off those same commitments and attitudes once we have left it. Perhaps even more important to this work, it is incumbent upon critical educators who mobilize Freirean insights to not only teach in pedagogical ways, but to write in pedagogical ways as well. Our theory must be coupled with practice, in order to live out the Freirean ideal of praxis:[4] action and reflection in equal measure on the world in order to transform it. This point is worth elucidating further.

There is perhaps no greater schism in teacher education than that which lies between theory and practice. The running stereotypic understanding of this schism often results in statements such as, "Theory is what they do at the university, here in schools we do practice"; or, "Teacher education is all about theory when it should really be about practice." While we will return to examining the ways this tension is mobilized as a part of the neoliberalization of education and assault on critical theory and social justice work in education in later chapters, for now let us focus specifically on why Freire emphasizes the notion of praxis so strongly. No practice is without theory. Even the most seemingly atheoretical position presumes a theory, a reasoning or justification, even if that theory is the utter rejection of all previous theories. The same can be said of practice: we are incapable of doing something without any kind of premeditation. Theory and practice must work in tandem, in equal measure; we must challenge narratives that say that universities create theories and people in their communities put those theories into practice. Instead, I insist that we maintain a commitment to both theory and practice, working to change our world through concrete practices informed by theories that come from the very people they are about. At times, this work requires us to question and reconsider previously held assumptions; it requires that we struggle with complex ideas and problems in order to define for ourselves what to do and how best we can serve the interests of the great majority of humanity. Only focusing on practice, or only focusing on theory, is empty work—we must strive for both at all times in our work and lives, and that is precisely what this chapter is about.

In an effort to define both for myself and for my readers what I am doing in this work, I have taken to referring to my method as Freirean Critical Study. What follows is my discussion of various elements of Freirean Critical Study in which I attempt to explicate a praxis-based orientation to my work as both pedagogue and writer.

Why Ideology?

I employ the concept of ideology here, not to argue that it is the single or only way of understanding our present political reality, but rather as a conceptual tool for understanding particular things about a given text or context. The best example of this concept, that is, employing a particular historical and theoretical understanding of particular elements of our present historical reality, comes from Michael Hardt and Antonio Negri (2000).[5] They write, "The end of the dialectic of modernity has not resulted in the end of the dialectic of exploitation" (p. 43). Hardt and Negri are here arguing that we take seriously both Marxist historical materialism as well as the insights of late twentieth and early-twenty-first-century theorists who reject a conception of absolutely everything as dialectical. Our present condition, in countries such as the United States, has become "postmodern,"[6] what Baudrillard (1994) elaborated as "hyperreality."

For Baudrillard, reality has become "more real than real"; cyberspace, telecommunication, and myriad other technological and economic advances have seen the commingling of reality and simulations of reality to the extent that for many, one cannot be distinguished from the other. Two examples will suffice to make this point. First, reality television shows, wherein the story lines play out on "real" peoples' lives yet are carefully edited, somewhat scripted, and designed to make the "real" lives they depict *more* real than the lives of those who sit at home viewing them. Yet often viewers cultivate relationships with the "characters" depicted, at times finding more solidarity in artificial relationships based on sharing in the experience of the show/performance than in their actual human interactions. Another example is the phenomenon so common with people of the millennial generation and those who are even younger: the need to post their most meaningful life events on social media in order to make them "real." This logic has produced a sense in which one is not really dating someone, for instance, unless their partnership is documented on Facebook and other such sites as "in a relationship." The logic would have it that one is not *actually* dating someone until it has been made "real" by posting it on social media—in virtual reality.

Still, we can and must understand oppression (exploitation, in Hardt and Negri's term) dialectically in order to understand not the essence of oppression, but rather its present historical work upon our lived experiences as human actors. Freire's (2000) dialectic of the oppressors and the oppressed gives us insight into understanding what Hardt and Negri are employing in their method of inquiry. The oppressors are only imaginable if we also imagine the oppressed, and so too the other way around. The oppressed are only the oppressed because of the existence of oppressors who actively oppress. For Freire (2000), this is where the insight that the humanity of the oppressor is caught up in the humanity of the oppressed derives from. In Freire's own terms,

> The discovery by the oppressed that they exist in dialectical relationship to the oppressor, as his antithesis—that without them the oppressor could not exist—[does not] in itself constitute liberation. The oppressed can overcome the contradiction in which they are caught only when this perception enlists them in the struggle to free themselves. (p. 49)

The "struggle to free" one's self is thus rooted in a conception of dialectics, yet allows room for other projects and practices, as the mere realization or naming of a dialectic will not transform our reality. It is in employing such an insight that Hardt and Negri (2000) incorporate into their own work insights from Marxist, Foucauldian, and other critical traditions that many have found incommensurable. Importantly, we must articulate where it is that we are beginning from in our own work, and we must do so in a way that places us in communion with critical traditions whose insights we employ in humanizing, liberatory ways (Freire, 2000). It is imperative that we employ every critical energy to articulate the ways in which human beings presently lead alienating and dehumanizing lives due to the presence and ongoing historical realities of oppressive ideologies: from racism to genocide, heterosexism and patriarchy to capitalist exploitation. And this means we must look to theories that speak not only to the dialectical nature of oppression, but also to theories of the struggle for liberation.

Any contemporary theorization of ideology must account for the critical black feminist conception of intersectionality (Casey, 2011; Crenshaw, 1992), which provides us the insight that we cannot understand oppressive systems (such as racism, heterosexism, patriarchy, and so on) independently, as if one did not inform, enmesh with, and shift through others. Thus, we must then concede that particular methods of inquiry, ways of positioning one's self, of *being* in the world (Ladson-Billings, 2006a) enable certain insights as it closes off others (Kumashiro, 2000). If it is oppression that we seek to abolish, however, and we can understand the dialectic of exploitation, of oppression, we would do well to not only justify such a method, but to employ it toward those ends that it seeks. In other words, we can focus our attention on particular issues so long as we maintain a critical stance that acknowledges the ways in which attention to a particular phenomenon is attention diverted from others.

Ideology, for our purposes here, follows in the tradition of Antonio Gramsci and Louis Althusser to articulate in particular the ways in which schools, educational leaders, and educational policy participate in and with ideology in an oppressive reality. Ideology can be understood if we understand Antonio Gramsci's (2008) conception of hegemony, of "the 'spontaneous' consent given by the great masses of the population to the general direction imposed on social life by the dominant fundamental group" (p. 12). Louis Althusser (2008) offers us a way of understanding how such a process is possible in his discussion of both Repressive State Apparatuses and Ideological State Apparatuses. He writes, "All the State Apparatuses function both by repression and by ideology, with the difference that the (Repressive) State Apparatus functions massively and predominantly by repression, whereas the Ideological State Apparatuses function massively and predominantly by ideology" (p. 23). Examples of Repressive State Apparatuses include the police and the military, which exercise brute force in order to control the population. Examples of Ideological State Apparatuses include churches, schools, political parties, and the media, all of which function ideologically. That is to say, they function from within a particular context and worldview, a way of orienting and understanding, which, (and this is crucially important) means they have a political dimension.

All of this is intended to carve out the terrain on which ideological critique is possible. White supremacy and neoliberalism are both ideologies as well as being ideological, and what the above conception helps us with is to position our aims for justice in both philosophical as well as political language. Ideological transformation is only possible in a context in which we take the concepts of ideology and hegemony seriously. That is, we will never be rid of ideologies, nor rid of hegemony, as peoples' experiences and contexts will always shape their views in complex ways that point to other conceptions that exist in a power relation to others' conceptions.[7] Our task is to co-author alternative and humanizing ideologies in an effort to bring forth a new hegemony of solidarity. This is precisely the aim of the later chapters[8] of this text, and thus we need to turn to another dimension of the method of Freirean Critical Study, the political nature of all teaching and education, in order to further develop what is at stake in the present method.

Democracy, and the Political Nature of Education

While it has been discussed above and in the previous chapter, the conception of education as inherently political occupies an important role in the method of Freirean Critical Study. This is coupled with a conception of democracy as a practice, as a way of being that acknowledges and acts on the political nature of all educational settings. It is imperative, from a Freirean (2006) perspective that we understand that

> [e]ducation is a political act. Its nonneutrality demands from educators that they take it on as a political act and

that they consistently live their progressive and democratic or authoritarian and reactionary past or also their spontaneous, uncritical choice, that they define themselves by being democratic or authoritarian. (p. 112)

So positioned, we are given two ways of being available as teachers: democratic or authoritarian. Each of these words is doing considerable work for Freire in this articulation, and thus it becomes important to explain this distinction both using Freirean insights as well as others whose work illuminates and enables this method.

Democracy, for Freire, is not merely a political theory or form of government but rather a practice, something that is lived. To this end, he defines what is needed to construct a "serious democracy, which implies radically changing the societal structures, reorienting the politics of production and development, reinventing power, doing justice to everyone, and abolishing the unjust and immoral gains of the all-powerful" (p. 118). For Freire, democratic teachers live *these* commitments out in their classrooms, in the ways they interact with students, but also in the ways they connect their work to their political aims. One who can be considered on the side of democracy is one who lives, who does, democratically. In the Freirean sense, it thus becomes antidemocratic, authoritarian to return to the above distinction, to not engage students in critically understanding societal structures, the means of production, and the ways in which existing systems of exploitation and control limit their full potential as human beings (Freire, 2000; 2006; Jansen, 2009). Extending this to the work of Freirean Critical Study, we must engage the above in our writing and theorizing of pedagogy, education, and society. We must live out in writing our commitments, as best as we can, and as modeled by authors like Freire but perhaps even more by folks such as bell hooks and others whose work engages the personal as political in praxis-oriented ways. Still, we need to better understand what is at stake in the concept of democracy, and how this impacts both critical teaching and critical inquiry into teaching.

When we return to two of the most important educational theorists from the United States, John Dewey and George Counts, we can gain further insight into not only Freirean conceptions of what it means to teach democratically, but also the dispositions that they both see as being central to teaching and to the very purposes of schools. Dewey (1916/2007), in *Democracy and Education*, details what he means by democracy, and for that purpose is worth quoting at length. He writes,

> A democracy is more than a form of government; it is primarily a mode of associated living, of conjoint communicated experience. The extension in space of the number of individuals who participate in an interest so that each has to refer his own action to that of others, and to consider the action of others to give point and direction to his own, is equivalent to the breaking down of those barriers of class, race, and national territory which kept men from perceiving the full import of their activity. (p. 68)

For Dewey, this must be our educative aim for the purpose of schools in a democracy: that they *be* and *practice* democracy. Thus, teachers are imagined as not only responsible for, but capable of such a practice, that this practice must entail commitments to abolish class difference, racism, and xenophobia becomes a way in which we can understand Dewey's conceptions of both the purpose of teaching as well as his conception of teachers.

Counts (1978), as a part of his text *Dare the School Build a New Social Order*, put forward the following as to what we ought to be striving for in schools if our commitments to democracy are genuine. He wrote,

> A society fashioned in harmony with the American democratic tradition would combat all forces tending to produce social distinctions and classes; repress every form of privilege and economic parasitism . . . strive for genuine equality of opportunity among all races, sects, and occupations. (p. 38)

Again, we see here the notion that commitments to democracy entail democratic practices: ways of being in democracy that affirm and support such a commitment. For Counts, teachers are not only political actors, they are perhaps the most critical actors in living democratically with regard to the ways young people learn about themselves and their world in schools.

We must, however, keep in mind that education on its own, or an individual teacher in her classroom with her students, cannot be responsible for the realization of each of these aims universally. To this argument, Freire (2006) writes, "It is true that education is not the ultimate lever for social transformation, but without it transformation cannot occur" (p. 69). Thus, we are left with a conception of teaching as inherently political which then entails that we ask questions of the political actions taken by teachers as well as those actions demanded of teachers by curriculum, standards, and the myriad other pressures and limits on teachers as authors (with their students) of their own curriculums. And of course, we must extend these commitments to critical inquiry into teaching as well, as best we can, and in ways that invite others into dialog and into practices of democratic learning and praxis. For educational practices and policies that are not democratic or, to go farther, stand in immediate contrast to democratic ways of being inside and outside of classrooms, a further analytical tool is essential in Freirean Critical Study: examining frames.

Framing

The ways in which ideas move in discourse, the symbols of and referential power in language, must be approached from a critical orientation that asks "Who is privileged?" and "Who is left out?" of every text and context. The notion of framing, as I employ it here, comes primarily from the work of cognitive linguist George Lakoff (2002; 2004) and contemporary educational theorist Kevin Kumashiro (2008), who employs Lakoff's conception of frames to examine the ways educational policy matters have become "common sense" in ways that privilege the Right. Kumashiro's use of Lakoff's theory represents an example of Freirean Critical Study in that in mobilizing Lakoff's work as a method of inquiry Kumashiro is able to better understand not only what is present or not present in a text, but also the ways in which what is present (or not) frames issues for the reader/interpreter of those issues.

Lakoff (2004) tells us that "frames are mental structures that shape the way we see the world" (p. xv). Frames function in political ways, because the ways in which ideas and texts are taken up by human actors have human consequences which thus entail conceptions of ethics: inherently political matters. To examine frames, or frames present in a given text or context, is to examine not only what is being said or communicated, but also the ways in which those texts and contexts function. Examining frames enables us to ask questions of a text and what is present to not only understand meaning or intent, but the political nature of the text itself and the frames it privileges or de-privileges, the images it constructs, and the metaphors and comparisons it evokes. Some examples, both from Lakoff and Kumashiro will help to make clearer what the method of examining frames entails and enables.

Lakoff (2004) gives us the example of the framing employed in the Rightist concept of "tax relief" and what such a frame functions to do. He asks us to

> [t]hink of the framing for *relief*. For there to be relief there must be an affliction, an afflicted party, and a reliever who removes the affliction and is therefore a hero. And if people try to stop the hero, those people are villains for trying to prevent relief. (p. 3)

Thus, in employing the notion of "tax relief" one employs the frames of "relief" as well as "affliction" and places both in relation to taxes. Lakoff argues that we can understand framing to be active and intentional political work and that in our present historical moment frames are more effective from the Right, with those on the Left often taking up Rightist frames and thus perpetuating Rightist policies. An example of this process is the use of family values metaphors (e.g., the Founding Fathers) for the nation that reinforce patriarchal "strict father morality" and undermine Leftist efforts at combatting heteronormativity and sexism.

Kumashiro (2008) uses Lakoff's concept of framing in terms of U.S. politics to examine the influence of Rightist think tanks and foundations on educational policy. In his work, he examines the frames of "standards, accountability, sanctions, and choice" with regard to schools to demonstrate how these frames "become linked together by a metaphor (the strict-father model) that makes the four frames inseparable from one another" (p. 35). The "strict-father model" is a concept from Lakoff (2002; 2004) to name the primary logic of conservative interests with regard to national politics. A strict-father model employs the logics of "family, self-sufficiency, and meritocracy" to argue that those who have not succeeded economically or otherwise have failed because of their own inability to work hard (Kumashiro, 2008, p. 35). Kumashiro shows the ways in which strict-father morality enables the dominant political and economic ideology in the United States as neoliberal capitalism. He notes that the strict-father family model is not only an ideology of conservative family values. Rather, free-market capitalist-oriented positions on schooling and education more broadly produce an ideology that links conservative family values explicitly with the needs and demands of the capitalist order.

In terms of framing, neoliberalism functions to place all social space and goods in subordinate relationship to the needs of the capitalist economy. In schools we can understand this process, to name merely one example, in the ways that the needs of students in classrooms become collapsed as synonymous with the needs of the capitalist economy (Casey, 2011). Neoliberal frames are evoked in classrooms to frame the need of students in economistic ways, for example, by focusing on students' eventual role in the economy (you'll need this to get a job), in making the United States "more competitive" with international economic rivals (economistic-patriotism), and more marketable to future employers (what the business community "wants"). I examine this in much greater detail in the chapters focusing on neoliberalism in education and the "professionalization" of the teaching force.

Pedagogical Theory versus Theorizing Pedagogy— Difficulties and Limitations

Thus far I have constructed a method of inquiry that takes as its starting point critical teaching. That is, the method of Freirean Critical Study is derived from the belief that our inquiry into the teaching act, and into education more broadly, cannot be divorced from our pedagogical commitments in the classroom. Thus, the three elements of Freirean Critical Study detailed above (ideology and ideological critique, the political nature of education, and framing) all correspond to critical (Freirean and culturally relevant) teaching acts: being explicit about the "culture of power" (Deplit, 2006) with students, creating space for student voice and the self-appropriation of knowledge, space for knowledge creation, for examining contexts and the political and historical forces that shape what we learn and how we learn it, just to name a few. These acts correspond to critical notions of how ideology operates on schools and society, how politics shapes and plays out in classrooms, and in the kinds of frames that we use to explain ourselves and the contents of our lessons. It is of course important to concede that teaching and inquiry into teaching are different, albeit interrelated acts. The act of teaching often happens before inquiry into said teaching, yet this inquiry informs both our theories of what we have done and what our future efforts ought to be. That critical teaching should form the basis of critical inquiry into teaching speaks to a political commitment that privileges teaching as an inherently intellectual endeavor.

Still, explicitly pedagogical theorizing, or pedagogical philosophy, has been critiqued by one of the most important critical theorists of the last century, Max Horkheimer, whose critique of instrumental reason plays a major role in the arguments mobilized later in this work. Horkheimer (1947/2004) writes,

> [When] philosophy is slanted for popular availability, i.e. its pedagogical character, nullifies it as philosophy. Theories embodying critical insight into historical processes, when used for panaceas, have often turned into repressive doctrines. Philosophy is neither a tool nor a blueprint. It can only foreshadow the path of progress as it is marked out by logical and factual necessities. (p. 112)

Horkheimer is here concerned with a particular kind of pedagogical philosophy in which critical insights are collapsed into manuals, into instructions, on how one ought to proceed. His insistence that philosophy "foreshadow" stems from the fear that philosophy itself can be instrumentalized and reduced only to its use as a tool, rather than its use in a philosophy of praxis.

It thus becomes imperative, especially given Horkheimer's importance, along with Theodore Adorno,[9] on what has become known as the critique of "instrumental reason," to specify the ways in which this text, which is both pedagogical and philosophical, is self-conscious enough to not position itself as a "blueprint" nor as a "panacea" but rather as a self-critical way of enacting the commitments of critical educators in inquiring into education, teaching, and those who teach. A Freirean response to this critique would go something like this.

Freirean Critical Study, with its explicit linkages and origins in critical teaching, constitutes a critical method of inquiry in the praxis of reading the world and the word. We must be cautious, however, as Freire was conscious, to not allow such a method to become a technology, merely something to be employed to achieve desirable results efficiently. Rather, Macedo and Freire (2006) "propose an antimethod pedagogy that refuses the rigidity of models and methodological paradigms" (p. xxiii). Such an antimethod pedagogy "frees us from the beaten path of certainties and specialties. It rejects the mechanization of intellectualism" (p. xxiii). Thus, my employing Freirean Critical Study as elaborated here is intended to enable an intellectually rigorous reading of the word and the world in a way that is grounded not on the bounded limits of a particular tradition in research, or even critical theory, but rather in the humanizing task of elaborating and theorizing the contexts in which we struggle to enable a radically democratic and humanizing education for all students. There is no one single path to justice, to abolishing white supremacy, or to a hegemony of solidarity; just as there is no single way of teaching in ways that are completely devoid of violence or oppressive connotations.

This is precisely the point Kumashiro (2009) makes when he writes that "No practice is always anti-oppressive" (p. 3). Something that is successful with one group of students can utterly fail with another, and we can never avoid every possible element of oppression in classrooms because we can never fully know every element of classrooms. And the very same goes for critical inquiry. We will always leave things out, our texts will always be bounded, limited, and partial. Yet with Freire's call in mind, to "reinvent" his work and ideas, we can bring to bear the whole of our engaged selves into our pedagogical work in the emancipatory spirit Freire detailed. My work here in elaborating my method of inquiry has been intended as an act of reinvention in the Freirean sense. I now move to detailing the Marxist foundations of this project, as both an accompaniment and addition to my method, before moving to the application of Freirean Critical Study in chapters 4 through 9.

THREE

Marx, Marxism, and Me

A class which forms the majority of all members of
society, and from which emanates the consciousness
of the necessity of a fundamental revolution, the
communist consciousness.

— *The German Ideology*

It makes poverty and property a *single whole*, which
it investigates *as such* to find the conditions for its
existence; an investigation which is all the more
superfluous as it has just *made* that whole as such and
therefor its *making* is in itself the condition for its
existence.

— *The Holy Family*

Critical black feminist scholar bell hooks (1994), in her series
of essays in *Teaching to Transgress*, describes her own process of
engagement with cultural and political theories in a deeply personal and powerful way. She writes,

I came to theory because I was hurting—the pain within
me was so intense that I could not go on living. I came to
theory desperate, wanting to comprehend—to grasp what
was happening around me. Most importantly, I wanted to
make the hurt go away. I saw in theory then a location for
healing. (p. 59)

31

For me, I would amend the first section of this quotation to read, "I came to Marxism because I was hurting." That is, in my work to understand the realities of white supremacy, I found over and over again that the history of white people's exploitation of people of color had a profoundly economic character. A simple narrative that white people are always already racist, and thus elaborated white supremacist principles for organizing society, is an oversimplification, to put it generously, and, more critically, functions today in ways that legitimate capitalist exploitation as merely or only racist in character. I was struck that our best arguments to show the "proof" of white supremacy, of de facto racism in our present context, almost always rely on economic figures and matrices. At the time of this writing, for instance, the overall unemployment rate in the United States stands at 8 percent, yet for black folks this figure is 14 percent, and the rate even higher for young black men in particular (Burke, 2013). These figures are empirical measures. These are objective statements on the reality of white supremacy, and the ongoing oppression faced by people of color. Yet these phenomena cannot be explained solely in racial terms. While there is no doubt that bigoted and hateful conceptions of racial others are absolutely in play in the unfair and unequal distribution of wealth and resources, white racism cannot explain this reality completely.

And so it was that I began to question why we almost always turn to socioeconomic status, wealth, and income to explain racism, without questioning how our economic system itself perpetuates racialized inequity. I asked myself, "Why is it that we think of the capitalist economic system as a neutral and impartial measure of (in)equality?" What would happen if we found within the capitalist system itself a profoundly dehumanizing and racializing project of legitimating the very means by which white supremacy maintains its hegemonic grip on the global order? When one begins asking questions of capitalism, there is no better place to turn than to the work of Karl Marx and scholars who have continued in the Marxist tradition. Here I provide an overview of Marx and Marxism.[1] My intention is not to be exhaustive in my coverage of the extensive body of work left by Marx. Rather, it is to be intentionally selective in the theories and concepts that most helped me understand capital and capitalism in both a material and theoretical sense. In what follows in this chapter, I move rather quickly through his body of work, highlight a selection of Marxist scholarship that advances Marx's work in critical ways for understanding our present capitalist reality, and attempt to address both common misconceptions and critiques of Marx, Marxism, and the political project of transformational praxis.

On Class(es)

While too few contemporary scholars have truly engaged Marxism in the field of education, or any other field for that matter, most people with some idea of Marx and Marxism can identify the two following class groups as central to Marxist theory: the proletariat and the bourgeoisie. The bourgeoisie are the propertied class, the owners of the means of production, representing and embodying the dominant and ruling hegemonic ideas. The bourgeoisie do not sell their labor, and are not wedded to receiving a wage from an employer on which to subsist. Rather, they buy the labor of others: the proletariat. The proletariat are the workers, the propertyless, who own their labor and must sell it in order to receive a wage and subsist. For Marx, these are the two objective historical classes, the two classes in dialectical relationship, where one calls the other into being.

There is great confusion for many in the contemporary United States, where virtually everyone identifies themselves as neither the owners of the means of production nor as proletarian, but as middle class. For Marx, the middle class exists, and we should note that by contemporary standards Marx was himself middle class, but the middle class importantly is not at the center of the fundamental tension and conflict that is the driving force of history: class struggle. This hinges on a dialectical conception of the forces of history: that two opposing forces in conflict create, through that conflict, ruptures and shifts in the course of history. This becomes much clearer when we think about the time Marx was writing in, the nineteenth century, in Western Europe.

The transition from feudalism to capitalism, for Marx, was a revolution. While it may come as a surprise, Marx credits capitalism with ushering in a heretofore unprecedented acceleration of goods and services, prosperity, and increase in the general well-being of

the majority of (Western European) people. The capitalist revolution, however, was a bourgeois revolution: the two classes in
conflict were the landed nobility and feudal lords versus the mer-
cantile and trading class.[2] The impoverished feudal serfs, whom we
can think of as most akin to sharecroppers in U.S. history, were
not the revolutionary class that brought an end to feudalism—
but, importantly, they certainly were a class. In capitalism, landed
nobility and feudal lords are replaced by capitalists, by the owners
of the means of production, and the class that is most in conflict
with the owners is clearly the workers. Thus, for Marx it is not
the case that there are only two classes, but rather there are only
two classes who are in dialectical tension to a great enough extent
to compel conflict and eventually revolution. And, understood in
dialectical terms, one class must abolish the conditions of its own
dehumanization: the class in opposition to it. Why does he think
this? For Marx, the revolutionary consciousness of the proletariat
comes from their alienation as workers, from the distance between
their labor and the products of their labor.

On Alienation and Surplus Labor

Marx's theory of alienation, complex as it is, can be understood
rather straightforwardly as follows: as a worker I produce goods
or services, but I do not own the products of my labor. Rather, I
sell my labor to the capitalist, who in turn pays me for my labor
and keeps for himself what I have produced to sell. The capitalist then sells the product of my labor, maintaining for himself the
maximum value possible, paying me the worker as little or as close
to a subsistence wage as possible. Marx's logic for this last point is
quite simple: from the capitalist's perspective, the worker requires
only what it will take to maintain her or him *as a worker*. In other
words, the capitalist only pays the worker what the worker needs
to live in order to be able to work. This is why in the most alienated positions in the economic order wages always skew toward
subsistence, the bare minimum necessary.

The workers feel alienated because of the distance between
their labor and the product of their labor. For Marx, this distance
exists because of the source of profit: surplus value and surplus
labor. Again, while this is a highly complex theory, and it should

be noted that many economists have come to refute this theory in our present era of financial capital,[3] we can understand it thusly.

Let's say the capitalist pays the worker an hourly wage, and the worker labors for ten hours a day. For the sake of this example, let's say the worker is building chairs. Surplus labor, and surplus value, exists when the necessary labor time to produce a good is less than the total time the employee works. Let's say in a ten hour workday the worker can make six chairs. The capitalist pays an hourly wage to the worker, but for Marx the source of profit lies in paying workers for only a portion of what they actually produce. For the sake of this example let's say three chairs have the equivalent value of the daily wage for the worker—so the worker sells his labor to the capitalist and is paid out of the money generated by the selling of these three chairs. But in the workday, the worker can make more than three chairs, twice as many in fact, yet the capitalist only pays the worker for the equivalent of three. Those three additional chairs the worker makes but does not receive the equivalent pay for constitute surplus value, profit for the capitalist.

This is a wildly oversimplistic example, and Marx spends literally hundreds if not thousands of pages in his writings working through example after example of this process. In my own conception of Marxism, the following conclusion becomes paramount, rather than the particular arithmetic: the source of profit for the capitalist rests on the worker's labor time and productivity exceeding what she receives as a wage in return. The worker, as we would expect, is alienated from the products of her labor then in two material ways: not owning said product, and producing more than is necessary to sustain herself, thereby creating surplus value for the capitalist who converts the surplus value into profit.

Use Value and Exchange Value

The labor theory of value, in Marxism, asserts that the exchange value of a commodity (think, for now, of price) is derived from the necessary labor time, and labor value objectified in the commodity. In other words, we should see every commodity as a material manifestation of labor, and price correlates to the amount of labor necessary for the production of the commodity. In this way, all commodities have a human character: not just in the sense that humans created them, but on the level of thinking about the *actual* person or people who made said commodity. This is why goods that are mass-produced are less expensive (typically) than those that are considered more "artisanally" made: because the exchange value of a commodity is derived from the labor that went into the commodity: and the less human energy that goes into a commodity, typically, the more surplus labor can be created (e.g., if it only takes four people to run a machine that produces twenty times what those four people could produce in the past, surplus value, and profit, goes up). All commodities, then, can be said to have two values: an exchange value, as we've been discussing, and a use value. Marx was interested in demonstrating that, to return to my earlier example, a chair is never just a chair: is never just its utility or usefulness. Rather, a chair is always also money, and we could list endlessly the various commodities and both their use and exchange value. The point is this: exchange value is derived from the labor of the worker(s) who made the commodity.

The worker, however, is exploited in the capitalist system in the following ways. First, workers *must* sell their labor, or starve. While the rhetoric of capitalism suggests a "freedom" of choice in employment, that freedom is bounded by the reality that one is free to choose where one will work but always in subordinate relation to the owners of the means of production and always in ways that alienate one from the products of one's labor. Workers are thus exploited systemically, coerced into selling their labor in order to survive, in the context of the commodification of literally every good and service. In this process shelter, food, and clothing—basic needs that must be satisfied for survival—all become commodities. These material human needs, in a capitalist society, can only be met by selling one's labor power, which in capitalism produces surplus labor and profit for the capitalist, thus exploiting the great majority of humanity to line the pockets of the owners of the means of production.

On Production, Labor, and What It Means to Be Human

Up to this point I have made frequent reference to the means of production, to what workers produce, and so on. What is often misunderstood in Marx is why a concept such as "owners of the means of production" is so powerful when one considers the fundamental question of what it means to be human. In *The German Ideology* Marx addresses this explicitly. What distinguishes the species *Homo sapiens* from all others is the uniquely human ability and proclivity to produce. Human beings make things, both material objects as well as concepts and ideals, but it is the act of producing that makes the human being a human. We can trace this back to (so-called) prehistoric times when humans created axes, spears, and other instruments to cut meat and cloth. In contemporary times, we see evidence of human production virtually everywhere, as in even the most remote places we so often find products of human invention and creativity. No other species produces things in such a manner, and this is why production for Marx is so central to his political commitments to emancipation and liberation.

Labor, so central to Marx, is thus what is necessary in the human act. One must labor to produce, and one must produce to be human. For Marx, this is then the fundamentally exploiting character of capitalism: human beings must labor in order to produce, but if they do not own the products of their labor, and further if they do not control what it is they produce, their human activity of producing not for themselves but for the capitalist is dehumanization par excellence. We should think of dehumanization very literally here: to be made *unhuman*, to be denied access to what it is that makes one human in the fullest sense.

In this way, we can better understand why the economic base, or the economic relations of a given society, are so fundamental to social life in Marxist thinking. A rather vulgar reading of Marx would suggest that there is the economic base, which determines all the aspects of the superstructure, which can be thought of here as more or less everything in society that is not primarily economic. Marx's argument is not that the economy determines absolutely everything, but rather that one can never understand *any* social phenomenon fully without consideration of the economic forces in play.[4] Economics, of course, in capitalism becomes the realm of production, which again is the uniquely distinguishing aspect of human beings in comparison to other species. Thus, we could rewrite the relationship of base and superstructure as the relationship of production to social life. And here, it should come into sharp relief that Marx is accurate to locate the vast majority of what constitutes us as human beings as our economic relation and positionality. Everything human stems from production, and one of if not the fundamental flaw of capitalism is that this creates the impetus for placing the needs of the owners of the means of production as the needs for all social actors. This is how the logic of "too big to fail" in relation to the great banking crisis of recent years would make perfect sense to Marx. In financial, speculative, capitalism, banks function as the primary owners of the means of production: the needs of the banks thus must become social needs.

A further comment is necessary on what is meant by the "owners of the means of production." If we maintain the line of thought that says production is what it means to be human, owning the means of production is owning the means of being human. This is a profound insight, because it means that in capitalist society workers are not only alienated and exploited, but they are quite literally cut off from their own humanity by being cut off from the products of their labor. This also means that owning the means of being human allows the capitalist class to dictate its own will as the will of all, as the will of the *real* humans. We should not be surprised, then, that the needs of banks become the needs of the federal government, which is imagined as acting on the needs of the people: owning the means of being human equates to owning what it means to be human. And this is precisely the stage we have reached: capitalism is normalized as the taken for granted, dehistoricized, and totalizing system of meaning that all human subjects must participate in in order to remain human.

On Commodity Fetishism

The commodity, for Marx, is a fascinating thing, because of what he believes is invested in every commodity: social relations. A commodity is never just a commodity, never just a thing, and, as we have discussed above, never reducible solely to its use value, to its utility. Instead, the commodity itself becomes a way of understanding the whole of the capitalist system through what Marx calls "commodity fetishism." The fetish[5] here is this: we typically experience commodities as things as such, as what they are, and thus conceive of the exchangeability of commodities as deriving from what they physically are. However, Marx compels us to understand that it is not in fact the commodities themselves that allow for exchange, but rather the "abstract labor" in any commodity that gives that commodity its exchangeable quality. An example can help make this more concrete. How is it that we can understand how many, let's say, forks equate to a chair, for purposes of exchange? For Marx, the answer is straightforward, yet intentionally hidden from view: what is being exchanged is not the forks for the chair, as no amount of forks in any capacity would ever be the same thing as a chair, and vice versa, but rather the abstract labor in the forks is exchanged for the abstract labor in the chair. They are exchangeable because they share the quality of having been made, having labor within them, and this labor is what is actually exchanged, for Marx, in the exchange of commodities. That both commodities are reducible to a monetary value begs the question of the source of said monetary value. Marx's answer is quite simply: labor. As we ignore the abstract labor in commodities, when we treat commodities solely as things, we fetishize the commodities as we lose any conception of the social relations imbedded in the creation of any commodity.

Any and all commodities contain within them the social relationships of worker and capitalist, of land and labor, thus, the whole of the capitalist system. It is precisely through fetishizing the commodity that consumers can and do perpetuate the exploitative character of capitalism, because we almost never consider the social context in which a given item was manufactured, who made it, what their working conditions were, what kinds of access to social services they had, and so on. We fail to see the inherently human quality in all things that are produced, and also the dehumanizing impacts of alienating workers from the products of their labor. When we consider land, in economic terms, we often talk about it as though it were the physical area itself, rather than the landowner who is figured and paid rent and so on. We could say the very same thing about the ways we think of machine-made goods, as though it were the machine itself we are paying, rather than the actual human beings who own or operate the machine.

Commodities thus contain within them evidence of the inherent conflicts that exist in capitalism, yet are almost always obscured from view.

What Marx Offers Us in the Twenty-first Century

Marx devoted his life, particularly after being thrown out of his home country in Germany and subsequently moving to England, to the study of political economy and the leading theories and theorists of his era. His early works can make for difficult reading because, for the most part, they are close and careful readings of the German Idealists, the Young Hegelians, whom Marx and Engels critiqued for placing more value in the realm of ideas than in the realm of material reality. Marx knew that we would never be able to only think our way to a truly human socialist or communist future, that real material action would be necessary. His later works are even more difficult, because they are an exceptional theorization of the whole of political economy in the nineteenth century and earlier, ranging across theories of money, value, labor, profit, and, of course, capital. It should be stated plainly that large portions of this work can be seen as no longer relevant given the developments of late capitalism, perhaps most notably the abolition of the gold standard since 1971.[6] While the work of this chapter thus far has sought to explain some fundamental insights contained in Marx's thinking, I wish to turn now to a more personalized summation of what Marx offers us as thinkers, pedagogues, and political actors in our present historical moment.

Marx believed that the political revolution that would abolish capitalism would only come about once the present productive forces had been developed as far as they possibly could be. The crises inherent to capitalism—and it should be made clear that recessions and depressions are not accidents in capitalism but rather a defining characteristic of capitalism as an economic system[7]—offer the potential for the working class in collective solidarity to take over the means of production. But this can only happen once capitalism's excesses and failures have been brought to their full force, their complete extent. In some ways, we could argue that Marx believed the only way we will abolish capitalism is through more capitalism. That is, only once capitalism has reached its full potentiality will the historical moment be ripe for a communist revolution. Since communism is often read as a dirty word in the U.S. context, a brief comment should be made.

Marx would not have considered the so-called communist revolutions of Russia, Cuba, China, Vietnam, and North Korea objective historical revolutions. No doubt, they were absolutely political revolutions, but as the previous mode of production had not reached its full potential in any of these countries, communism there was essentially doomed from the very beginning. The fact that none of these countries ever fulfilled the first task of communism—to abolish the nation-state and political borders—means that we should not conflate the USSR and what Marx meant by communism. In the modern era there has never been a wholly communist society—and one might argue that even in the United States, arguably the most fully developed capitalist economy in the world, capitalism has not yet exhausted its full potentiality and thus not led to revolution.

Marx is then very much still relevant, and it should be noted that the collapse of capitalism is not understood as an inevitability, as though one day we will look out of our windows and say, "Oh, capitalism is over." It takes human actors to make human history, and Marx believed that violence is inevitable in this process. Still, one would be right to say that if Marx's theories of money no longer take into account the present global standing of fiat money,[8] and, further, if we still have yet to reach the point where capitalism has developed to its full potential where "workers of the [entire] world unite" to overthrow the existing regime of production, then the obvious question should be: What use is Marx?

Plenty, I would reply, because his fundamental insights into capitalism and the owners of the means of production remain just as true, if not more so, today than in his time. There is nothing natural about capitalism, and while it has brought with it the largest expansion of human freedoms in recorded history, it has utterly failed to bring about the just reality so many people crave. Capitalism necessitates exploitation, because the owners of the means of production are incentivized to do everything at a profit, to maximize efficiency rather than human freedom, to place the needs of shareholders ahead of the needs of employees and consumers, and to constantly grow and expand at the expense of both humanity and the natural environment. In this way, capitalism functions to maintain conditions of poverty by keeping wages as low as possible in the pursuit of maximizing profits.

No one can deny the existence of poverty, yet few would entertain the notion that the labor theory of value offers insight into how poverty is maintained. Removing ourselves for the moment from Marx's painstaking work of documenting mathematically how his theory works in practice, we can attempt more simply to understand poverty on a global scale. Imperialism was primarily an economic project, and was chiefly concerned with taking wealth and resources (which would be converted into further wealth and capital through the process of exchange) from subordinated countries back to Western nations. The creation of the wealth of the West, including the United States, must be understood not merely as an accumulation of wealth, but rather as the forceful *taking* of wealth, quite literally robbing millions upon millions of people. This process continues today in the form of global capitalism wherein workers are no longer solely in competition with their neighbors but with the whole of the human race. The labor theory of value can then be imagined as even more relevant than ever, for if a subsistence wage in the Global South is half of what it is in the Global North, the capitalist is able to derive more profit from the surplus value produced by the worker who is being paid significantly less than what the product of the worker's labor is worth. Marx thus devised a theory that predicted, and can explain, the phenomena of globalization and outsourcing a century before these processes took hold.

But perhaps the most important insight from Marx that we should maintain in our thinking about the present realities of global capitalism is the political praxis of dialectics. First, we must understand the dialectical conception of capitalism itself. The various "successes" of capitalism, and again Marx is very clear that these are numerous, are coupled with the very problematics that undermine these apparent successes. What does this mean? Capitalism necessitates constant growth and expansion. This can be in the form of increasing the size and scope of a business, the profit of a business, the financial operationalization of capital in a business (e.g., General Electric now derives a majority of their profits from their investment banking, rather than from producing electronic goods [Moore, 2011]), and many other examples we could list of what it means for a business to "grow." The inherent conflict is this: with the constant demand to expand, the various expanding entities come into conflict not only with each other, but with the larger system itself. Rivalries, competition for profits, and the constant pursuit of growth undermine the long-term stability of the capitalist order, creating crises such as the home mortgage and investment bank catastrophe of the last few years. Further, the quarterly profit reporting system places emphasis on short-term gains at the expense of stability. Thus, firing a mass of workers with millions of dollars invested in training them makes sense (and profits) one week, but not the next. Practices such as these cause the constant dips and peaks that characterize any capitalist economy.

Marx's logic further enables us to identify the conditions for the existence of the proletariat premised on the existence of the capitalists. Better put, if one seeks to abolish the condition of proletarian "wage slavery" one must abolish the conditions under which the proletariat have come into existence, in opposition to the capitalists. If we wish to abolish the condition of poverty, we must abolish that condition which necessitates poverty, the greed of the capitalists. For one small group to hold immensely more wealth than the vast majority of the peoples in the world, a vast number of oppressed and marginalized people must exist. And thus we cannot abolish poverty while maintaining capitalism and the private ownership of property. The two need each other. In fact they only exist because of the existence of each other.

On Ideology and False Consciousness

There is a need to explain further the concept of ideology as it was introduced in the previous chapter in relation to Marx's own theories. The particular phenomenon of people who, while they are not themselves capitalists, support capitalism or internalize capitalist logics represents an immensely important group in the maintenance of capitalist hegemony. Marx explains these people as experiencing a form of ideology known as false consciousness. For Marx, in its most simple form, ideology can be understood, as he puts it in *Capital*, as "they do not know it, but they are doing it." Ideology, then, is seen as a kind of guiding force obscured from view so as to maintain the dominant order. It is an ordering of consciousness, a means by which knowledge is filtered through and brought into existence along existent lines of perceived reality. Ideology functions to legitimate and demonize, often without reference to how or why a particular phenomenon ought to be viewed from a particular ideological viewpoint.

Perhaps the easiest form of ideology to recognize in our contemporary vernacular is the notion of "common sense." One almost never asks the question, "common for whom?" This is ideology at work: a framework for understanding in predefined ways. False consciousness is imagined in opposition to proletarian consciousness, or consciousness of the dialectical relation of capitalist and proletarian, wherein, in order to abolish one, the other must be abolished. A worker who imagines herself as a capitalist, so this theory would go, is experiencing false consciousness, because her class position locates her as proletarian, as a worker, yet she rejects this positionality in claiming instead a bourgeois identity.

In contemporary times, however, this conception of ideology is perhaps no longer sufficient to explain our present reality. For example, we can think of people who are committed to redressing the ecological crisis, and who adopt the use of reusable water bottles yet do not advocate for meaningful reform of carbon-producing industries. These people know that our present rates of pollution are unsustainable for many species on Earth, yet they do not act on this knowledge in ways that will eliminate the largest polluters, and focus instead on individual rather than systemic or structural actions. Slavoj Žižek's (1989) work enters here, and he claims that we should reformulate Marx's original dictum, "They do not know it, but they are doing it," as, "They know very well how things really are, but still they are doing it as if they did not know" (p. 30). As Žižek's work is concerned with the intersection of Marxism and Lacanian psychoanalysis, he describes our present reality of ideology as "ideological fantasy." Leaving aside the psychoanalytic elements to Žižek's argument, we can see here perhaps a better conception for the usefulness of the theory of false consciousness. We are constantly beckoned to act "as if," in the face of capitalist reality: as if capitalism is truly natural, as if our governments truly represented the will of the majority of the people, as if our actions have no larger impacts, or conversely, as if our individual actions are all that matter (e.g., "I'm not racist, therefore America is good," etc.). All of these elements of capitalist ideology—or more precisely, of the ideology of those who in capitalism are not themselves capitalists yet position themselves as supporters and defenders of capitalism—mold the experience and beliefs of its adherents into the dominant ideological form of capitalism. And this, in classical Marxist terms, is false consciousness: acting against one's own best interests to serve dominant interests.

On Some Common Criticisms of Marx

Up to this point, we have been concerned primarily with Marx on his own terms, and, with only a few exceptions, with treating his ideas in a generous sense to better understand the complexity and depth of his theory. It becomes necessary, however, to engage some common criticisms of Marx as a way of positioning my own use of Marxist concepts in the subsequent chapters addressing white racial identity and white supremacy, neoliberalism in teacher education, and elaborating an anticapitalist antiracist pedagogy. I will note that Terry Eagleton (2011) has written an entire book responding to common criticisms of Marx, titled *Why Marx Was Right*, in which he begins each chapter with a criticism and then responds. It is not my intention to cover every criticism of Marx, as this would likely require several additional books. Rather, I will here respond to three criticisms that, in my own working-through of them, have helped me formulate my own particular iteration of Marxism as I apply it both to my work as a scholar and as a teacher educator. The three criticisms are as follows: (1) Marxism is determinist and does not allow for agency; (2) Marxism is essentialist; and (3) Class is no longer relevant as a site for identity construction and political movement.

To respond to the first criticism, that Marxism is determinist and denies agency, we should first consider what Raymond Williams (1977) has argued in his *Marxism and Literature*, that "[a] Marxism without some concept of determination is in effect worthless. A Marxism with many of the concepts of determination it now has is quite radically disabled (p. 83)." Williams is calling attention to the need for both a conception of determinism but also for theoretical space and room for human actors to *act,* to engage in their world. For Williams, this can be accomplished by distinguishing two kinds of determinism, first, "the setting of limits," and second, the exerting of "pressures" (pp. 86–87).

When we consider the theory of determinism, we often approach it solely from the position of the setting of limits, of an outside force controlling and disabling human agency and what is possible. We should be careful, however, to make sure that we not lose sight of the very real processes that function this way. There are definite limits, not only physical, but political, social, etc., that are maintained both by brute force and coercion. Yet to totalize these, to reify the limitations imposed from without as what is meant by determinism, and then to claim that there is a deterministic character to Marxism would negate Marxism as an emancipatory project. Thus enters the exerting of pressures. A way of thinking about pressures is to imagine these as being exerted from the bottom up, whereas the setting of limits occurs from the top down. Pressures might include doing well in school (or not) depending on one's social context and community. What becomes important is that we understand that it is not solely the ruling elite who determine the life chances and outcomes for all, but that marginalized communities themselves have their own expectations for participation and membership. They also have the capacity to abolish the conditions that maintain their oppression.

Still, at the center of all of this rests the actual human actor, to whom Marx is never willing to deny agency. In fact, it is quite the opposite, as it is only through the *action* of a people, not merely thinking of but engaging in praxis, that societal transformation is possible. Eagleton (2011) sums this up well, remarking that we should understand Marx not as a determinist, but as a historical determinist who, rather than reading the events of recorded history merely as random, reads them instead as functioning with a particular shape and character. There is good reason he has very little to say about what a communist reality will consist of, because it has not been determined, but rather will be defined by the people who create such a reality.

Regarding the second criticism, Marxism is accused of essentialism typically in the following way: there are only two classes (or at least only two that matter for "history") yet reducing people solely to their class position denies their complexity as human actors. Thus, in this line of criticism, "proletarian" is an essentialist category. We can treat both this criticism and the third critique—that class is no longer relevant as an organizing principle for social action—with help from Teresa Ebert and Mas'ud Zavarzadeh (2007). They ask, Have poststructural critics become more worried about essentialism than about capitalism? Scholars such as Frederic Jameson (1991) and Stuart Hall (1997), according to Ebert and Zavarzadeh (2007), have conflated "cultural logic," in Jameson's terms, with the materialist logic of class.[9] These writers, and other poststructuralists,[10] have argued that developments in late capitalism have produced culture as a material reality and that consumption and production (of culture) are "no longer distinguishable" (p. 38). Everything, in other words, is now cultural. Thus, any claims at an objective universal reality are seen as culturally biased and essentialist. The collapsing of multiple or all cultures into a single framework, like the Marxist notion of class, functions to ignore cultural difference and thus essentializes all peoples into, in this instance, a Eurocentric conception of how our present society functions.

Such a stance, however, obscures the material ways in which class position (relation to the means of production) functions to produce culture. Of course, culture has and ought to have significant meaning for people. But to argue that culture has replaced class as the most impactful condition for peoples' material conditions works to normalize capitalism and capitalist processes as they impact both identity formation and a person's material reality. Ebert and Zavarzadeh reason that if this is the case, there is no need for any further discussion of anticapitalism, as the abolition of capitalism must be understood as a project that exceeds and exists outside of identity claims because class is an *objective* reality that cuts across cultures. They write,

> Class . . . is a property relation; this means class differences are produced at the point of production where surplus

labor is extracted from workers and not in the market. The market does not produce wealth; it simply distributes what is produced elsewhere, and the elsewhere is where labor power produces surplus labor. (p. xvii)

Ebert and Zavarzadeh thus work to show that class cannot be reduced to culture, and that such a practice, making class cultural, obscures the material relations of owners and workers. Owning a home does not make one a capitalist, but buying and owning the labor of others does. We cannot fall back on thinking of class as an attitudinal phenomenon (Eagleton, 2011) as though classism were what we were seeking to abolish. Marxism is not a critique of snobbery, it is a critique of the actual material relations that function to dehumanize. It is thus not essentializing to say that someone sells their labor in order to live if it is objectively true, and one's class position has little to do with how one feels about said class position.

Marxism in Postmodernity

Jorge Larrain (1995) has examined these and other poststructuralist criticisms of Marxism to develop a Marxist critique of poststructuralism as it functions in support of and alongside capitalism. He writes, of poststructural theory, "No other ideological form seems to be better suited than post[structuralism] to defend the [capitalist] system as a whole, because it makes of chaos, bewildering change, and endless fragmentation the normal and natural state of society" (p. 288). What poststructural discourse fails to acknowledge is that this chaos and fragmentation is brought about by market forces in the capitalist economy. That our reality has become more chaotic as it has become more capitalist does not disprove or discredit any of Marx's insights. In fact, it makes them all the more important. Larrain goes on,

What is new about neoliberalism is that it counts now on the post[structuralist] philosophical outlook as a powerful ideological ally which seeks to convince people that it is impossible for human beings to act politically with effect on society as a total entity . . . this is a most dangerous and insidious ideology which can only protect the interests of the ruling class (p. 288).

These are serious criticisms, and in some ways can be read, especially by poststructuralists, as a classical Marxist trope: anyone who disagrees with Marxists is on the side of the ruling class.

It is not my intention to make such a claim in this work, as I employ a number of poststructural insights in both my theoretical work and my pedagogy in teacher education classrooms, albeit in critical ways that seek to combat the tendencies in such work to normalize or naturalize capitalism. Rather, I wish to call the reader to reconsider what for many has become a taken-for-granted assumption in both social theory and in educational scholarship: that the existence of multiple cultures makes it impossible for us to make claims that are empirically true for all peoples across culture. I argue that we should heed warnings of essentialism and Eurocentrism that these scholars offer, but should not fall into the trap of thinking that because of cultural difference we can make no objective claims for material reality. I am calling for others to (re)engage with Marxism, not in order to become dogmatic but in order to rethink and reevaluate the dogmas we carry with us already.

The relevance of Marx for our work in the twenty-first century stems from his insights into the dynamics of capitalism that create the crises we continue to experience. It stems from his theorizations of commodity fetishism that we continue to misperceive, perhaps to an even greater extent than before, the social relations imbedded in every commodity. And it stems finally from Marx's insistence that regardless of our aspirations, we must begin from our present reality, from really existing women and men in specific contexts, in order to move toward one another in solidarity to transform our oppressive capitalist order and to realize true humanization.

The work of Marx reminds us, especially those of us committed to antiracism and other social justice efforts, of the constant influence of the economic base on social life. So often, particularly when we are discussing white supremacy and white privilege as they manifest in our contemporary experience and daily interactions, we find ourselves at a loss for a course of action. While we can identify privilege, we rarely have concrete answers to the relatively simple question, "What do we want white people to actually do?" If we constantly seek economic measures with which to understand oppression, we must not allow the economy or economic pressures to function as a taken-for-granted neutral system. Yet this is precisely what we do when we fail to appreciate the explicitly capitalist nature of white racial identity in the United States.

I now turn to an examination of white racial identity as it has functioned historically, to make these connections more concrete and to demonstrate how the maintenance of white supremacy functions to maintain the cultural logic of capitalism.

FOUR

White Racial Identity in the United States

A Conceptual History

History does nothing, it possesses no immense wealth,
it wages no battles. It is *man*, real living man, that
does all that, that possesses and fights. . . . History is
nothing but the activity of man pursuing his aims.
—*The Holy Family*

The purpose of commerce is not consumption, but the
gaining of money, of exchange values. This doubling
of exchange—exchange for the sake of consumption
and exchange for exchange—gives rise to a new
disproportion.
—*Grundrisse*

One could argue about the relative worth of whiteness scholarship, or, scholarship that seeks to better understand white racial identity and the ways in which the ongoing legacy of white supremacy continues to materially impact the lives of people in the United States. Like many disciplines before it, whiteness studies is moving into a kind of lost moment—the various conceptual stances taken up by many are incommensurable with others, yet all claim the same goal: to abolish white supremacy, to establish and

51

live out racial justice in profoundly humanizing ways. The ways in which one might live out an antiracist white identity, as a white person actively working against systemic racism, seem too numerous to list. Yet there are those in the field of whiteness studies that would argue that no white person, even one committed to social justice and actively engaged in antiracist struggle, is capable of not being racist, or of not being in racist ways. "All white people are racist," this logic goes. I work in this chapter to unpack such a stance through an examination of the history of white racial identity in the United States.

Some have reached the conclusion that all white people are always and will always be racist and advocated the "abolition" of the white race, wherein people we now deem as white would become raceless beings and people of color would be able to maintain their own racial identities if they so chose to (Ignatiev and Garvey, 1997).[1] Others might posit that because to be white makes one racist, we must abolish the structures and discourses of racism in order to live worthier lives, all the while knowing that we are incapable of living outside of these structures and discourses (Applebaum, 2011).[2] While these conceptions of white racial identity and antiracist action are detailed much more extensively in the next chapter, I begin in this way to carve out the terrain on which both this conceptual history and the critiques in the following chapter emerge.

More and more, it seems that most whiteness scholarship has given up on white people being able to live in ways that would reduce or end structural racism. Why is this the case? Why do I and so many other white educators feel they are incapable of living out their commitments to social justice given both the White Privilege and Race Traitor[3] theories of whiteness and white racial identity? How did whiteness studies reach such a state? And what new theories are necessary to make the prospect of living in worthy ways again possible to those of us who live and move in the world in white bodies, grew up in white homes, and culturally belong at least in part to a group we've historically imagined as the white race?

The next two chapters take up a selection of whiteness scholarship over the past thirty years to understand first the history of whiteness and white racial identity in the United States. How is it that people from across Europe became imagined as one race in the United States, and how did that race come to think of itself as superior? Next, I explore what this history can tell us about our present reality of whiteness by focusing on white racial identity. If whiteness is a standpoint, where is that standpoint and how have theorists come to conceptualize what "being in white ways" does to those engaged in the being? In a way, this chapter can be approached as a kind of literature review; however, I prefer the term *conceptual history* here to refer to this work. My aim in this chapter is to trace the origins, myths, and lived experiences of whiteness and white people in the United States throughout history.

The Juridical Construction of Whiteness in the United States

Famed American political scientist Rogers Smith (1997) offers what is perhaps the most concise way of understanding U.S. history with respect to whiteness and white supremacy. He tells us,

> When restrictions on voting rights, naturalization, and immigration are taken into account, it turns out that for over 80 percent of U.S. history, American laws declared most people in the world legally ineligible to become full U.S. citizens solely because of their race, original nationality, or gender. (p. 15)

His emphasis in this passage—on voting, naturalization, and immigration—offers a way into conceptualizing the historical literature on whiteness in the United States.[4] Much of Smith's statistic, that more than 80 percent of U.S. history has been characterized by racist, xenophobic, and sexist conceptions of citizenship, stems from a U.S. law passed in 1790, which declared,

> That all free white persons who, have, or shall migrate into the United States, and shall give satisfactory proof, before a magistrate, by oath, that they intend to reside therein, and shall take an oath of allegiance, and shall have resided in the

United States for one whole year, shall be entitled to the rights of citizenship. (referenced in Jacobson, 1999, p. 22)

Of course, the term *white* and its racial significance had a much older history of usage in what would become the United States, in the form of colonial laws that would eventually serve as the basis of state laws once the United States was established. These initial whiteness laws are where we can first see a legal basis, thus a material cause, for the cultural logic of white supremacy.

While they were significantly fewer in number than those of African descent, many of the first slaves in what would become the United States were people we would consider white today. Poverty often resulted in European men "indenturing" themselves to work as unpaid laborers across the Atlantic in the colonies for an agreed-upon amount of time. While the prospects for someone willing to sell themselves into slavery are difficult to imagine as any kind of "privilege," it is important to keep in mind that much of the origins of White Privilege stem from this aspect of the indentured servitude system: it was not permanent, and the children of indentured servants did not (automatically) become indentured servants themselves. Both of these elements of the indentured servitude system mark it as structurally different from the practice of enslaving Africans, who experienced a permanent form of slavery with the understanding that any children they had would also be enslaved (Lopez, 1997). A few more words about this dynamic are worth mentioning.

Virginia law, in 1662, declared that all children born of African American women who were slaves would inherit their mother's racial (and legal) identity. This law prevented children born of white male slave masters and black female slaves any possible claim to their white father's wealth, family, or racial privilege. It also marks part of the unique character of slavery in the United States: the eventual abolition of the transatlantic element of the slave trade, although it persisted much longer in Brazil.[5] These two critical elements, the practice of white slavery in the United States coupled with colonial race laws, provide us the clearest places to look in order to understand where our present conceptions of both white racial identity as well as white privilege come from.

In 1640, Massachusetts became the first colony to officially legalize slavery, despite its presence in many other colonies before officially becoming a part of colonial law (Lopez, 1997). Other colonies formulated their own laws to differentiate between slaves who were seen as "white" and those of African descent, and to differentiate how these slaves were to be treated. An example of such a law that was common across the South, where white and black slaves worked together, allowed white slaves to beat black slaves, but not the other way around (Thandeka, 2006). And in the course of these whippings, it was stipulated in the same slave laws that white slaves were not to be beaten with their shirts off, while for black slaves no similar right was available (Thandeka, 2006). Thandeka theorizes that these laws functioned to protect the interests of the white elite by creating a "psychological allegiance to the elite through abuse: the right to abuse those below them and a constraint on the abuse meted out by those above them" (p. 46). Over time it became clear that white slaves or servants were capable of becoming a kind of middle manager for slave owners, thus creating the positions that would eventually become institutionalized in state laws that mandated how many white workers must be present dependent on the number of black slaves on a particular plantation (Thandeka, 2006). After Bacon's Rebellion in 1676, an interracial rebellion along class lines involving free and enslaved black and white people, Virginia instituted even harsher slave codes with the intention of thwarting future cross-racial solidarity among slaves. This fear of cross-racial solidarity eventually led Virginia and the other colonies/states to stop importing indentured servants from Europe in favor of slaves from West Africa. Thandeka notes that by 1660 it had become more profitable to import slaves from Africa, as indentured servants were to receive fifty acres of land after their time of service. Black slaves, while they cost double the price of indentured servants, would live out their entire lives in bondage, as would all of their children, and thus as disease rates decreased and life expectancy grew in Virginia and the other colonies, black slaves made for a more lucrative long-term investment (Thandeka, 2006). These practices and racial laws were not repealed until the abolition of slavery two centuries later.

While the Thirteenth, Fourteenth, and Fifteenth Amendments to the United States Constitution abolished the legal codes that governed the treatment of slaves, and the laws that allowed white people the right to hold them, there remained legal protections for whiteness. Naturalization and citizenship requirements would not be amended until 1952 to include peoples not considered "white" (Jacobson, 1999). In fact, there was an explosion of explicitly race-based laws that followed the abolition of slavery in the United States, known collectively as Jim Crow.[6] Jim Crow laws enabled white people to segregate their neighborhoods, their schools, and their workplaces, as well as many other social spaces. These laws created what so many white people living in the United States claim to have experienced: a sense of distance from people of color, a result of the suburbanization and urban ghettoization processes of the post–World War II United States (see Jackson, 1987). Today, these same distancing processes are continuing in the complexities of gentrification and the resulting diversification of suburban cities close to urban centers, many of which are experiencing dramatic demographic shifts in their schools (see Gay & Howard, 2000; Lipman, 2011; Watkins, 2012 for more on how these phenomena impact schools). Other juridical constructs, such as homeowners' associations, zoning ordinances, and redlining, continue to function in ways that privilege whiteness and white peoples to the detriment of people of color.

It is of critical importance here to note that the origins of whiteness, as described above, do not begin by elaborating the "most esteemed race" and their "natural right" to wealth, a project far more common in white nineteenth-century social science on race, which I examine later in this chapter (Watkins, 2001). In fact, whiteness was invented to create a false sense of solidarity between impoverished white servants and their property-owning (both in land and human capital) white masters. By a false sense of solidarity, I mean that the material lives of white plantation workers (first indentured servants, and later paid middle managers) were actually far more similar to the lives of black slaves than they were to the white elite. Intended to thwart class solidarity, the initial whiteness laws in the U.S. have had a ripple effect still present today in the common practice in the United States of identifying first along racial lines, and only secondarily along class lines (Wilson, 1978). In order to undermine the class consciousness of white servants that might lead them to understand themselves as existing in solidarity with black slaves, as happened in Bacon's Rebellion, black people became slaves in a way white people could never be: because it was written into law. And later, in the nineteenth century, when the working conditions of poor whites still should have placed them in solidarity with black slaves, their meager wages and oppressive work schedules were always subject to comparison with those of black slaves and always found superior—at least they were being paid.

Sociohistorical White Racial Identity Development

Among the very first texts published in what has become the field of critical whiteness studies was David Roediger's (1991/2007) *The Wages of Whiteness: Race and the Making of the American Working Class*. Roediger tells us, early on in that work, that "[t]he white problem" is "the question of why and how whites reach the conclusion that their whiteness is meaningful" (p. 6). So positioned, whiteness for Roediger is a problem of meaning making, tied explicitly to class and economic relations. As part of his historical tracing of how European immigrants came to be seen as white over the course of the nineteenth century, we learn that much of white racial identity development among Northern industrial laborers stemmed from the ability of white working men to imagine themselves in contrast to two important nonwhite groups: Native Americans and enslaved African Americans. In comparison to Native Americans' purported "laziness," white men thought of themselves as hardworking, and this hardworking disposition was central to what it meant to be white. Always having the reality of slavery with which to compare one's own life and wages, white industrial workers would often evoke the imagery of slavery as they positioned themselves as "wage slaves" or even "white slaves" (Roediger, 2007). Importantly for Roediger, these stances were taken up not as a critique of slavery, but rather as a way of marking out a life for white workers that made them *racially* better, simply by not being black. Their low pay reduced them to the status of blacks, and this was the true injustice.

Roediger also troubles the commonsensical historical assumption that white working-class antiblack (racist) sentiment stems from job competition with African Americans. Instead, he found scant evidence of such a stance previous to the Civil War. Rather, what is far more interesting for Roediger, in order to understand white working-class racial identity, is the popularity among working-class white people of minstrelsy and minstrel shows. For Roediger, minstrelsy functioned to mock white aristocrats while also offering the opportunity to commiserate, in some ways along class lines, with black Americans. Emerging out of what had been African American festivals and performances, notably Voting Day celebrations; minstrelsy became a form of entertainment for white workers that functioned to diminish intraracial differences among whites. Their un-blackness became a unifying feature that collapsed European ethnicities into one homogenous white race. Caricatured and brought to life in front of them by other white men in blackface, the otherness of blackness functioned to diminish the racio-ethnic differences among whites. Minstrelsy accomplished this because of its ability to cut across ethnic, class, and religious lines. This was also precisely the desire of the Democratic Party of the time, which sought to unify Northern white workers and Southern slaveholders under one party with one central unifying principal: white blood, white entitlement, and white unity (Roediger, 2007).

It is from this conception of minstrelsy that we can best understand what Roediger means when he evokes W. E. B. DuBois's (1903/2005) notion that whiteness could function as a "public and psychological wage" that would work to legitimate low pay for whites while reinforcing white superiority. For DuBois, this was central to why white workers and black workers were incapable of reaching a class-based unity in the South to oppose their (mutual) white bosses. But Roediger takes DuBois's insight farther to argue that part of what this psychological wage accomplished, alongside minstrelsy, was a way for white workers to imagine black people as their (whites') former selves.

In immigrating to the United States, working-class Europeans surrendered past ways of being in order to make themselves more like white elites, who shunned working-class ways of being and living. These past ways of being, including such things as traditional festivals and celebrations and drinking alcohol at lunch, were surrendered in order to become *more* white, and the practices that were no longer sanctioned for newly whited European immigrants became stereotypes of black promiscuity and drunkenness. This surrender saw those elements of life that European immigrants felt they had to give up to survive in the United States inscribed[7] on the bodies of black people. Black people became what the white European immigrant secretly both despised, either in themselves or their former selves, and longed for (Ellison, 1995; Lensmire, 2011). Roediger (2007) concludes from this that "[b]lackness and whiteness were thus created together" (p. 95). Whiteness so created cannot understand itself absent what Toni Morrison (1993) has theorized as the "dark Other."

For Morrison, whiteness was invented out of blackness in such a profound way that one cannot imagine whiteness absent the presence of what she calls "Africanism." Morrison writes, "Africanism is the vehicle by which the American self knows itself as not enslaved, but free" (p. 52), and further, "Nothing highlighted freedom—if it did not in fact create it—like slavery" (p. 38).[8] Here we see Morrison's argument for the link between whiteness and white racial identity to blackness and both real and imaginary conceptions of slavery.[9] Freedom for Morrison is at the heart of what white racial identity meant for European immigrants, but she is diligent to continually call out the ways in which such an idea of freedom must be premised on an example of un-freedom in order to carry any meaning itself. Whiteness *needs* blackness, and a less free or un-free blackness at that, in order to understand itself as free. For Morrison, the white American preoccupation with freedom is a way of understanding the desire for slavery and the "life of regularized violence" against people of color that remains in place in our present era. In other words, for Morrison, white people need examples of what is not white in order to understand themselves as white, and in the white imaginary as detailed by Morrison through her analysis of (white) American literature, this need for violence is a need for reassurance in the white mind that the white self is what it claims to be: free, innocent, and good.

Even long after the abolition of slavery, there is still a need for white people to carve out the image of an "other" against which they can construct their own belonging and identity. While it is beyond the scale of my present argument and analyses, one can easily read into this the work of Michelle Alexander (2010) and the vast overrepresentation of people of color, especially African Americans, who are incarcerated in the United States. To this point, Alexander highlights the finding that there are currently more black people in prison than were enslaved just before the Civil War. She further documents the ways in which the War On Drugs has functioned to criminalize black men in particular (the other as criminal), and the ways in which the media perpetuates the notion of the black man as dangerous and criminal to legitimate the vast expansion (and profitability, for prison owners) of incarceration. We could thus claim, following Morrison's logic, that there is something about the white desire to understand itself as "free" that necessitates the maintenance of an un-free, un-white other from whom to arrive at self-definition through negation (i.e., "That is not me, therefore I am the opposite of the 'other,'" and so on). In other words, we still have an "un-free" racialized caste in our present era; the project of white racial identity formation is still premised on understanding itself as free, and thus on marking others as un-free.

The larger insight here, of whiteness being completely enmeshed with blackness, of whiteness being invented out of blackness and conceptions of the free and un-free, offers us a way of understanding another historical account of white racial identity that builds on this important point from Morrison. Matthew Frye Jacobson's (1999) *Whiteness of a Different Color: European Immigrants and the Alchemy of Race* serves as a welcome complement to Roediger's work. Like Roediger and Morrison, Jacobson is interested to understand how whiteness has come to be imagined and is shaped by blackness and conceptions of blackness. Extending his historical analysis beyond the nineteenth century, Jacobson finds that the main function of Jim Crow laws on European immigrants was to have a mass whitening effect on European ethnic groups who experienced "probationary whiteness." This probationary whiteness can be understood by considering the cases both of Irish Americans and Jewish Americans, both groups highlighted in Jacobson's analysis.

Both groups, on their initial arrival to the United States, were not yet white but emerged later as part of a larger conception of whiteness premised on the idea of nonblackness as the defining criterion for membership in the white race. Jim Crow served to make everyone who was not black white(r), which Jacobson shows by examining naturalization cases wherein people from the Middle East and East Asia sought to prove their whiteness (and thus fitness for legal citizenship) based on the premise that they were not black. For Jacobson, Jim Crow is the historical era wherein we can trace the declining significance for European Americans of locating themselves as descendants of a particular European ethno-national grouping. If the sign on the drinking fountain, or the immigration form, offered only two choices—black or white—the nuance of an identity such as German Catholic was minimized through the project of maintaining an apartheid system wherein there were only two social locations available. The various sub-appellations, if you will, of whiteness came to lose their social significance as larger historical organizing processes (such as main-taining racial segregation) collapsed all European ethnicities into one newly homogenized bloc: white folks.

Like Roediger, Jacobson sees minstrelsy as central to under-standing this whitening of Europeans' ethnicities. He theorizes that in blacking up, Jakie Rabinowitz/Jack Robin (a minstrel actor) becomes no longer "a Jew" but a white man playing a black man. With blackness as the ultimate contrast, white racial differences melt away, and minstrelsy is a site to understand how this process is possible.[10] Jacobson also spends time examining the invention of the Caucasian race and the ways in which the concept Caucasian came to be seen as more "scientific." As eugenics came to hold sway in white research on race, the need to legitimize and jus-tify a superior white race again functioned to mitigate differences across European ethnic groups. The great insight of Jacobson's work stems from his ability to demonstrate over and over again that, throughout U.S. history, whiteness has been imagined out of blackness, and that whiteness has had material benefits for those who have been able to successfully move from the status of "pro-bationary whiteness" into being a part of the white race.

The Science of White Supremacy:
Nineteenth and Early-twentieth-century Scholarship on Race

The invention of the term *Caucasian,* and its peculiarly enduring legacy,[11] represents a linkage between Jacobson's work and that of William Watkins (2001) whose text *The White Architects of Black Education* provides what is perhaps the most far-reaching yet eminently readable treatment of scientific racism and its impacts on education in the United States. Of particular interest to us here is his treatment of what he has termed "scientific racism," a term used to refer to many of the earliest studies in what would become the social sciences. We learn that the term *Caucasian* was actually coined by Johann Friedrich Blumenbach, in 1781, as he "considered White [*sic*] people as beautiful as the southern slopes of Mount Caucasus" (p. 27). Blumenbach, like others of his time such as the United States' own Thomas Jefferson, was convinced even before the theory of Darwinism that black people occupied an evolutionary place closer to chimpanzees and gorillas than to white people. Jefferson's use of the term "oranootan" to describe black men is evidence of such belief, and these racialized and white supremacist standpoints were brought into conversation and alignment with later insights in the social sciences drawn from Darwinism.

In the mid-nineteenth century the notion that black people actually were a separate and distinct species from whites gained traction. This view was held and written about by such notable scientists as Louis Agassiz and Samuel George Morton, both of whom held multiple degrees in biology and medicine respectively. The real import for latter social science research on race was that Agassiz and those that followed his methods and models came to conflate social traits with (so-called) biological traits. This led to conflating differences in culture, habit, intelligence, and ability with differences in physiognomy and biology (Watkins, 2001). It is here that we can see the origins of biological determinism that would prove to be the most pervasive racial logic to emerge entering the twentieth century. It is important here to call attention to the status of these researchers and the legitimacy such "studies" brought to the practices of white supremacy and slaveholding in particular. As Watkins shows, these "scientists" gave "scientific and medical legitimization" to white supremacist logics though "medical journals, conferences, and lecturers that embraced their themes" (p. 33). With the rise of Social Darwinism, these positions hardened, and more and more studies of everything from "skull size" to "hair thickness" were used to continually assert the dominance of the white race against all others. Social Darwinism provided the conceptual theory, and studies abounded to reaffirm the notion that white people truly were more fit for governance, civic participation, and the "good life."

Out of Social Darwinism emerged eugenics, a science that took the tenets of social Darwinism to heart in arguing for heredity as the cause of virtually every social characteristic. And scholars such as Francis Galton advanced the scientific bases for white supremacy even farther by adding mathematical and statistical analyses to underscore the findings that one could rank order races, and that social characteristics stemmed from biological inheritance. This sophisticated logic allowed white scientists to ignore every aspect of socialization. In the case of African Americans, slavery, lack of access to health care and adequate nutrition, and a host of other social factors we could list here were ignored as scientific inquiry was concerned solely with the ways in which genetic inheritance led to behavior and ability. Watkins points out that these "hereditarian" views of intelligence have endured, citing Herrnstein and Murray's (1994) infamous[12] The Bell Curve, which argues straightforwardly that black people have a lower IQ than white people and that this gap in IQ is the cause for racial inequity in society. These authors make these claims despite the many studies that have negated the biological determinist conception of race by documenting that there is more genetic diversity within any single race than across races (Watkins, 2001).

This "scientific racism" has had an enduring impact on white racial identity, an impact that many have failed to interrogate in whiteness studies of contemporary white populations. It is easy for us to argue that nineteenth-century studies that argued that hair density is a sign of intelligence is just an example of antiquated racism and move on. However, we must consider the impact of such work in context, that is, what it meant and represented to those for whom it was meant to be read, and what it meant in the history of the development of the social sciences. While this again points to a project that is larger than the scope of my present interest, white racial identity, we must be clear that these blatantly white supremacist studies were cutting-edge, peer-reviewed science at the time, and in many cases were some of the founding studies of the social science disciplines of anthropology, sociology, and psychology. Galton's legacy of bringing mathematic certitude to these studies, that is, bringing mathematic certitude to white superiority, cannot be overstated. While I will return to a critique of what the legacy of mathematical certitude and data-driven decision making means in the context of both pedagogy and teacher education more broadly, two points need to be made here. First, these studies allowed *reasonable* peoples to find white people superior to all others, or to find Native Americans and black people inferior, not out of hatred, jealousy, or contempt but purely in light of "data." While a white person may well have been able in the nineteenth century to recognize their co-humanity in the face of a black person, the science of the day was clear: they are fundamentally different, and whites are fundamentally superior. Second, these studies legitimized economic practices that relegated black people in particular to the lowest echelons of the economic hierarchy, both during and after slavery. Watkins's term for this is "accommodationism" wherein black people moved out of slavery but occupied the very same position economically as they had before. Scientifically informed white people *knew* that black people would not be able to "handle" their freedom as white people could, and they participated in creating educational and vocational accommodations that would slowly bring black people into the mainstream economic fold, knowing all along that this would never be fully possible given the innate differences in ability, aptitude, and personality that so much of the science of the day "proved."

Other Defining Historical Moments
in the Shaping of White Racial Identity

Up to this point I have focused almost exclusively on the formations of white racial identity in opposition to blackness, or to an invented "other" against which white people could compare themselves in their identity construction process. I have also been concerned primarily with the nineteenth century, which, while extremely important to our present reality of white supremacy as well as our present conceptions of white racial identity, remains incomplete if I do not highlight a few more defining moments in the shaping of white racial identity in the United States. I present them here in an effort to present other histories and narratives that operated and are operating alongside the white-black identity formation process detailed above.

In 1871, the U.S. federal government abolished the standing law that granted Native American tribes their rights as sovereign nations. This meant that what had previously been treated as indigenous land, which the federal government could not intrude on, became land for potential white settlement. As a part of the larger ideological project of Manifest Destiny, the recently victorious Northern armies in the Civil War were sent west to fight Native Americans, establish reservations and new laws surrounding Native use of their indigenous lands, and bring Native Americans under rigid structural control. Nowhere was this process more stark than in the institution of Native American Boarding Schools, in place in some areas until the early 1980s, that worked to systematically undermine indigenous ways of being, indigenous languages and epistemologies, and to bring Native peoples into a subordinate relationship to the larger capitalist project of the United States (Wallace-Adams, 1995). For many white people, Native Americans function as an "other" against which they can construct meaning and identity. The displacement of Native peoples and their enduring presence especially in the Western United States has created for many whites an additional group of people from whom they can differentiate themselves and understand themselves as "better off" (or just simply "better") by comparison.

The fastest growing racio-ethnic group in the United States are Latin@s,[13] who have experienced both in the past and present an immense amount of bigotry and oppression fueled by white supremacy. In the twentieth century, before 1954, more than 1.5 million "Mexicans" were deported from the United States. More than half were U.S. citizens, the bulk of them driven out during the Great Depression when competition for work was especially high. In our present historical moment of economic recession and high joblessness, we have seen again the very same process: deportation rates are up, in fact, 2011 saw the highest deportation numbers in history (Silverlieb, 2011) with more than 350,000 people kicked out of the country.[14] We can see here a clear example of how closely joined the aims of white supremacy and the capitalist economy are, a point that will be returned to in greater detail in chapter 5. For now, we can attribute the above to the following, albeit naive, conclusion: when competition for jobs is especially high, more people are deported. In terms of white racial identity formation, we can take from this once again an "other" against whom white people can imagine themselves in opposition. Latin@ peoples are increasingly scapegoated as responsible for the loss of jobs in the face of the current economic crisis. This scapegoating, as mentioned earlier, functions as an othering process that many white people participate in as a process of solidifying their own sense of self, their own sense of whiteness.

I provide these two brief examples to acknowledge the complexities of identity formation. While the historical content of this chapter has demonstrated the ways in which whiteness and blackness have become enmeshed with one another, the creation and maintenance of others is a process that goes beyond white and black peoples. In chapter 6 I return to the creation and maintenance of others in our present historical moment as a part of my discussion of the intersections of whiteness and nationalism. For the purposes of the argument of this chapter I wish only to suggest that while the primary other against which white racial identity is constructed is a black other, there are many other racio-ethnic others that white people can and do construct their identities from. Whiteness studies needs to do more work to untangle these complex processes and question the ways in which nonblack racial others function in the creation of white racial identities.

Whiteness as Standpoint: White Racial Identity Presently

Whiteness became a legal privilege before the United States was an independent nation. The laws surrounding whiteness, while shifting over time, have continued to give benefits to white people at the expense of people of color. Today we can think of examples of this in areas such as zoning laws, redlining,[15] gerrymandering, and the ways in which schools and school districts are assigned (Lipsitz, 1995). While no longer including the discourse of "whites only," we still live in a society beset with laws that work to privilege white people. But do these laws truly privilege all white people? This is the question that I will seek to answer next, but first we must understand how the history of whiteness and white racial identity presented here impacts our present conceptions of whiteness in our own historical moment in the United States.

Ruth Frankenberg (1993) defines whiteness early in her work *White Women Race Matters* as, "a location of structural advantage, of race privilege . . . a 'standpoint,' a place from which white people look at ourselves, at others, and at society. . . . 'Whiteness' refers to a set of cultural practices that are usually unmarked and unnamed" (p. 1). George Lipsitz (2006) similarly provides the definition of whiteness as "the unmarked category against which difference is constructed. . . . Whiteness never has to speak its name, never has to acknowledge its role as an organizing principle in social and cultural relations" (p. 1). This conception of whiteness, as a conceptual standpoint coupled with material advantage, has come to be the dominant way in which whiteness scholars approach the study of white racial identity and the ways in which white people live in and make meaning of a white supremacist reality. Thinking about how such an understanding of white racial identity is possible, it is helpful to better understand some of the more nuanced elements of these two and other authors' insights into white racial identity.

Returning to Frankenberg (1993), in her study of white women's conceptions of race and their own racialized identities, she notes that we can understand U.S. racial discourse in three moments: "essentialist racism, color- and power-evasiveness, and race-cognizant reassertions and reorientations of race difference" (p. 140). Here, the three moments move chronologically. First is a conception of race as biologically fixed and directly limiting agency based on racial dispositions and "natural" characteristics of a particular racial group. Here we can think of the nineteenth-century race theories discussed above as an example of biologically determined, "essentialist racism." The next moment is characterized by attitudes of assimilationism and accommodationism, historically emerging out of Reconstruction. We can think here of examples of this second moment in the sense that Watkins (2001) discusses as the goals for philanthropists in the creation of black education immediately following the Civil War. The aim of these "white architects of black education" was to gradually allow black people to improve their social condition, but in a way that would maintain the racial hierarchy and unequal access to power (p. 1). The third and final moment of race consciousness, which Frankenberg

(1993) credits the civil rights movement for cementing in our racial discourse, is her notion of reorientation of racial differences. An example of this discourse can be found in critiques of color blindness. In opposition to white people who claim "I don't see color," the reorientation of difference acknowledges skin color as a social reality and that such arguments for color blindness function to belittle peoples of color.

The most important insight from Frankenberg on these different moments, however, is that white people—in this case the white women who were a part of her study—have access to *all three* moments of race discourse and use all three at different times and in different contexts. Frankenberg notes, "The challenge in talking about white women thinking through race is capturing the correct balance between their 'entrapment' in discourse and their conscious engagement with it" (p. 140). She wants us to note here that while we can understand racial discourse historically, historical discourses that predate our present moment are still available to white people to use to understand and explain their own conceptions of race and racial identity. And as white people, we use all three all the time: believing in biological determinism ("they're just better athletes"), avoiding race-talk ("he's got dark hair and brown eyes"), and socially just inclusive language ("black men experience stereotype threat").

In many ways and, as Frankenberg notes for a number of her participants, many discoursal moves, the ways in which white people refer to people of color, function not so much as antiracist discourse but as face-saving strategies to avoid sounding racist. George Lipsitz's (2006) seminal work on the "possessive investment in whiteness" offers us further insight into the present state of structural racism and how individual white people's own attitudes and conceptions of racial oppression do not necessarily have structurally significant results. While the great success of Lipsitz's work is to document the concrete laws and practices that enabled the system of white supremacy to take shape, he is also successful in demonstrating how individual white people's attitudes about individual people of color cannot constitute the full extent to which we understand systemic white supremacy and structural racism. To this end, he writes, "Whites may or may not be openly racist in their personal decisions or private interactions with others, but

they nonetheless benefit systematically from the structural impediments to minority access to quality housing, schools, and jobs"
(p. 46). Put more simply, it does not matter if an individual white
person is racist or not, racism still exists at a structural level, and
thus we must not only engage individual white people but engage
societal structures as well to understand the full scope and scale of
white supremacy.

Lipsitz also offers us a powerful insight into the ways in which
the possessive investment in whiteness becomes attached to other
investments in identity among white people. In a compelling section titled "Whiteness and War," he shows the ways in which
Ronald Reagan as president was able to attach other "psychic and
material investments" to the investment in whiteness in order to
present an intersectional identity that would rely on the possessive
investment in whiteness in order to realize neoliberal and neoconservative aims. Specifically, Lipsitz tells us that Reagan was successful in locating whiteness alongside masculinity, patriarchy, and
heterosexuality. So positioned, Reagan was able to position the
civil rights movement, women's movement, and queer movements
as all anti-American—as threats to what made (white, Christian,
male) America great in the past, rather than pointing to capitalist exploitation as the cause for declining wages and rapid infla-
tion. For Lipsitz, most white people feel a kind of helplessness in
the face of corporate power and are encouraged by white elites to
"relieve the pressures of their lives by scapegoating people with
non-normative sexual identities, different religious beliefs, immigrants, and communities of color" (p. 116). We can see here direct
parallels to the ways in which white elites encouraged the possessive investment in whiteness by creating artificial privileges for
white slaves over black slaves (Lopez, 1997; Thandeka, 2006) as
well as the psychic process of scapegoating in minstrelsy (Ellison,
1995; Roediger, 2007).

What is most striking from Lipsitz's (2006) work, then, given
my historical tracing above, is that whiteness continues today to
be a tool of power for white elites in order to compel solidarity
among working-class white people with the owners of the means
of production who continue to exploit them. People of color and
other marginalized peoples are scapegoated, despised, and longed
for still today. This is central to understanding white racial identity,

and shows the ways in which the important historical work of critical whiteness studies remains central to imagining ways to mobilize white people for antiracist action.

To add further complexity to the current state of theory on white racial identity, Shannon Sullivan (2006) offers a Deweyan account of white racial identity as habit. Central to her work is the notion of "ontological expansiveness," which she locates as imperative to understanding the ways in which habit enables new insights into white ways of being. She writes, "[T]o be a white person means that one tends to assume that all cultural and social spaces are potentially available for one to inhabit," and further, "Instead of acknowledging others' particular interests, needs, and projects, white people who are ontologically expansive tend to recognize only their own" (p. 25). Thus, for Sullivan, being white comes with white habits and so an important element of whiteness scholarship should then be to uncover those habits to find ways in which white people can "unlearn" ways of being that do violence to people of color or that maintain oppressive systems. While she is careful not to locate all white people as being ontologically expansive, her larger notion of white habits and the difficulty in being able to stand outside of and away from one's own habits in order to understand them is an important caution to white people committed to social justice. She provides us with the troubling insight that the extent of systemic racism might be that it is *in* us as white people in ways that we are as yet incapable of knowing.

Katerina Deliovsky's (2010) work in *White Femininity* also showcases the complexity of white racial identity, and here she argues that whiteness is an explicitly masculine system of power and control. Deliovsky asserts that white women are caught in a double bind: they are privileged in race and oppressed in patriarchy. These intersectional systems of oppression, and the intersectional identities that they are caught up in, for Deliovsky, rely on "compulsory 'white' heterosexuality." She writes, "What it means to be a 'good girl' within European family relations is oftentimes connected with issues of compulsory 'white' heterosexuality and racial solidarity" (p. 58). In other words, part of what it means to belong to one's family, in the case of white women, is to present one's self in heterosexual ways that do not create tension with notions of (hetero-patriarchal) white racial solidarity. Further, Deliovsky theorizes that it is by participating in racism that Europeans prove they are white, or at the very least are able to "climb the white ladder by defending whiteness" (p. 68). Part of this defense, for white women, is to be docile feminine "good girls" in the eyes of their fathers and to not cast doubt on the relative whiteness of their families. Whiteness in this instance is then seen, as Lipsitz (2006) sees it, as an investment. But importantly for Deliovsky, it is something that can be understood as contested for those Europeans experiencing Jacobson's (1999) "probationary whiteness." White women thus must behave in a certain way or else risk undermining the work of their families to be white.

Emerging from these works, taken together, is a conception of whiteness as contested terrain, as possessive investment, and as caught up in competing historical discourses that do not move neatly in linear fashion but rather are reappropriated and reinvoked in moments of crisis or in moments where "probationary whiteness" becomes visible. Certainly each of these theorists agrees that whiteness entails a form of privilege, but importantly in each of these cases this privilege is relative and caught up in multiple systems of meaning that can serve at times to enable opportunities while simultaneously closing off others. The instability of whiteness and white racial identity become clear in these accounts, something that much of the whiteness literature in teacher education seems to not have paid sufficient attention to (Lensmire, 2011). I believe the primary cause of the inability of so much whiteness theory in education to adequately acknowledge the complexity of white racial identity stems from two of the leading schools of thought in whiteness studies: Race Treason and White Privilege.

FIVE

The Impossibility of Whiteness

On White Privilege and Race Treason

The individual considers as his *own* freedom the
movement, no longer curbed by a common tie or by
man, the movement of his alienated life elements, like
property, industry, religion, etc.; in reality, this is the
perfection of his slavery and his inhumanity. Right has
here taken the place of privilege.

—The Holy Family

Today the man who has nothing is nothing, for he is
cut off from existence in general and still more from a
human existence, for the condition of having nothing is
the condition of complete separation of man from his
objectivity.

—The Holy Family

"White complicity," defined by Barbara Applebaum (2011) in
her book *Being White, Being Good*,[1] is the claim that "white people, through practices of whiteness and by benefitting from white
privilege, contribute to the maintenance of systemic racial injustice" (p. 3). This claim, that all white people are complicit in the
perpetuation of white supremacy through their benefitting from
white privilege, serves as the primary analytic insight from which
she elaborates a "white complicity pedagogy." From the earliest
pages we learn that Applebaum is interested in understanding how

it is that even well-meaning white people—"good" white people, to use the book's title—are complicit in perpetuating racial inequity. She is interested in showing how our present conceptions of responsibility fail to capture the depth of the white complicity claim, because they are overreliant on "modernist" conceptions of guilt for wrongdoing that an individual has consciously done. She thus argues that our present theories of responsibility fail to adequately take account of white complicity and the ways in which whitely ways of being, regardless of intentions, reproduce white privilege and structural racism.

I begin this section by discussing Applebaum because I am convinced that without both the White Privilege and Race Traitor theorizations of white racial identity and white supremacy, her project would not be possible. Applebaum does not set out to prove that all white people are complicit in the perpetuation of structural racism. Rather, this is the point from which she *begins* her analysis. Understanding both the Race Traitor and White Privilege claims thus becomes imperative in order to grasp the conceptual work Applebaum is doing and what her theorization of white racial identity means for white people committed to social justice. Further, in the spirit of Freirean Critical Study, we must examine her first point of departure: that all white people are always already racist.

In the subsequent sections of this chapter, I first delineate the theories of both Race Treason and White Privilege before providing a synthesis of what will be shown through the subsequent tracings of these theories: that both misunderstand the causal relation between privilege and oppression, and thus fail to provide a comprehensive praxis for white antiracism. Finally, I offer my own pedagogical theorizing of contemporary scholars of color who have put forth what can be considered a more generous (and pedagogical) account of white racial identity. If our true aims for antiracist work with other white people are genuine—if the purpose of whiteness studies scholarship and theorizations of white racial identity is actually to mobilize white people for antiracist action—then we must find ways in which the material realities of white supremacy can be understood, theorized, and acted on in order to transform our present reality. The stakes are truly this high, as any white person who has struggled to answer, "I know I have privilege, but what do I *do*?" can attest. This is a more sophisticated question than it may first appear, and I will return to this "problem of enactment"[2] later on.

Race Treason: Abolishing the White Race

Whiteness studies in general have struggled, according to Moon and Flores (2000), to articulate a "liberatory whiteness and/or white identity" (p. 99). Another way of putting it is this: the field of whiteness studies is divided on what such an identity would rest on, how it would know itself as liberatory. For the Race Traitors (see Ignatiev, 1999; Ignatiev & Garvey, 1997), any inkling of an identity that considers itself white is unavoidably a problem, and should be resisted, as Race Traitors advocate, instead, the "abolition of the white race." Drawing largely from Marxist and historical analyses of whiteness, typified by Ignatiev's (1999) *How the Irish Became White* as well as from the now defunct journal *Race Traitor: Treason to Whiteness Is Loyalty to Humanity*,[3] the Race Traitors believe that we will never be able to realize racial justice until the white race no longer exists. Rather than seeing racism, or even the social construct of race as the primary causes of structural white supremacy, my reading of the Race Traitors is that they instead believe that it is the white race, as such, that is the cause of racialized injustice.

In place of positioning themselves as white, Race Traitors advocate an identity of being nonwhite, some even going so far as to advocate the appropriation of "blackness" or black ways of being to distance one's self from participation and membership in whiteness (Moon & Flores, 2000). The Race Traitors advocate such a position because of their belief that whiteness and the presence of whiteness are incapable of ever imagining a positive white way of being in relation to people of color. In fact, it is precisely the *white* character of white ways of being that cannot ever be brought in line with commitments to justice for all peoples, regardless of race. Whiteness simply cannot exist, if there is ever to be racial justice. White people must cease to become white, this logic goes, so that once there are no longer white people there will no longer be white supremacy. An example of this can help. In the first-ever

issue of *Race Traitor*, in an article dubbed simply "Editorial," with
no authorship credited, we learn that what white people need to do
is to cause difficulty for those who enforce our socioracial logics
and laws (police officers, in this example) to know who is or is not
white. The "Editorial" reads,

> But if enough of those who looked white broke the rules of
> the club to make the cops doubt their ability to recognize a
> white person merely by looking at him or her, how would it
> affect the cops' behavior? And if the police, the courts, and
> the authorities in general were to start spreading around
> indiscriminately the treatment they normally reserve
> for people of color, how would the rest of the so-called
> whites react? (reprinted in Ignatiev & Garvey, 1997, p. 13)

"Breaking the rules" here refers to white people asking police officers why they are only getting a warning when being pulled over,
or other ways of calling attention to racial injustice and the various
ways white people typically avoid harsh treatment in the realm of
law enforcement. A possible suggestion is to have a bumper sticker
that reads "Avenge Rodney King" (p. 13).

Race Traitors celebrate John Brown—at one point in the "Editorial" he is referred to as "the transcendent John Brown"—as the
model for white abolitionism. Brown is known in U.S. history for
his unsuccessful raid on the federal armory at Harper's Ferry in
1859, a raiding party composed of both white and black people
seeking to overthrow the regime of slavery through armed insur-
rection. Brown is perhaps most celebrated in the Race Traitor's
theory because of his belief in armed rebellion, and of course the
fact that he was a white man who stood in utter opposition to the
ruling ideology of his time: white superiority, black inferiority,
and the racial hierarchy that allowed for and enabled slavery. The
authors of the "Editorial" believe that "a new Harper's Ferry is
being prepared. . . . When it comes, it will set off a series of trem-
ors that will lead to the disintegration of the white race" (p. 13).[4]
The Race Traitors' desires for action, for white people to actively
"break the rules" of whiteness, cannot be questioned.

Such a stance toward white racial identity, and to antiracism more generally, can be a potentially powerful practice and

positioning for antiracism, as demonstrated by the educational-
ists Zeus Leonardo (2004) and Christine Sleeter (1995). We must
understand a white racial identity project that is just a few years
older than Race Treason (the first issue of *Race Traitor* came out
in 1992), White Privilege, to understand fully the need for the new
abolitionism. After summarizing White Privilege, I work to theorize both projects by calling attention to what they share in their
fundamental assumptions about oppression, privilege, and white
racial identity.

White Privilege: Unpack Your Knapsacks, Racists

In a mediated culture that constantly portrays white people as
heroes, as affluent, or even simply as normal, we can and must
acknowledge the ways in which most white people are the beneficiaries of at least some form of racial privilege. In much antiracist
writing on the concept of white privilege and the divestment of
privilege (see Case & Hemmings, 2005; Lawrence, 1997; McIntosh, 1988; Wise, 2008; 2009) white people are imagined as indi-
vidually benefitting from the history and present reality of white
supremacy, now understood and presented as white privilege. This
shift, from white supremacy to white privilege, can be thought of
historically as a result of the "official" juridical end of sanctioned
white supremacy with the civil rights legislation of 1968. Once de
jure segregation and discrimination had been outlawed, however,
de facto segregation and discrimination followed in its wake. The
new importance of zoning, redlining, and homeowners' associations in protecting racial discrimination and access to services took
on a new guise: white people experienced privilege in a society
that still felt very much as though it was set up to maintain white
wealth, interests, and ideals.

Peggy McIntosh (1988), who coined the phrase *white privilege*
and first elaborated the contents of this privilege, wrote:

> I see a pattern running through the matrix of white privi-
> lege, a pattern of assumptions which were passed on to me
> as a white person. There was one main piece of cultural
> turf; it was my own turf, and I was among those who could

control the turf. My skin color was an asset for any move
I was educated to want to make. I could think of myself
as belonging in major ways, and of making social systems
work for me. I could freely disparage, fear, neglect, or be
oblivious to anything outside of the dominant cultural
forms. (p. 3)

McIntosh elaborated privileges[5] that she felt she received as a white
person that her friends and colleagues of color did not. She was
moved to examine these privileges after reflecting on the ways in
which her male colleagues often distanced themselves from culpability in maintaining sexism and patriarchy. She felt these men were
unaware of their "male privilege," of the ways in which society
rewards men to the detriment of women and men's ability to not
think about issues of gender and gender discrimination other than
when they elected to do so. She then worried that she was doing
the very same thing with regard to race, and about her own relative
racial privilege in a society as beset with white supremacy as it is
with patriarchy. Thus, the now classic list of privileges came into
existence, and the concept of White Privilege has been central to
work in the field of whiteness studies ever since.

McIntosh's initial whiteness text, "White privilege and male
privilege: A personal account of coming to see correspondence
through work in women's studies" contained a list of forty-six
privileges McIntosh believed she received in her daily experience.
While she is careful in her work to call attention to the ways in
which racism is a structural phenomenon that cannot be reduced
solely to the level of individual white actors, it seems that far more
often whiteness work that mobilizes McIntosh focuses on the list.
My first experience with McIntosh, in fact, included only her list
of privileges, containing twenty privileges taken from the original text. I was in a teacher education course, in my first year of
undergraduate work, and after we went outside and lined up we
were instructed to take one step forward if the privilege read by
the instructor applied to us. We each evaluated the statement and
then reacted, with the white students, especially the white male
students, taking more steps than the students of color. At the time,
I remember thinking that McIntosh was right, and that I had a
great deal of privilege.

In subsequent years, McIntosh's work has spawned an entire conference, The White Privilege Conference, held annually, where "1,500 [people] attend from more than 35 states, Australia, Bermuda, Canada, and Germany" (White Privilege Conference official website). Her work has also led to the SEED (Seeking Educational Equity and Diversity) professional development program wherein thousands of teachers have taken up critical examinations of curriculum and pedagogy in the context of systemic oppressions. In the academic literature on whiteness, Ladelle McWhorter (2005) perhaps puts it best when she writes, "No thorough overview of Whiteness Studies ever omits reference to Peggy McIntosh's article 'White Privilege: Unpacking the Invisible Knapsack' (1989)" (p. 545). A Google Scholar search of this article's title produces 2,980 results, seemingly proving her point that one cannot talk about whiteness without McIntosh and her list of privileges.

I wish to make clear, before proceeding, that McIntosh and the Race Traitors should be commended for their work in advancing not only the field of whiteness studies, but for their work to carve out the terrain of antiracism in the face of white supremacy. While my criticisms that follow are direct and at times biting, we should celebrate those who have devoted considerable time and energy to combatting white supremacy, both in their writing and in their lives. Thus, I wish to position myself in solidarity with these projects, and offer the following as a critical interrogation that seeks to advance this work farther with a new conceptualization and attention to praxis in antiracism.

White Privilege and Race Treason: Misunderstanding Oppression

For me, the essential flaw in the Race Traitors theory is this: whiteness is not something individual white people are capable of manipulating. Lipsitz (2006) has demonstrated this with his discussion of the differences between most white people's intentions and the presence of structural racism. He writes, "Whites may or may not be openly racist in their personal decisions or private interactions with others, but they nonetheless benefit systematically from the structural impediments to minority access to quality housing, schools, and jobs" (p. 46). Regardless of belief or intention, white people are themselves caught up in the cultural logics, discourses of power, signs and frames of domination present in the very phenotypic edifice of whiteness. And each of these things makes individual actions to "rid one's self of whiteness" more than impossible because whiteness does not exist on the individual body but on the collective bodies of white people, a shifting and complex cultural as well as racial group (Applebaum, 2011). That is, while whiteness is indeed a possessive investment (Lipsitz, 2006), it is not an individual investment but rather a collective and communal investment in the ways Deliovsky (2010) showcased in her example of "good white girls." Whiteness and the logics of white supremacy operate both inside and outside of individual white people. Addressing only one will not eliminate the other. This is how multiple forms of whiteness and white ways of being are possible (remembering Sullivan's (2006) notion that not *all* white people are necessarily ontologically expansive): the ways in which white people internalize and act on the externalized reality of white supremacy vary. At the same time, if we are to understand whiteness as something we can both recognize and understand, we must ask how both an affirmed and committed white supremacist and an affirmed and committed socially just white person can still be understood as manifestations of the same racial group, how they are both *equally* white.

In the simplest sense, the signifiers of white domination are carried by all white people: in our hair color and texture, the shape of our facial features, the clothes we wear, and so on. Whether or not we are on "the side" of people of color, we look like those who seek to do them harm even in our present reality. And so we are left with an impossibility that white scholars of whiteness seem to insist on repeatedly: that white people become "good," if for no other reason than to be able to locate one's self outside of and away from the "bad whites" who are committed white supremacists. Confessing one's own racism has become a kind of trope in whiteness scholarship authored by white academics, as if in calling themselves out as imbued with racism or as beneficiaries of white privilege there might yet be conceptual space for them to exist in a way that decouples them from complicity in whiteness (Applebaum, 2011). Such a move, of white authors calling themselves racist, does little more than serve to position them as "good" in the sense of the newly reimagined ways in which to be a "good" white person is to confess one's own racism.

The worthy elements of the Race Traitor position rest on their understanding of whiteness as an overarching system, as a process of meaning making and power in a raced society. The notion of abolishing this system is worthy if one understands whiteness as a systemic reality responsible for the exploitation and oppression of people of color. This position is mistaken, however, as whiteness does not exist solely as power, but rather as a signifier of power. Whiteness reinforces the colonialism, imperialism, and capitalism of those who created and lived out (live out) the realization of these projects to gain immense wealth from the subjugated masses. Yet it was not whiteness that gave rise to capitalist exploitation, nor the capitalist enterprises of the transatlantic slave trade, colonial expansion by Europe to the rest of the world, and so on. Whiteness did not invent the desire for wealth; it enabled the justification for the realization of this desire to be concentrated in ways that would protect the powerful and position those in power as more like some than others.

Educationalist John Dewey made a very similar observation in a speech he delivered in 1922 in China with the title "Racial Prejudice and Friction." There, he argued that race "is a sign, a symbol, which bears much the same relation to the actual forces which cause friction that a national flag bears to the emotions and activities which it symbolizes, condensing them into visible and tangible form" (as quoted in Sullivan, 2006, p. 35). Sullivan goes on to explain this point, and Dewey's theory of racial friction, in more detail. She writes,

> The actual forces causing friction are political and economic. Race prejudice, or the aversion to people who are of a race different than one's own, do not cause the friction in one's relationship with them. Race prejudice instead is the effect of that friction brought about by other causes. (p. 35)

In this formulation, then, race stands in as a sign for "political" and "economic" conditions, and racial prejudice stems from attributing these conditions with the sign of race. We read race in others, and infer meaning in relation to the political and economic realities that undergird our interactional experiences with others. Whiteness, then, functions as a sign for political and economic realities—but it does not fully encapsulate these conditions, or explain them in any rich detail. It merely stands in for, takes the place of, the complex material conditions of systemic white supremacy.

Abolishing whiteness without the abolition of the systems that created it will not result in a more just reality. It is essential here that we keep in mind, again, the point from Hardt and Negri (2000), discussed in chapter 2, that "[t]he end of the dialectic of modernity has not resulted in the end of the dialectic of exploitation" (p. 43). In other words, we can and must understand oppression (exploitation, in Hardt and Negri's terms) dialectically: wherein the part and whole, the master and slave (to use the famous Hegelian example), oppressors and oppressed are understood as calling their opposites into being. This move, of understanding oppression dialectically, enables one to understand that rather than attempting a theoretical departure from whiteness, its "abolition," we must understand that oppression is not contingent on whiteness or white supremacy to function. Whiteness and oppression are not dialectical opposites; abolishing one will not result in the abolition of the other.

Rather, oppression, understood dialectically, consisting of the Freirean (2000) oppressors and oppressed, allows for a radical solidarity the Race Traitors seek across present racial lines. This solidarity cannot come about through the abolition of whiteness, however, because such an abolition is only possible if that which is signified by whiteness were to be abolished. The only way to abolish whiteness would be to abolish its meaning, its functioning referential power, something that is impossible to do through discourse absent a radical redistributive ethic of justice and solidarity that cannot be located and legitimated by our present conceptions of race as such, race on its own, in a de-historicized vacuum. Our possessive investment is too great, and the stakes too high.

It is as though the Race Traitors believe we have already arrived in a moment of radicalism where race itself is pliable enough to be reformulated. Such a moment would require that virtually every social code would be capable of being reformulated on the side of justice. This cannot happen until that which is signified by whiteness (e.g., oppression, colonialism, and private ownership) is abolished, and while the rhetoric of the Race Traitors contains evidence of such a project, their conclusion remains incapable of realizing the world they imagine.

When we examine McIntosh (1988) and her list of forty-six privileges, which she elaborates as evidence of the ways white people experience white privilege, what we see is that despite her efforts to contextualize white supremacy and structural oppression as systemic realities, the operationalization of antiracism in this schema rests solely at the individual level. That is, white privilege reduces whiteness to actions and benefits for white people *as individuals* rather than understanding white supremacy as an ideology of collective oppression, as a scapegoating project to protect the material wealth of white elites (Lipsitz, 2006). This logic is assuming something about whiteness' essence, the nature of whiteness. It assumes that at a fundamental preracist level white people are/were good and that racism and racist ways of being and speaking in the world are something that has been internalized by white people in order to safeguard (at times consciously, at other times unconsciously) their own relative privilege and power. But Applebaum (2011) makes clear that the white complicity claim does not allow any white person to not support structural racism, because they are the beneficiaries of privilege whether they like it or not. All white people have privilege, is the fundamental tenant of the White Privilege discourse. Whether or not all white people have *the same* privilege does not seem to be a worthy question.

Yet white privilege is not what gave rise to the transatlantic slave trade, colonialism, Japanese internment, and the myriad other examples we could list here of brutal racist acts by white peoples in recent history. Rather, white privilege is an *effect* of structural oppression and the enduring legacy of white supremacy. Leonardo (2004) engages this by offering his own list of white supremacist events throughout history to call attention to the need for not only an interrogation of white privilege and individual manifestations of said privilege, but also to the systemic reality of white supremacy. His fear is that in focusing solely on white privilege, we lose the historical understanding of the causes of this privilege. Still, he tells us in the article, he believes McIntosh and her list of privileges represent an important entry point for white people to learn about whiteness in contemporary society. He even shares that he continues to teach with her "Invisible Knapsack" piece. This work, while representing an important insight into the limits of white privilege as envisioned by McIntosh and others who follow in the line of white privilege theorizing about whiteness, fails to interrogate the inherent problematic in starting somewhere other than the beginning—in maintaining that the idea of white privilege must function as a kind of gatekeeping mechanism a white person must pass through before being able to understand, or even examine, the history of white supremacy and the role of race and racism within the larger phenomenon of oppression.

We can make this critique more visible with explicit examples. The privilege of whiteness was not what led white Virginians in the seventeenth century to stipulate what kinds of beatings slaves could legally receive based on race, as discussed earlier (Lopez, 1997). Rather, fear of cross-racial solidarity among slaves led elite whites to create specific laws to differentiate between slaves of African descent and those of European descent. These elite whites were able to create laws to guarantee their privileges as owners of capital, both human and monetary. But it was not their privilege that enabled them to completely dominate the lives of those whom they owned. Rather, it was their power, sanctioned by law. The privilege of being able to make and enforce such laws existed outside of whiteness in its initial iteration. It was brought into whiteness as a project of ideological coercion, to obscure the causal and originary roles of power, wealth, and entitlement. Homogenizing all white people into a group of oppressors functions, perhaps more than anything else, to mystify those social actors who created, enabled, and profited from the system of white supremacy to the point that one can only refer to all white people as upholding and maintaining the racist regime we presently experience. For those who consciously created and maintain this system, this is a profoundly useful means of control—obscuring the culprits, making all white people guilty and thus, none of them.

This final point can be explained further with a turn to the work of Hannah Arendt (1987) and her critique of "collective responsibility" in the case of the German people after the Holocaust. Arendt is worried here that a logic that argues that "everyone is guilty" quickly slips into "everyone is equally guilty" and thus obscures the actual wrongdoers to make them indistinguishable from everyone else. She writes of this point, that the cry of

We are all guilty . . . has actually only served to exculpate to a considerable degree those who actually were guilty. Where all are guilty, nobody is. Guilt, unlike responsibility, always singles out; it is strictly personal. It refers to an act, not to intentions and positionalities. (p. 147)

While it is, of course, problematic to extend theorization regarding Nazis and Nazism to white people in the contemporary United States, we should take seriously the similarity between the claims advanced by both Race Traitors and White Privilege discourses that all white people are complicit in the maintenance of white supremacy. If all white people are racist, using Arendt's logic, then we will be unable to differentiate between committed white supremacists (whom I often refer to more vernacularly as "old-school racists") and white people who harbor no ill will toward people of color but simply exist in social space as white. While this fails to answer the question of whether or not all white people are racist, it does showcase the political problematic of blaming all when some clearly have done more harm. In fact, this is precisely the kind of logic that White Privilege brings to bear on white slaveowners in seventeenth-century Virginia: making all white people guilty for the crimes of a powerful but small subset of white people makes it much harder to identify those who are actually most responsible.

And the logic of privilege in particular functions in the same way. If all white people have white privilege, this quickly slips into all white people have equal privilege, once again obscuring the difference between those who maintain power and control through racist practices and attitudes and those other white people who do not find it difficult to buy hair care products or to see themselves represented positively in history books. Those who are not oppressed, or perhaps those whose oppression is manifestly less severe than others, receive the relative privilege of not suffering or suffering less than others. To call white slaves who were able to keep their shirts on while receiving beatings "privileged" hardly seems appropriate, yet this is precisely what the logic of white privilege would have us believe. The criterion for racial privilege in much of McIntosh's (1988) work appears to be simply determining whether one's life is relatively less marred by oppression than racial others. And so, in seventeenth-century Virginia, white slaves who were able to keep their shirts on for beatings were more privileged than black slaves who could be beaten on their bare backs. Does such a privilege, which importantly in this example comes with beatings regardless of race, constitute a meaningful entry point for mobilizing white people for antiracist action in the twenty-first century?

White privilege, as an idea or logic, fails because it overemphasizes privilege itself rather than the cause of privilege. Or better put, rather than what privilege symbolizes. We can see here a similar kind of logic to that exercised by the Race Traitors: the advocacy of the abolition of a piece of whiteness still rests on the notion that whiteness is the cause of that which we seek to end. The kinds of privileges white people receive are imbued with the various other systems of meaning in their lives, contingent upon their subject position in relation to society. To elaborate the ways in which a white woman is privileged, to ask her to do this as antiracist action in and of itself, leaves out the intersectional ways in which she is both privileged and marginalized in a society as imbued with racism as it is with patriarchy (Deliovsky, 2010). Her race may well place her in league with the dominant and powerful, but her gender places her in solidarity with all other women in ways that cut across both race and class.

Whiteness as sign, as referent, is unidirectional[6] regardless of an individual white person's standing in the spectrum between committed white supremacist and committed socially just white actor. Whiteness always symbolizes power, dominance, privilege, and at times normalcy.[7] There is no preracist white person; white people were invented (imagined) out of racism, so the logic of both the Race Traitors and White Privilege advocates goes. Thus, changing what white means, whether it is in the divestiture of privileges or in renouncing one's own whiteness completely, these projects are incapable of moving us forward toward justice because they are manipulating the wrong thing. It is to the signified of whiteness—the nature of dominance, power, and privilege—that we must turn our attention as committed white actors engaged in the pedagogical and political work of becoming more fully human and seeking justice in our world (Freire, 2000). We must make not whiteness itself, but that which whiteness has enabled historically and continues to enable, a thing of the past. Specifically, we must abolish white supremacist logics that protect the material interests of the extremely wealthy at the expense of the great masses of humanity. In the United States presently, the richest four hundred people have more money than the bottom 150,000,000 (Moore, 2011). This present reality of radical economic inequity was not created by whiteness, even though people whom we now understand as white created it and continue to benefit most from it.

While causal arguments are always difficult to make, especially in theoretical or conceptual discourse, it should appear clearly here that privilege is not the cause of oppression, but rather an effect. Privilege is one of the effects of oppression, and we could list many others here: dehumanization, discriminatory logics and practices, loss of past ways of being and belonging, and so on. Privilege deserves to be treated alongside these other effects of oppression, rather than singled out as the defining character of white racial identity and the primary means by which white people and others can work against structural white supremacy. We must shift our gaze beyond privilege, to find the truly heinous thing lurking behind it, oppression.

To conclude my discussion of both the Race Traitors and White Privilege advocates, we can return to Applebaum (2011) as a recent example of the mobilization of these discourses in theoretical research on white racial identity. Beginning from the stance that all white people simply by being white receive privilege and therefore perpetuate structural racism serves to attribute so much power to whiteness that it reduces the complexity of white identity to a conception of white people merely as embodied privilege. Whiteness scholar Timothy Lensmire (2011) sums up my fears of what such a starting place means for our endeavor to mobilize white people for racial justice. He writes,

> White people are racist, down deep. But the deep down is not monologic or finished. We ignore this complexity and conflict at our own risk—at the risk of failing to see openings to concrete work that we can do as individuals and groups to combat racism; at the risk of slowing rather than accelerating educational and political efforts for social justice. (p. 115)

I now turn to authors who are re-theorizing white racial identity in powerful ways that "accelerate" our efforts for social justice by providing an account of whiteness that sees white people as more than merely embodied privilege, while accounting for the very real material privileges whiteness has historically enabled for white actors.

A More Generous Account of White Racial Identity

The Reverend Thandeka, a Unitarian Universalist minister, offers what is perhaps the most striking critique of white privilege; as demanding confession from white people for the original sin of racism. Thandeka (1999), in a speech delivered to the Unitarian Universalist Association General Assembly, shares how the belief that "all white people are racist . . . no black people are racist" and that "whites must be shown that they are racists and confess their racism" is tied to the biblical story of Adam:

> Through Adam's sin in the Garden of Eden human nature was corrupted—a doctrine linked to the Trinitarian claim that only through the death of Jesus and with the assistance of the cleansing work of the Holy Spirit can human nature be saved. In every age, Christian theologians have found new language to explain this doctrine. The antiracist doctrine is just such a recent example.

What Thandeka is referring to here as "antiracist" can be seen as existing in direct lineage to McIntosh's (1988) conception of white privilege and the subsequent growth of a literal economy of antiracist speakers, workshops, programs, and conferences. Thandeka sees all of this work as actually hindering real material progress toward ending racism and oppression. Instead, she told her assembly, "The simple truth is that most middle-class white persons, including UU's, are not part of the economic ruling elite in this country. They have not amassed structural power and control. Our UU antiracist rhetoric, however, claims that they have." She concludes with the example of Dan, a white man.

Although he is not a racist, Dan might make a confession of racism to a UUA antiracism trainer because this would be the only way to mollify the trainer and also because racism is the only category he would have to express a far deeper loss and regret: his stifled feelings and blunted desires for a more inclusive community.

This move on the part of Reverend Thandeka, of calling out Dan's "stifled feelings and blunted desires," references theorizations of white racial identity that have been largely absent from theorizations of whiteness by scholars in the Race Traitor and White Privilege traditions.

David Roediger (1998) reminds us that the first scholars of whiteness and white racial identity were African American writers and philosophers. There, in works by those such as Ralph Ellison (1995), we find accounts of whiteness that do not hide the details of the brutality of torture and murder known as lynching. But we also find an account of the pain of living in such a way, of living with lynching as spectacle, as part of a cultural and racial act of solidarity among whites, and yet against their own conscience, their humanity. Whiteness scholarship has largely ignored any account of what white racial identity means to white people on a psychosocial level. That there can be pain in those who are seen as only privileged is a radically humanizing thought. It requires that we think of white people first as human beings, and only secondarily as caught up in the systems of cultural meanings and discourses known as whiteness. This is precisely what Thandeka (2006) accomplishes in her book, *Learning to Be White: Money, Race and God in America*.

Thandeka (2006) begins her book with stories in which white adults recount the moments when they first realized not only that they were white, but also that there were expectations of them from their parents to *be* in certain ways in order to keep their parents' love. Examples include a young boy who invited his friends who lived next door to join his birthday party and later learned that he had somehow made a mistake, because his parents were uncomfortable that the friends were black. Or a young woman who invited her favorite teacher home for dinner with her parents, who were shocked that the man was black and made her feel she had done something wrong by not telling them his race before. These are examples of what Thandeka theorizes not (only) of racism, but of intrawhite racial abuse, leading to white shame.

Thandeka's conception of shame stems from the recognition of brokenness (a concept complemented by Jansen (2008; 2009; discussed below). She writes, "[T]his self [a white self in a white supremacist society], seeing its own brokenness, feels shame" (p. 108). This feeling of shame, Thandeka argues, is a critical piece of what it means to be white in our society. White shame entails certain emotive responses, resulting from the "failure of the self to live up to its own ideals" (p. 108). In other words, moments when young white people revert to excluding others based on race in order to keep their parents' love—which means the same thing in this theorization as maintaining membership in their own racial group—and thereby produce the feeling of shame. Further, she writes, "the feelings of shame-filled dejection, apathy, and depression have been brought on by the self's failed attempt to live up to its own notion of an *ideal self*" (p. 108; emphasis in original). For Thandeka, once we find ourselves in this state in which we cannot reconcile the demands of participation in whiteness and choose in opposition to it, we cannot help but feel shame. This shame stems from the portion of ourselves, she tells us, that is, "not 'theoretically white'" (p. 75), the portion of ourselves that has been abused and made white by "adult silence to racial abuse" (p. 24). We are broken as we learn what it means to be a part of white society, breaking becomes almost a rite of passage that we can never speak of, for if we did, we would be returned to this moment and state of our own shame.

Thandeka's work is especially powerful in addressing the pervasive notion of "white guilt" that so often manifests in discussions of whiteness, particularly among white people who believe, many from past experiences, that the purpose of such discussions is to make white people feel guilty. Thandeka's theory of white shame responds to this sentiment in a powerful way. She writes, "Guilt, by contrast with shame, is a feeling that results from a wrongful deed, a self-condemnation for what one has done . . . shame results not from something one did wrong but rather from something wrong with oneself" (p. 13). We experience guilt when we have actually done something, and on reflection we feel guilt when we deem that act to have been wrong. The oft-cited resistant white person's trope of "but my ancestors didn't own slaves" is a response to a failure to disentangle guilt and shame. If we are asking white people to interrogate what it means that people who looked like them owned other human beings the way one might own a car today, we should not be surprised when the resulting conversation centers around notions of guilt, and why this guilt feels like the wrong reaction, given the very likely truth of the claim that no one in their family ever did own slaves. Simply saying, "This isn't meant to make you feel guilty" does not actually get us away from guilt. Rather, what is needed is an alternate descriptor that accounts for the genuine feelings of being flawed, and Thandeka's conception of white shame does precisely this.

We feel shame when we recognize the moments when we, as white people, have had to choose to maintain the love of our white family members at the expense of solidarity with marginalized others. The test for this process is very easy, and I have asked this question many times at the various lectures and talks I have delivered on white racial identity and white supremacy since first encountering Thandeka's work. I ask those in attendance to raise their hands if they have ever not called attention to a racist or otherwise offensive act or speech act for fear that their relationship with the offending party would suffer. Inevitably, every hand goes up.

This account of shame is complimented by Freire's (2000) contention that, "As the oppressors dehumanize others and violate their rights, they themselves also become dehumanized" (p. 56). In other words, there is a certain giving up of one's humanity in the act of oppressing another, which we can imagine in much the same way as Thandeka has elaborated in her concept of white shame. There is an important point to make about placing these two theories, dehumanization and shame, side by side in this manner. Neither Freire nor Thandeka is interested in demonstrating in any way that all white people are actively oppressing racial others. What they are interested in accomplishing, however, is to show that in the act of confronting one's ideal self and recognizing one's own failings, one is dehumanized and feels shame. In many ways, Thandeka's account of shame provides new insight into pedagogical opportunities to mobilize white people for anti-racist action by providing a richer account of Freire's conception of dehumanization in the form of white shame.

The notion of dehumanization, of not being fully human, is a point of entry into South African scholar Jonathan Jansen's (2009) notion of brokenness as central to the experience of what it means to be white in a white supremacist society. Jansen compels us to approach others as broken as part of a pedagogical project he has called "post-conflict pedagogy." This pedagogical stance—that is, approaching white people as able learners, as agentic beings—again serves as an important elaboration of the links between Freire and Thandeka. If we can imagine the demands of critical pedagogy[8] as the basis from which we ought to understand white people, what new insights into white racial identity might become available?

This was Jansen's (2009) interpretive stance for his work in Pretoria, South Africa, to understand the white racial identity of white Afrikaners who came of age after apartheid. From his time as the first black dean at the University of Pretoria, Jansen uses the personal stories of his experiences working with Afrikaners to theorize both the present state of white racial identity and how we can mobilize white people for antiracist action. For Jansen, this is possible based on our present state of brokenness. He defines brokenness as "the idea that in our human state we are prone to failure and incompletion, and that as imperfect humans we constantly seek a higher order of living. Brokenness is the realization of imperfection" (p. 269).

Among examples of this realization he offers first the story of a poor white father who breaks down in tears as he confesses he does not have the money to pay for his daughter's tuition at university to become a teacher. Jansen shares that this was the moment when he recognized the Freirean conception of the ways in which our humanity is caught up in the humanity of others. He was able to recognize the likeness between himself and the two white people in his office. Likeness in this moment stemmed from recognizing a moment of vulnerability, a moment of brokenness that was shared by all involved. For Jansen, such moments reveal our true humanity because they bring us closer to one another through the shared experience of brokenness in the face of our oppressive reality. This recognition is essential to Jansen's pedagogical and political project of reconciliation in South Africa, but the insights are important to understanding whiteness in the U.S. context as well.

When we take each of these three theorists' concepts together—Thandeka's account of white racial identity formation coupled with her theorization of white shame, Freire's concept of dehumanization, and Jansen's ideas of brokenness—we are left with a much different conception of whiteness and white racial identity than those of the White Privilege or Race Traitor theories. We find the human consequences of oppression in Thandeka, of living in systematic oppression and knowing that we are conflicted in allegiance, and that as a result we feel shame. Much the same way that Roediger (2007) discussed the ways in which European immigrants had to surrender pieces of their cultural (then seen as ethnic) heritage in order to become white, white people today who do not harbor white supremacist beliefs are broken by their own failure to live up to their ideals in the face of structural white supremacy. Even as Amanda Lewis (2003) is right to point out that we have race inscribed on us from our very earliest days on earth, with our racial group printed on our birth certificates, we must also connect the plight of the European immigrant and the plight of the young white child. Both sacrifice wholeness to become white. And becoming white means living with shame.

Putting It Together: What a Generous Account of White Racial Identity Enables Pedagogically

For the past few years, I have spent a great amount of time thinking about the profundity of a quote from the Reverend Harvey Johnson: "The white race cannot tell when they began to be known as such" (as quoted in Roediger, 1998). In some ways, I imagine the field of whiteness studies to be attempting to answer this challenge one hundred years after it was first issued. But rather than think about what the Reverend Johnson meant in terms of what we ought to be researching historically, I choose to read this quote as a pedagogical call. We need to help white people better understand how it is that they are white, how such a thing was/is possible, and what it means for them to live out their commitments to other human beings. Demanding that, before we can do any of this, these white people must find evidence for and confess their own racism, flies in the face of critical pedagogical commitments to honor the knowledge learners bring with them to their work in classrooms. In this way it is possible, if for no other reason, to reject the Race Traitor and White Privilege discourses simply on pedagogical grounds. It is conceptually impossible for me to honor the humanity of my students if I cannot imagine them as anything other than racists. And for this reason, in addition to those I've detailed above, it becomes imperative that we elaborate a theorization of white racial identity that accounts for the material causes and effects of white supremacist capitalist hetero-patriarchy (hooks, 2003) in ways that do not overly determine the pedagogical outcomes of antiracist work with white people.

Jansen's (2009) argument for the need for a pedagogical stance that entails a conceptual and political crossing "towards one another" becomes one such way of better understanding the stakes of and need for a theory of white racial identity capable of allowing room for those white people who seek social justice to both understand themselves and the conditions under which they struggle. We must include in any theory of white racial identity the ways in which white people experience relative racial privilege. But we cannot allow ourselves to think that this is truly what makes them human beings, as if white people are *only* racist. And if we are willing to concede that white people are human beings, we must then ask how is it that we can begin the pedagogical task of learning about whiteness and oppression so that we can mobilize people whose commitments to antiracism are sometimes profound, so that they can live out those commitments in powerful ways. How else can we live and teach critically in humanizing ways?

Whiteness scholars in education need to be reminded what it is they believe students are capable of in P–12 classrooms in comparison to how they conceptualize their own students. Karen Lowenstein (2009) showed evidence for this in her work to review the literature on multicultural teacher preparation of white teachers. She found that the research has assumed and promoted a deficit lens, wherein young white women are depicted as deficient learners about diversity. If our present theorization of white racial identity leaves us unable to imagine our white students as capable, I would charge that the pedagogy that follows such a disposition is not living up to its humanizing potential.

Summing Up

The above tracing of the theories of Race Treason and White Privilege, followed by the more generous theorizations of white racial identity formation, can be summarized and positioned as a series of problems. Here I present these problems with brief summative comments to underscore the arguments presented above.

First is the problem of individualizing collective experience. If we demand a conception of systemic racism and structural white supremacy as global phenomena, we cannot reduce these complex systems to individual manifestations by individual actors. White privilege fails over and over again to mobilize white people for anything other than confession, because at the level of the individual, confession is quite literally all they can do to address their individual cases of relative racial privilege. Confession comes to function as the antiracist act itself, and lends itself to the second problem.

The second problem is one concerning solidarity, and how a white person is imagined as being able to work against racism. For Race Traitors, this person must cease to be white for their work to have transformational value and meaning. The white person must, with other formerly white people, abolish the white race, and thus be fully on the side of people of color. But of course such a project is untenable, because regardless of political standing or beliefs about people of color, white people have experienced a simultaneous whitening and homogenizing in the context of the United States after Jim Crow. This point can be made more simply: white people from the United States are not European, but still do have a culture. And this culture cannot be reduced solely to racism, as though white people were only racist. White people must struggle for justice as white people, with all the complexities and contradictions that entails.

The third problem is the relationship between privilege and oppression, or what the target for antiracist work with white

people ought to be. Both White Privilege advocates and Race Traitors locate whiteness (which can be read as synonymous with white
privilege here) as the cause for the unjust treatment of people of
color. But whiteness, as was illustrated in the previous chapter, was
a concept invented to legitimize oppressive conditions and generate wealth and power; not the other way around. Scientific racism follows the practice of slavery; it did not invent it, but rather
sought to legitimate white supremacy after white supremacy had
already come into existence. Thus, asserting that whiteness as such,
or privilege as such, is the cause for injustice completely ignores
the history of white racial identity formation in the United States.

Fourth, and finally, is the problem of mobilizing white people
for antiracist action. Declaring all white people always already racist represents a pedagogical orientation that is steeped in a deficit
frame. That is, white people are seen as deficient at race relations
or multiculturalism, rather than as learners who bring their own
experiences and knowledges to the project of working against
white supremacy. We often make the mistake of treating white
people who have little experience thinking through issues of race
and racism as resistant racists, rather than as learners. We would
never fault someone who had not taken geometry for not being
proficient in their first efforts in a geometry course; why do we
insist on faulting white people for not being proficient in their
first efforts to understand what it means to be white in a white
supremacist society and what this means for them as social actors?
My answer to this question is that many antiracist educators, and
especially advocates of White Privilege and Race Treason, have
failed to approach white people pedagogically. That is, as learners,
with resources for their learning and a desire to understand their
world in sophisticated and complex ways.

There are many more scholarly accounts and theorizations of
white supremacy and white racial identity that are not featured
here, and of course additional problems that I have failed to detail
in this summary. And while it is important to never stop theorizing our reality and the context in which we struggle for justice,
I would argue that studying whiteness for the sake of studying
whiteness is largely empty work. And if one's theory of whiteness
is incapable of mobilizing white people for socially just action, or

makes one incapable of engaging with others in humanizing ways, then we ought to reject it for those reasons alone.

I have attempted here to lay out a conception of white racial identity that honors the history of whiteness and white supremacy, as well as the complex realities of white racial identity and racial privilege. I have argued against theories that I see doing more harm than good for the cause of racial redistributory justice. It is my hope that such work enhances the critical project of mobilizing white people for antiracist action.

SIX

Whiteness, Nationalism, and Neoliberal Capitalism

It may seem peculiar, in this relation between labour and capital, and already in this first relation of exchange between the two, that the worker here buys the exchange value and the capitalist the use value, in that labour confronts capital not as *a* use value, but as *the* use value pure and simple, but that the capitalist should obtain wealth, and the worker merely a use value which ends with consumption.

—*Grundrisse*

The separate individuals form a class only insofar as they have to carry on a common battle against another class; in other respects they are on hostile terms with each other as competitors. On the other hand, the class in its turn assumes an independent existence as against the individuals, so that the latter find their condition of life predetermined, and have their position in life and hence their personal development assigned to them by their class.

—*The German Ideology*

Mitt Romney, the Republican Party candidate for president in 2012, makes for an excellent entry point into understanding the intersections of whiteness, nationalism, and neoliberalism in our present political reality in the United States. The first presidential

99

election in the Tea Party era saw someone whom many viewed as an "establishment" Republican figure win over the vast majority of his party, Tea Partiers included. Romney's primary campaign strategy, repeated many times in stump speeches across the country, celebrated his record as a businessman, and argued that what the United States needed most was a president who would govern like a businessman. A sampling of this rhetoric will suffice to make the point, taken from a speech on August 14, 2012, in Chillicothe, Ohio:

> I spent twenty-five years in business, and I know what it takes for the private sector to create jobs. I know why jobs go away, what it takes to bring them back, and what we must do to make America the best place in the world for entrepreneurs and innovators and job creators. My five-point plan will bring more jobs and more take-home pay for middle-class Americans.

Again and again, Romney referenced his experience in business as what made him the most viable candidate, and from the *Wall Street Journal* to the U.S. Chamber of Commerce, businesses seemed to agree that a businessman in the White House was what was needed. Of course, the "private sector" spokespeople—business owners, executives, and managers—have good reason to support a candidate who supports their positions. But what about the masses who supported Romney who were not at all a part of the capitalist elite? Why did they want a businessman in the White House?

It appears that in recent years the role of the president, even the entire purpose of government, has shifted into advocating for U.S. global financial interests. Obama emphasized the role of small businesses seemingly just as often as Romney during the campaign; both candidates positioned their views on education in explicitly economic terms,[1] along with rhetoric on the increased "competition" facing the United States. These phenomena are indicative of what critical theorists have dubbed neoliberalism.

Neoliberalism can most easily be understood as the application of business logics to those areas of society that are not businesses themselves. Emerging out of the post–World War II era of pro-business expansionism and anticommunist efforts, neoliberalism

[v]alues competitive markets and the freedom of individual choice within them, and devalues governmental or cultural attempts to redistribute resources or accountability. Thus, it often manifests in policies that reduce governmental regulation of trade, increase the privatization of public services, and support the growth of businesses. (Kumashiro, 2008, p. 36)

Organizations such as the International Monetary Fund (IMF), the World Bank, and World Trade Organization (WTO) can all be seen as advancing neoliberal aims of "fiscal austerity, privatization, market liberalization, and governmental stabilization" with the aim of advancing the growth of capitalism (Kumashiro, 2008, p. 36). In neoliberalism, market-based logics become neutralized as "common sense," areas of society previously deemed public become private, and the needs of the economy are placed above any and all other possible needs of a society. Thus, in neoliberalism, we should not be surprised that the role of the president has become likened to the role of the CEO, and that the primary charge of the government is to support and protect the growing of the economy. This is, in ideological terms, how one can understand the Wall Street bailouts, the logic of "too big to fail," and the ways in which the U.S. president is evaluated largely on economic terms, on whether or not he grew the economy.

But to understand the particular ways in which whiteness, nationalism, and neoliberalism coalesced around the figure of Mitt Romney, we need to examine the historical formation of the Tea Party in the runup to Romney's candidacy and eventual loss to Obama. We must also, however, develop a theory of nationalism and the intersections of race and nationalism in particular, to develop this theory fully. Thus, in this chapter, I provide a brief historical tracing of the Tea Party's formation before reviewing the theoretical literature regarding nationalism and racial identity. After returning to the Tea Party to demonstrate the processes of nationalist and racialized inclusionary and exclusionary practices, I place Romney's candidacy in relation to former Republican presidential candidate Pat Buchanan's (2011) work in his *Suicide of a Superpower*.[2] Buchanan positions the Republican Party as "The White Party" and decries the loss of "traditional American values" in light of the shifting demographics of the United States, which will lead to white people no longer constituting a majority of the population in the coming decades. In this chapter, then, I attempt through the example of Romney and the Tea Party to demonstrate the ways in which nationalism, whiteness, and neoliberalism are constantly shaping and reshaping one another. This will provide a national context for subsequent chapters that deal explicitly with education.

The (Almost Entirely White) Tea Party

On April 15, 2009, the date federal income taxes were due in the United States, thousands of people across the country gathered to protest against the Obama administration in light of the economic recession, which had (and continues presently) seen millions of people lose their homes and jobs. The protesters referred to the various gatherings as "Tea Parties," a historical reference to the prerevolutionary Boston Tea Party, which saw white Bostonians disguised as Native Americans sneak aboard a British trade ship and dump tea into the Boston Harbor to protest against the colonial British government. The Tea Party Protesters, or Tea Partiers, as those who participated in the tax day and subsequent rallies, campaigns, and elections have come to be called, comprised 18 percent of the U.S. population according to a *New York Times/* CBS poll published in the *Times* on April 14, 2010. That same poll "found that only 1 percent of Tea Party supporters are black and only 1 percent are Hispanic. It's almost all white" (Blow, 2010).

The supporters of the Tea Party movement "tend to be Republican, white, male, married and older than 45" (Zernike & Thee-Brenan, 2010). Further, "white Tea Party supporters are twice as likely as white independents and eight times as likely as white Democrats to believe that Barack Obama was born in another country" (Blow, 2010). The Tea Party protesters, at the height of their activism, carried signs bearing slogans such as, "Don't spread the wealth; spread my work ethic" and "I Want My Country Back!" But there were also signs and slogans bearing openly racist sentiments, such as, "The Zoo has an African lion and the White House has a lyin' African," featuring a picture of a male lion. Clearly such an association was intended to call attention to Obama's blackness, his "Africanness" as central to his depiction as a liar. African people are liars, is the message communicated through such a sign. There has in fact been so much critique of the Tea Party movement's racist discourse that one more recent Tea Party sign read, "It doesn't matter what this sign says, you'll call it racist anyway" (Buchanan, 2011).

Of course, that a group is almost 98 percent white does not necessarily make that group a white supremacist organization. In fact, the main motivation for Tea Party supporters is the belief "that the policies of the Obama administration are disproportionately directed at helping the poor rather than the middle class or the rich" (Zernike & Thee-Brenan, 2010). Still, if a group who is organizing on principles of U.S. nationalism as well as class solidarity is being accused of racism, we need to attempt to understand not only what those claims mean for the movement, but also what they mean for the very construct of nationalism in the United States. That is, we need to ask not only about Tea Party supporters, but also about nationalism itself in the United States and the relationship between whiteness, white supremacy, nationalism, and capitalism.

On Nationalism and the Nationalist Need for Racial Others

The formation of national identities, and of nationalisms, is extremely complex and far more varied than a simple deterministic understanding based on citizenship in a nation-state would lead us to believe. Puri (2004) writes, "National identities do not have any inherent essence, but are defined in opposition to another" (p. 15). There can be no national identity possible if there are not exclusionary processes available to distinguish insiders from outsiders. To illustrate this, one need only think of a simple binary: either you are one of us, or you are not. There can be no national identity without those who are outside the nation to demarcate insiders from outsiders. While this point will be elaborated further pertaining to the creation and maintenance of both internal and external racial others in the United States, it is important to understand the various others against which a national identity may be constructed.

Aminzade (2013) writes, "Although *all forms* of nationalism are xenophobic to some degree in that they entail exclusionary boundaries distinguishing citizens from foreigners, the forms and targets of exclusion vary considerably" (p. 25; my emphasis). In fact, there are many categorical identities against which a given nationalism may create its other. Xenophobic responses to others' sexual orientation, gender, social class, and religion have created and maintained various facets of nationalism that seek to maintain the "otherness" of the national outsider as well as a sense of homogeneity and cohesion in the national body (Calhoun, 2004; Puri, 2004).[3] That all national identities must be formed and maintained in response to real or perceived others means that inherent to any form of nationalism is the tendency to exclude. To expand on this point even further, without exclusionary processes there would be nothing to keep national identities bounded. Just as nation-states create artificial political boundaries to demarcate their own territory from others', so the same process works ideologically in nationalism. And just as international borders are policed and protected, so too are the borders that demarcate belonging to the nation.

We can thus understand nationalism and the formation of nationalism as a process whereby some national identities are constructed in opposition to others, and not, as much of the rhetoric of nationalism would have us believe, in reified traditions likened to kinship and descent (Calhoun, 2004). While lineage and family history certainly inform nationalism, one's national identity is forged moreso by those who are excluded from the nation than by those who actually exist within it. The United States is an ideal case to help understand this point. As the product of a nation that emerged from colonialism with a wide variety of ethnic groups from myriad backgrounds and cultures, U.S. nationalism could not rely solely on primordial histories to solidify the national body. While the war with Great Britain by which the United States gained its independence and became a sovereign nation has become a watershed in a "widely remembered past," it created the impetus for defining U.S. nationalism as anti-British (Calhoun, 2004, p. 33). That is, the foundation of U.S. nationalism stemmed from its opposition to the competing nationalisms of those who were still loyal to the British government as colonial citizens (internal others), as well as the British soldiers and government (external others). Part of the task of understanding nationalism as a process of inclusion and exclusion is also to understand that those who are included and excluded in the national identity shift over time. Thus, the history of the U.S. War of Independence can be remembered today as a simple binary of us against them, when in fact "us" was far from being one single unified group.

Nationalism and race thus intersect in myriad ways across different contexts. Manzo (1998) writes, "Nationalism may invent, ignore or dissolve racial boundaries. . . . But nationalism is racial when it treats permanent difference . . . as alien, threatening, and a problem to be solved" (p. 19). Manzo believes that nationalism cannot exist without the "twin concepts" of nation and alien and that these two concepts inform one another in any and all nationalisms. Colonialism and colonial legacies are largely responsible for the salience of race in nationalisms, even to this day (Winant, 2001). We can understand this in the context of the United States if we position white plantation owners as colonial masters, who forged a false sense of solidarity between themselves and European servants to prevent cross-racial unity along class lines in the era of slavery. Colonial race relations often created multiple races, and subsequent postcolonial nationalisms often are forced to reconcile (invented) racial hierarchies and the same processes of nationalism that they struggled against during colonial rule.[4] While racism and white supremacy were part of colonial legacies, the creation and maintenance of the racial other has become a central animating concept in nationalisms from Rwanda (Mamdani, 2001) to Australia (Manzo, 1998), and of course here in the United States (Morrison, 1993). A question that remains unanswered, however, is the role racial others actually play in nationalisms.

To this end, A. W. Marx (1998)[5] tells us that in the case of the United States, "Institutionalizing common prejudice against blacks reinforced white nationalism" (p. 12). He theorizes that intrawhite conflict, in this case rather oversimplified as referring to that between Southerners and Northerners in the Civil War era of the United States, necessitated legal responses to create and maintain a racial other in order to build intrawhite solidarity. White conflict can be reconciled if whites can agree on the subjugation of some-one who is seen as nonwhite. The important differences between blackness and whiteness, in this case, are utilized to remind whites of their shared identity.

The effects of such processes, for A. W. Marx, are twofold. First, solidarity is built among competing white groups. This can take the form of groups of European immigrants appropriating white discourse and acting to oppress people of color out of defer-ence or allegiance to the white collective, which they are attempting to join through participating in the maintenance of white suprem-acy. The very presence of nonwhite racial others has a whitening effect on all those who are not clearly part of the subordinated racial group, as was discussed in chapter 4. The Jim Crow South whitened everyone who could not be considered African American in a simple racial binary system where laws only applied to whites and blacks, creating only two possible identities (Jacobson, 1999; A. W. Marx, 1998). The second effect of the process of institu-tionalizing oppression against a racial other, however, is that the marginalized other also is able to build unity in response to the institutionalized oppression. In the case of the United States, black unity was built on opposition to state-sanctioned white suprema-cist laws at the same time that white unity was built on maintaining said laws.[6]

Whiteness and nationalism thus operate in tandem to accom-plish primarily two things: to maintain the racial hierarchy and thus race-based solidarity, and to maintain national identities that will sustain nationalisms through the maintenance of racial others. In the context of the United States, African Americans represent an internal other against which whites construct their identities and thus know themselves to be white. As the state has an interest in maintaining its own power, conflicts among powerful social actors must be mediated, and the ideology of nationalism coupled with the racial ideology of white supremacy operate side by side to pre-serve the status quo. That is, with commitments to the nation built on whom the nation excludes as well as a racial identity defined by those who are not a part of the racial group, whiteness and nationalism can become so deeply entangled that it can be dif-ficult to tell where one ends and the other begins. Jim Crow can be understood as a solidarity-building and reconciliatory move, allowed by Northerners to persist in the South in order to maintain white cohesion. We can understand this in terms of nationalism and the need to protect the state from further conflict, and we can also understand this in purely racial terms: a white supremacist society legislating the oppression of people of color. However, it should appear clear that to treat Jim Crow as solely racial or solely nationalist misses the extent to which whiteness and nationalism overlap, intersect, and inform one another.

It becomes impossible to tease whiteness and nationalism apart in the context of the United States because of the overwhelming similarity between the two concepts. Both create others against which identity formation takes place. Both maintain solidarity by exclusionary practices preventing others from being included in the group. Both are historical creations, authored by human actors to serve particular political, cultural, and social demands. And finally, both are constantly being reinvented and renegotiated to accommodate shifting desires and needs.

The Tea Party Movement's Whiteness and Nationalism

If the racial other against which whites in the United States have constructed their identity (Morrison, 1993) now occupies the White House, it is not hard to imagine the visceral pain some white people are feeling. Surely Obama's presidency, and now his second term in office, means that something has truly changed about what it means to be a "real" American, and thus, who they are. Despite the clearly white-supremacist implications of such thinking, my reading of whiteness earlier must be theorized alongside the Tea Party movement to understand not only the racial context of the movement, but also the extent to which the Tea Party movement is a response to forces far greater than the individual participants who populate the protests.

To accomplish this, it is useful to start with a specific example of Tea Party discourse:

Dee Close, a 47-year-old [white] homemaker in Memphis, said she was worried about a "drift" in the country. "Over the last three or four years, I've realized how immense that

drift has been away from what made this country great,"
Ms. Close said. (Zernike & Thee-Brenan, 2010)

In this short description and quote, we can actually see the ways in
which nationalism and whiteness coalesce in the Tea Party movement. Namely, Ms. Close is harkening back to a time that has
passed when this country was "great," presupposing that this is
no longer the case. She uses a very vague term, "drift," to explain
what has made the country no longer great, and also points to just
the last "three or four years" in which the fall from greatness has
seemingly taken place. If we contextualize this individual woman's
statement with larger national processes in the time frame she is
talking about, since 2006, we can point to the midterm electoral
victory of Democrats in the United States Congress as the potential cause of the "drift" Ms. Close is worried about. Zernike and
Thee-Brenan (2010) write, "While most Americans blame the Bush
administration or Wall Street for the current state of the American economy, the greatest number of Tea Party supporters blame
Congress." It should not be surprising, then, that Ms. Close as a
self-identified supporter of the Tea Party movement points to the
last time Congress shifted hands as the start of the period of "drift"
that has seen the country fall from "greatness."

Yet we must also attempt to contextualize Ms. Close's response,
in terms of both whiteness and nationalism, from a national perspective. The Democratic victory in 2006 spurred social conservatives who were not opposed to George W. Bush and the two
ongoing conflicts (wars) in Iraq and Afghanistan to resist their
newly elected representatives. Appropriating nationalist discourse,
they accused the new Congress of wishing to usher in socialism,
raise taxes, and harm small businesses. Right-wing pundits, writers, and leaders encouraged these fears in order to build solidarity
and a base from which to campaign for the presidential election of
2008. Of course, 2008 saw Democrats take even more seats in both
houses of Congress and also saw the election of the first African
American president in U.S. history, Barack Hussein Obama. Less
than four months after Obama was sworn in as president, the Tea
Party Tax Day protests took place.

From the above narrative, we can trace nationalism in action,
from the congressional elections of 2006 all the way up to the

election of Obama. Tea Party members unified and built solidarity in opposition to the Democratic Party and manufactured notions of what that party represented. Some were literally fearful for the future of the country, their country, which helps us position the power of national identity in the movement as a whole. The impact of such monumental legislation as the Wall Street bailout and health care reform served to build solidarity among those who opposed the new Congress on ideological grounds.

That same opposition, however, becomes manifested in opposition to those who are not considered part of the inclusive national group. As violent military conflicts and drone bombings rage on in the Middle East and North Africa, the most widely visible external racial others are Muslim men of color. We should not be surprised, then, that so many in the Tea Party movement cling to the belief that Barack Obama was not born in the United States. As an African American man, who spent time in Indonesia (a Muslim country) and whose father was Muslim, Obama represents not only the dark internal racial other but also the external racial other who is portrayed widely in the media as hating the United States "for our freedom." It is not only that Obama is not white, it's the extent to which he is not white that brings him into conflict with what the Tea Party sees as U.S. values. We can thus understand why so many Republican and right-wing pundits used Obama's middle name frequently in the runup to the 2008 election: Hussein is, of course, the name of the former dictator of Iraq whom the U.S. government overthrew, a name synonymous with a racial other that allows me as a white person to understand myself as white by virtue of my not being Hussein.

Understood this way, the charges of racism and white supremacy levied at the Tea Party movement are not surprising. Yet what the reading above enables is a more expansive reading of the Tea Party as white and as nationalist. It is fully possible, as the above discussion has indicated, that a nationalist rhetoric contains within it discourse that is meant to maintain the exclusion of racial others. The Tea Party movement, as an almost all-white movement, is not a white supremacist movement because of who is in the movement; it is a white supremacist movement because of who is excluded and how that exclusion has come to be practiced. Harkening back to a remembered past, even if it is as recent as ten years ago, harkens back to a time just like today in which a white supremacist society maintained racial hierarchy to preserve and maintain the status quo. As challenges to the remembered past present themselves, human actors informed by both racial and national identities respond to threats by building solidarity in exclusionary processes.

The Tea Party movement can thus be seen as a highly visible manifestation of a process that has operated in the United States since before the country's independence. As long as nationalisms and races are in conflict with one another, there is no possible way to separate whiteness, white supremacy, and nationalism. This is because nationalism necessitates other nations and nationalisms, just as white supremacy necessitates those who are seen as not white. These processes are enmeshed with one another so that the necessitated difference of one can function for the other. That is, in the creation of a nationalism, a racial other can be made as a national other, and thus said nationalism can function to maintain both national as well as racial others. We should not be surprised if a nationalist project in which nearly all participants are white were racist; indeed, we should be surprised if it were not.

The Romney Candidacy: Neoliberalizing Racio-Nationalism

The early primaries for the Republican presidential nomination were dominated by Tea Party victories, first for Michelle Bachman who had delivered the first-ever Tea Party rebuttal to Obama's 2011 State of the Union Speech, and later for Rick Santorum, who then became the leading oppositional candidate representing more "conservative" Republicans over Romney. By December 3, 2011, the Republican candidate pool consisted solely of white people,[7] and by the next month solely of white men.

Of course, for a party that is more than 90 percent white, we should not be surprised that the candidates the majority of the party's members support are those whom they see as like themselves: white folks. In 2008, then–Democratic National Committee chair Howard Dean, in an interview with National Public Radio, made the following remark: "If you look at folks of color, even women, they're more successful in the Democratic Party than they are in the white, uh, excuse me, in the Republican Party" (ABC News,

2008). While many Republicans, including Republican National Committee chair Mike Duncan disputed Dean's comment, saying that "[h]is efforts to divide Americans are an insult to all our nation's citizens and have absolutely no place in the national dialogue" (ABC News, 2008), former Republican presidential candidate and cable news commentator Pat Buchanan responded differently. In his *Suicide of a Superpower* Buchanan devotes an entire chapter to "The White Party," which he begins by discussing the Dean "gaffe." Buchanan (2011) writes, "[T]he Republican Party may be fairly described as the white party" (p. 329). His evidence for this is compelling, as he cites 2008 presidential election results in which "91 percent of McCain voters were Christian, and 91 percent were white. White Christians are the Republican base" (p. 336). While the 2012 election is still being analyzed in detail, we do have access to exit polling figures that give us an idea of the racial distribution in the 2012 electorate.

In 2012, 93 percent of African Americans, 71 percent of Latin@s, and 73 percent of Asian Americans voted for Obama (Edison Research, 2012). The only racial group that Obama did not win a majority of was white folks, only 39 percent of whom voted for him. The electorate in 2012, according to the conservative Brookings Institute, was comprised of 71 percent white folks, 12 percent black folks, and 11 percent Latin@s (the remaining electorate was lumped together into "other races" in this data set) (Frey, 2012). So what do these statistics mean? Buchanan and Dean are right; the Republican Party is and remains the white party.

For Buchanan, these results stem from the shifting demographics of the United States electorate. He cites, for example, that in 1976 90 percent of the votes cast were cast by white folks. "Had John McCain run in 1976 instead of 2008, not only would he have won, he would have won the popular vote before a single non-white vote was cast" (Greener, 2009, quoted in Buchanan, 2011). But of course, it is not 1976, and now, "White Americans, who provide nine out of ten Republican votes every presidential year, have fallen to less than two-thirds of the U.S. population and three-fourths of the electorate . . . people of color vote Democratic—in landslides" (p. 338). Projecting these results into the future, by 2020 white voters will make up 66 percent of the electorate, meaning that "A GOP presidential candidate could then win the same 60 percent of the white vote the GOP won in 2010 [in the midterm elections] and still be 10 points away from a tie in the popular vote" (p. 338).

Buchanan reads all of this as an attack on "traditional American values" and in particular as an attack on white Christian men. Buchanan repeatedly returns to the demographic projections that white people will cease to be the majority of the U.S. population by 2042. He extends this analysis into other chapters that focus on the marginalization of white Catholics, the former greatness of the Grand Old Party, and the eventual disappearance of the white race altogether. It is not necessary to go into the details of these other arguments to understand Buchanan's central point; rather, the following will suffice:

> Half a century after Martin Luther King envisioned a day when his children would be judged "not by the color of their skin, but the content of their character," journalists of color are demanding the hiring and promotion of journalists based on the color of their skin. Jim Crow is back. Only the color of the beneficiaries and the color of the victims have been reversed. (p. 150)

Here we find the tired claims of "reverse racism" so common in contemporary discourse on the declining significance of race and of the need to repeal Affirmative Action and other measures designed to increase access and opportunity for historically marginalized peoples. We can refute this with one sentence: according to the U.S. Census Bureau, in 2012, white people have twenty-two times more wealth[8] than black people and fifteen times more than Latin@s (Luhby, 2012). If reverse racism or discrimination against white people is real, it certainly isn't working very well.

To return to Romney then, we can make the following claims based on the above discussion. First, Romney's party is truly the white party, 90 percent comprised of white people. Second, more people of color are in the electorate than ever before, and as a result maintaining a majority of the white vote is no longer enough to be elected president. Third, as a result of no longer being able to count on only white votes, Republicans (and conservatives of the various stripes we could list here) project their dissatisfaction with rhetoric that fewer white people equates to fewer opportunities for white people and thus creates the need to "take back *their* country." I need now to place all of this into context in light of the above discussion of nationalism, and further to understand how capitalism functions in this process.

White Capitalist Nationalism

It is important here to remember the origins of the conception of white people. Whiteness was invented to legitimate the exploitation of people of color, and to place white people who were not the owners of the means of production in solidarity with those who were, under the banner of the white race. If whiteness was then invented to legitimate what we can understand as a fundamentally capitalist project—the accumulation of wealth through the creation of capital via surplus labor—we could rightly say that whiteness has always carried with it a kind of economic mobility. If the owners of the means of production are white, and if, while I am not an owner, I am also white, I can think of myself as having at least some form of economic security in knowing that the economic system is set up, if not for me, for people who look like me to be successful. The Tea Party's rhetoric, and often blatantly racist pronouncements, speak to this larger history of whiteness. What the white people in the Tea Party movement are responding to largely is their own notion that whiteness no longer guarantees much of anything in terms of security and well-being.

Buchanan identifies much of this in his chapter titled "The End of White America." While his conclusions that white people are now facing a Jim Crow–style regime of segregation and discrimination are wildly unfounded, his evidence to support such a pronouncement has resonance for many white people, Tea Partiers or not. With specific regard to the great recession at the turn of the decade, the employment statistics give us important insight into why whiteness is seen as under threat. If we take the thesis of Buchanan as "white men are now being discriminated against," the following statistical findings as they concern specifically both men and white men can be viewed as supporting such a thesis at first glance. However, upon closer examination, we find instead that the processes and practices of capitalism itself, not some new racial order, are the ultimate culprit for so many white men's loss of employment, economic standing, and sense of self.

Buchanan notes that by mid-2009, "unemployment among women had reached 8 percent, but among men it was 10.5 percent, the largest gap ever recorded by the Bureau of Labor Statistics" (p. 128). Men, thus, are worse off than women in terms of employment—imagined here solely as having a job and not taking into consideration either wealth or earning potential. With specific regard to male construction workers, we learn that "unemployment rose in the Great Recession to 19.7 percent, while illegal aliens held 17 percent of all construction jobs, up from 10 percent in 2003" (p. 128). Buchanan cites data from the Pew Hispanic Center to make this point, and here we see again that men face an unfair burden, but that this burden is compounded by loss of jobs to undocumented immigrants, who, whether accurately or not, are always imagined in this argument as people of color, as nonwhite. Buchanan goes on, "In the second quarter of 2010, foreign-born workers gained 656,000 jobs. Native-born workers lost 1.2 million jobs" (p. 128). Again, the argument goes that people of color are taking the jobs of white people. When we consider specifically so-called "blue-collar" workers, we learn that these men have "suffered 57 percent of all job losses in the recession" and that they "make up only 11 percent of the workforce" yet "constitute 36 percent of those who have lost jobs" (p. 129).

The following narrative becomes apparent: men are no longer more likely to be employed than women, and men are more likely to lose their jobs to someone who is not like them, someone who is not white, particularly in traditionally working-class, blue-collar occupations. White nationalism requires the maintenance of others, of an excluded population, so as to define and find meaning in those who are included. As so much of our identity in the United States is constructed out of our occupation ("What do you do?" is often the first question asked when meeting someone for the first time, and always refers to employment), losing one's job can mean much more than losing one's economic security. It can mean losing one's sense of self, of identity, of who we are and what we care about. If we can tell ourselves a story that we lost our job because of someone else—who is not like us, and does not look like us, and is not a member of our nation—we can feel a sense of nationalism defined in the negative. We reach for a positive identity to compensate for our loss of self-worth, and loss of the means of maintaining our material needs. We wrap ourselves in our nation through nationalism and thus participate in the exclusionary process of maintaining said nationalism.

The question of whether or not the capitalist economic system itself is the cause of the disparities listed for white men is never entertained in Buchanan's text. But we can and must seek to extrapolate the ways in which white nationalism, as characterized by Buchanan, is inherently caught up in naturalizing and mystifying the exploitative nature of capitalism. "The immigrants took my job," functions on the side of capitalism in at least three ways. First, it naturalizes the capitalist economic system itself as a taken-for-granted, always-already phenomenon that is fundamentally just and meritocratic. The white worker has a natural right to his job, in this line of thought, and the market system is undermined by undocumented laborers entering the workforce of another country. Second, it fails to investigate the causes for immigrant labor in the first place. Nationalism in the United States, by constantly insisting that we live in the greatest country on earth, we are the best, and so on, creates an illusion that the primary reason someone would immigrate here is to take a piece of the pie, to take what is rightfully ours. But if we imagine, just briefly, the experience of a Northern Mexican man whose family had been farming corn for generations but who could no longer find a market for his products once NAFTA[9] came into effect and the price of imported corn made his own local crop obsolete, we should not be surprised if he sought to work in the country responsible for his no longer being able to support himself. The important thing here is this: undocumented immigration is an effect of the global capitalist system, of the need for constantly greater profits without regard to local communities and actual human needs. Third, and perhaps most critically, in lamenting that "immigrants took my job," there is never any engagement with the owners of the means of production who actually did the hiring and firing, or laying off as the case may be. That is, we misrecognize the agentive actor in the process if we blame the person of color rather than the capitalist, the owner of the means of production.

Thus while at first it can seem a reach to declare that the sentiment "The immigrants are taking our jobs" functions on the side of capitalism, it should be clear that this is in fact the case. White nationalism, with its need to exclude racial others, creates the possibility for the white actor to never question how it is that the economic system is not set up for her benefit. By scapegoating people of color and immigrants, white nationalism naturalizes the capitalist system and goes so far as to blame the people who are marginalized by the very same system for their own marginalization, rather than indict those in power who actually made the decisions to hire, fire, and invest in the first place.

White nationalism, then, functions today in many of the same ways it did in seventeenth-century Virginia, where European indentured servants were granted the status of "white" in order to legitimate and naturalize the accumulation of wealth by the white owners of the means of production. Understanding the loss of one's job in solely nationalist and racialized terms obscures from view the ways in which the system itself (and those who actually control it) functions to limit opportunities and protect the interests of the ruling elite. It is here that we can see why exorbitantly rich people such as the Koch brothers have an interest in funding Tea Party candidates and initiatives that seek to maintain the narrative that it is not capitalism that is the cause for so much of the dehumanizing experience currently being suffered by so many white people, but rather the "other," the "not-us" against whom we define ourselves. Nationalism in the United States functions to legitimate capitalism, and offers scapegoats for both those in power and those not in power to point to and, in solidarity, imagine themselves in opposition to.

Electing a businessman to the White House, as a representative of the white party, makes perfect sense for a white nationalist capitalist project like the Tea Party. We can see in Mitt Romney the complete manifestation of wealth, power, and prestige: traits that we long for, especially as white people in the United States. White people were asked to imagine themselves as a racial group so as to obliterate any possible class-based solidarity movement for transformation that might lead to white elites losing their wealth and power. If we fail to understand that it is precisely the accumulation of wealth and power that dehumanizes, we risk universalizing the aesthetic of capitalist accumulation as the natural course of human history, of progress. In nationalism, we demarcate those who ought to be or deserve to be in power from those who do not, thus further distancing ourselves from our comrades across the globe who face many of the very same hardships experienced by white people in the contemporary United States. And as white people in particular, we do this at our own peril. Whiteness, and membership in the white race, is a false bill of goods, a form of capital that represents such a pittance, such a small drop in the vast ocean of power and control, and yet has the extraordinary function of legitimating suffering for the sake of profit.

Tea Partiers have every right to be angry, as does Pat Buchanan, but in directing their anger toward people of color and nationalist "others" they further entrench themselves in the very ideology that creates their suffering. Thinking of the Tea Party merely as racists is not only unhelpful, it is an oversimplification that those of us on the Left make to our own peril.

While both major political parties in the United States are unabashedly wed to capitalism, we can still find in the example of the Tea Party evidence of resistance and a potentiality for coalescing around common aims. What is needed is for the great majority of people in the United States to realize that it is not necessarily their (lack of) luck or skills that has led to their marginalization and feelings of being slighted, but rather the capitalist economy, which places its need for profit and efficiency ahead of the actual human needs of women and men. Capitalism never functions for the needs of all, and nationalism rationalizes this by emphasizing who is to be included and excluded rather than focusing on the need for such inclusions and exclusions. Nationalism, in much the same way as racism, stands in the way of abolishing capitalism because it makes of capitalism the natural state of affairs rather than a perverse warping of what it means to be fully human.

SEVEN

Professionalizing the Teaching Force

Neoliberalism and the Complicity of Teacher Education

Capital therefore takes no account of the health and the length of life of the worker, unless society forces it to do so. Its answer to the outcry about the physical and mental degradation, the premature death, the torture of over-work is this: Should that pain trouble us, since it increases our pleasure (profit)?

—*Capital*

In reality I possess private property only insofar as I have something vendible, whereas what is particular to me may not be vendible at all. . . . If [my frockcoat] becomes tattered, it can still have a number of features which make it valuable *for me*, it may even become a feature of me and turn me into a tatterdemalion. But no economist would think of classing it as my private property, since it does not enable me to command any, even the smallest, amount of other people's labour.

—*The German Ideology*

Yesterday I received a message from a student, a young woman who is pursuing her undergraduate degree in elementary education, in which she offered up in just a few short sentences one of the most powerful critiques of teacher education I have ever heard.

She had asked me to send her an article I had mentioned in class, Cynthia Brown's (1987) overview of Freire's method of literacy instruction, "Literacy in 30 Hours." After I had sent her the article, she sent this message:

> Thank you very much! Risking the curse of the compliment, I feel like I should let you know that this class has made me realize how much better it is to be informed on your own initiative, rather than learning only what you "have to know." Perhaps an obvious statement, but the latter seems to be all that we are worried about most of the time. Anyway, I appreciate your help, have a great week!

I do not include this message here as evidence of my own abilities in the classroom, but rather wish to position the ensuing examination of the movement to professionalize teaching in relation to this young woman's experience in her other teacher education courses. Learning what one "has to know" as opposed to being "informed on your own initiative" here represents critique of the dominant logic of teacher education programs: teaching future teachers the "scientific basis" for their work in classrooms, teaching them what they "have to know" in order to be "effective."

My student was calling attention to the realization of efforts made by leading teacher educators for the past thirty years[1] to professionalize teaching and teacher education. And importantly, she was critical of what this has meant for her as a learner. In being complimentary regarding a course that is oriented in direct opposition to the idea of a "scientific knowledge base of teaching," of "effectiveness" or "efficiency" as the goals of working with young people in classrooms, she is critiquing the attitude of teacher professionalization that offers less meaning and fewer opportunities for the self-appropriation of knowledge. And I agree with her. However, it is not enough to declare that the creation and maintenance of a scientific knowledge base for teaching creates learning conditions that emphasize understanding of bare minimums in preference to self-motivated inquiry in teacher education. We must slow down and examine the history of the professionalization movement alongside other contextual forces.

In this chapter, I work primarily from David Labaree's (1997) critique of the professionalization movement in his chapter "Rethinking the Movement to Professionalize Teaching" to first trace the origins and aims of the movement and those most involved in its creation. Next I deepen and extend Labaree's discussion of the ideological presuppositions of the professionalization movement to call attention to the ways in which neoliberal capitalist logics of instrumental reason pervade the discourse and practice of the new "professionalized" teacher education. I then turn to the ways the professionalization movement has functioned in support of neoliberal aims for education, in some ways willingly and in other ways unintentionally, to elaborate a picture of the current state of teacher education in our present neoliberal historical moment.

The Holmes Group and the Carnegie Task Force: The Origins of the Professionalization Movement

In 1983, the National Commission on Excellence in Education authored a report titled "A Nation at Risk: The Imperative for Education Reform." The report declared that schools in the United States were failing to actualize the expectations placed on them, and indicated that the United States' competitive edge in economics was being eroded because of our "failing" school system. The authors suggested that more standards and accountability were necessary for teachers and students, that the school day should be longer, and that teachers should be compensated based on their performance in the classroom, using market-based incentives rather than seniority as the basis for teacher salaries. The stated "primary motivation" for these recommendations was the finding that SAT scores had dropped in the twenty years before the report. In *The Manufactured Crisis*,[2] Berliner and Biddle (1995) showed how these data can be explained primarily as evidence of the success of Affirmative Action movements to increase the number of women and people of color taking the SAT as a part of applying to colleges and universities. White male students maintained the same scores, in some years actually improving from the past, but as more people who had traditionally been denied access to universities began to take the test the overall scores declined.

Still, "A Nation at Risk" cemented in the U.S. imagination the need to address our "failing schools" and this included teacher educators. In 1986, three years after "A Nation at Risk," two reports were produced by groups of leading scholars and deans to elaborate a vision of how to address the apparent "failures" of education, and the historically low status of teachers. The Carnegie Task Force on Teaching as a Profession's report was titled *A Nation Prepared: Teachers for the 21st Century*. The task force was made up of "an elite assortment of public officials, executives, leading educators, and teachers union officials under the sponsorship of the Carnegie Corporation of New York" (Labaree, 1997, p. 129). The other report was titled *Tomorrow's Teachers* and was authored by the Holmes Group, "a consortium of the deans of colleges of education at about one hundred leading research universities" (p. 129). Both groups argued that for teaching to improve, it needed to be seen as a profession, like other professions such as law and medicine. Teachers were to be trained specialists, possessing a unique set of skills backed by research and best practices known as the "scientific knowledgebase" for teaching.

To accomplish this, the reports argued for the need to enhance the professional education of teachers by replacing traditional undergraduate programs that resulted in teacher certification with graduate level courses in "what the Holmes Group calls the 'science of teaching'" (p. 130). The model for a professional teacher education program was to include undergraduate courses in subject matter before the graduate-level work of teacher education, to further be enhanced by "an extended clinical internship in a 'professional development school,' analogous to a teaching hospital" (p. 130). Medical education was the explicit model to be employed in the new teacher education, as medicine was seen clearly as a profession, and thus making teacher training more closely resemble the training of doctors would add legitimacy to the profession of teaching. Teaching was to be seen as a set of specific skills and practices that professional teachers knew and were able to use based on their engagement with and learning of the "scientific knowledgebase" on teaching.

A second major component of both reports was their advocacy of a new hierarchy of teachers within schools, the creation of what the Carnegie Task Force called "lead teachers" and what the Holmes Group called "career professionals." These teachers, after demonstrating their abilities in the classroom to be those of an elite teacher, would receive higher pay and increased responsibility in their schools. While they would still be primarily responsible for their own classrooms, they would also serve as peer-coaches and mentors for teachers in the lower tier, have more control over curricular decisions, and be involved in teacher education programs at the university level. The formation of the National Board for Professional Teaching Standards, which Labaree points out is, again, modeled on medicine, could function as the body that would grant this more elite status to expert teachers.

Labaree is not content to see these groups' reports merely as products of the specific time in which they were created, the early and mid-1980s. Rather, he explores the historical genealogy of the professionalization movement, to place it in context alongside the history of education and teacher education in the United States. First, he tells us, "Whereas the 1960s and 1970s were marked by a push for more equity in schools, with attacks on racial segregation and [social] class-based tracking, the early 1980s brought a shift in the direction of excellence" (p. 135). With the threat of declining economic productivity looming, as evidenced by the drop in SAT scores, teacher professionalization can be seen as a response to the shift away from social mobility as the primary organizing principle for public education and toward social (mostly economic) efficiency. This economic imperative for education manifested alongside the formation of neoliberal ideology, and resulted in both reports arguing for an explicitly market-based approach emphasizing "individual initiative and unfettered competition" as necessary measures to improve and professionalize the teaching force (p. 137). Teachers were to have an economic incentive to professionalize, to pursue National Board Certification, as opposed to past education reform initiatives that had been historically more bureaucratic, more focused on top-down reforms rather than teacher-led initiatives, and less individualized (see Kliebard, 2002). This was thought to have the impact of increasing teacher autonomy, a focus of both reports.[3]

Labaree wants us to understand the historically feminine character of the teaching force in the United States. He sees the professionalization movement as emerging out of the successes of the feminist movement, which had created more opportunities for women to pursue studies and careers in fields that had previously been closed to them. For Labaree, teaching needed to professionalize or risk losing these young women who in previous generations had seen teaching as one of the most viable occupations for college-educated women. He writes, "Professionalization offers the teacher a way to escape identification with the unpaid uncredentialed status of mother" (p. 138). Yet there is a patriarchal character to professionalization, as the formation of a scientific knowledge base that is abstracted and removed from the specificities of daily experience and classroom practices has the possibility of ignoring the inherently political nature of teaching and the feminist insight that "the personal is political" (hooks, 1994). The scientific knowledge base for teaching can be seen as a move away from traditionally female attributes that many would desire in teachers, such as empathy, nurturance, and attention to others' feelings and experiences. In response to fears over these "feminine" aims, the scientific knowledge base risks abandoning the many positive aspects of feminist approaches to teaching in place of a rigid, calculated, and male conception of what teaching and learning ought to be. Labaree writes, of the Holmes Group and Carnegie Task Force,

> They argue that this profession should be grounded in a scientific knowledge base, arranged competitively into a meritocratic hierarchy, and focused on the task of increasing subject-matter learning. Apparently thinking of teaching's femaleness as unprofessional, the professionalizers seem to be trying to reshape the female schoolteacher in the image of the male physician. (p. 139)

Labaree thus encourages us to read professionalization as de-feminization, and question the extent to which the move to professionalize can function to harden already existent imbalances in power. He notes that school administrators were seen as professionals long before teachers, and of course the overconcentration of men in administrative roles should be seen as support for Labaree's fears.

Yet, beyond the feminist problematics associated with professionalization, Labaree sees the professionalization of the teaching force as an outgrowth of the professionalization of teacher educators more generally. As normal schools transitioned first into teachers colleges and later into state colleges and universities, teacher educators saw their title and status shift from that of a high school teacher to a university professor's, all in the course of the twentieth century. Much as teachers are increasingly viewed as having a lower status in comparison to other professions requiring postbaccalaureate training and credentials, so teacher educators are seen as having a lower status in the university compared to professors in other disciplines. The exception to this, by and large, has been educational psychologists. Labaree writes:

> Since the turn of the century, education psychology has been one area within education schools that has been able to establish itself as a credible producer of academic knowledge [and] thus establish its faculty as legitimate members of the university professoriate. (p. 145)

This is why we should not be surprised that so many in the professionalization movement "began with applying the methods of educational psychology to the problems of teaching" (p. 145). We thus must explore how the ideological underpinnings of educational psychology operate within and upon the movement to professionalize teaching if we are to understand fully what is at stake in such a movement.

Formal Rationality, Instrumental Reason, and Positivist Science in Education

Labaree sees the professionalization of teaching movement as emerging from the need for teacher educators to overcome their relatively lowly status vis-à-vis their academic colleagues, both in the university at large and even within their own colleges of education. The need for legitimation has resulted in teacher education coming to embrace what Labaree calls "formal rationalism," an ideology attributed to the beginning of the modernist period and typified by Descartes and Newton. He writes that formal rationality

[e]mphasizes formal logic over rhetoric and proof over argumentation; it focuses on the development of abstract principles rather than the study of diverse, concrete individual cases; and it concentrates on constructing timeless theories grounded in the permanent structures of life rather than exploring the shifting and context-bound problems of daily practice. . . . It constitutes the core of what we think of as the scientific method. (pp. 148–149)

Teacher education, from the 1960s on, has sought to draw on this position regarding inquiry, believing rightly that those forms of research that are most highly rewarded by the academy, and those most used by legislators and those in power to make social policy decisions, employ the scientific method, modeled on positivist science and educational psychology.

To break with Labaree, we should go farther in our analysis. It is one thing to identify formal rationality and positivism as causal ideologies that help to explain the logics of the professionalization movement. But we must go farther to examine the ways these ideological precepts function on the side of the status quo, on the side of neoliberal capitalism and white supremacy in our present oppressive reality. To do this, the work of Max Horkheimer is especially helpful in articulating the limits of formal rationalism and the ways in which these limits obscure critical insight into the economic system itself. Horkheimer was primarily concerned with the ways in which reason has been instrumentalized; the ways in which reason has shifted from being a faculty of the mind to being a tool or technology to be used in pursuit of ends that may or may not themselves actually be rational, good, or just. Reason itself is empty in terms of morality and ethics when it is used purely instrumentally. This is how the Nazis were able to use the logics of reason and efficiency to devise and justify the most effective ways of eliminating an entire race of people: the mathematical formulas themselves were rational, the means of executing their aims were efficient, but of course their purpose was abominable. Reason and its application in positivism offer us only data, only that which is to be evaluated but never the most worthy criterion for how it ought to be evaluated. To cite an example that is more appropriate to teaching and teacher education, instrumental reason can tell us exactly how well a particular student did on an exam, and it can even tell us how accurate the exam was in testing the information the exam was designed for, but it can never tell us *why* we should be teaching something or *why* some things should be on the test rather than others; instead, it posits that we test in order to be scientific, as though such a way of being offered anything other than merely more science. This is why reason must be approached critically, and, further, why any attempt to collapse teaching into a form of instrumental reason fails utterly to address the political nature of teaching: the why of it all. A closer engagement with Horkheimer will help make this more transparent.

Horkheimer begins his critique of positivism with the admission that for many people around the world there is little lost in the declining significance of philosophy and philosophical thought. Scientific thought, seen as more concrete and objective, has taken over in capitalism. The scientific method itself becomes its own philosophy, its own religion, and its own myth. Horkheimer (1947/2004) writes,

> According to the positivists, what we need is abundant confidence in science. Of course they are not blind to the destructive uses to which science is put; but they claim that such uses of science are perverted. . . . The objective progress of science and its application, technology, do not justify the current idea that science is destructive only when perverted and necessarily constructive when adequately understood. (p. 40)

What Horkheimer is aiming at here is to problematize the assumed benevolence of science as such. Science itself is neutral, from the positivist perspective. It is deemed objective and immune from any flaw save those that human beings bring to bear on it. Horkheimer goes on to argue that "the positivists" "adapt philosophy to science, *i.e.* to the requirements of practice instead of adapting practice to philosophy" (p. 41). In other words, presupposition and intuition are to be abandoned; any form of knowing that does not conform to the scientific method is seen as lacking, as less worthy, and at best as not trustable.

While it may strike the reader as extreme, the example of Nazism represents precisely what Horkheimer wishes to critique. The Nazis utilized many elements of the scientific method, in heinous experiments on human beings, in testing their propaganda materials, and in any other number of examples we could cite here. The question they inspire is a rather simple, if explosive, one: If the Nazis employed science and the scientific method for their brutal project, how can we hold the scientific method up as the highest (or only) means for discerning truth or fact? Science is neither on the side of liberalism nor authoritarianism, to use Horkheimer's terms, but rather must fall back on the self-evident principlethat the answer to any critique of science is more science. This is why capitalism is never situated in opposition to science and the scientific method: because science as technology can be applied to reality in any context, just or unjust. The same principles apply to concentration camps that apply to commercial factories, in terms of how they ought to be run, how to maximize their efficiency, and so on. For Horkheimer, this is why science can never define for us what we ought to be striving for, but rather is limited to being a means to an end that it cannot evaluate in human terms, in ways that can clarify its function for humanization, liberation, or any other number of the nonpositivist social aims that so many of us, positivists included, claim we desire.

Returning to formalized reason, Horkheimer wants us to consider the peculiar ways in which "an activity is reasonable only if it serves another purpose. . . . In other words, the activity is merely a tool . . . it derives its meaning only through its connection with other ends" (p. 25). Here we can enter into the reality of high-stakes testing as perhaps the clearest example of instrumental reason in practice in contemporary education in the United States. The tests themselves measure academic achievement, which is imagined out of the results of the test (and past tests) and normed accordingly, so that questions are evaluated based on a sufficient number of students conforming to the statistical logics of normal distributions, and so on. The purpose of the test is always to evaluate learning, and increasingly now for evaluating teacher efficacy in the complex mathematical formulas of value-added assessment models. And we need the tests, to tell us how students compare to one another, and how teachers compare to one another, so that we can do more tests to continue to refine the most efficient way of learning, and so on. But learning what? The test thus can only derive its meaning through its relationship to other ends; the test has value insofar as it correlates with or impacts future events. More and more, tests function to solidify the idea of tests themselves as always already, as self-evident, and as commonsense. Further, such testing can come to stand in for more student-centered interventions in the "achievement gap/educational debt"—testing becomes the intervention, as though more results and more tests (more science) will automatically yield more socially just ends (Ladson-Billings, 2006b). And so it is that testing takes up more and more of the school year, with the idea being that all of these additional tests will improve student performance on the tests that matter most, which only ever have to justify themselves in relation to the apparent need for tests in the first place. Thus, certain tests are deemed better or worse than others without ever questioning the notion of what the tests might ever actually offer us if our aims for education were more sophisticated than simply the mastery of an arbitrary set of skills and facts for memorization.

Milton Friedman, Vouchers, and the Origins of Neoliberal Education

Of course, this state of affairs is taking place in the context of neoliberal capitalism, and as such it must be understood as a part of larger, nonscientific but instead political goals regarding the future of public education. Since "A Nation at Risk," the Right has sought to maintain its position that public schools ought to be made private and placed in competition with one another through a national voucher system (see Kumashiro, 2008). Examining the logics of vouchers is then a possible way of orienting ourselves to the ideological constructs and frames operating in neoliberal education policy. As famed Chicago School economist Milton Friedman (1962) defined them, school vouchers are a system in which

> [g]overnments could require a minimum level of school financed by giving parents vouchers redeemable for a specified maximum sum per child per year if spent on

"approved" educational services. Parents would then be free to spend this sum and any additional sum they themselves provided on purchasing education services from an "approved" institution of their own choice. The educational services could be rendered by private enterprises operated for profit, or by non-profit institutions. The role of the government would be limited to insuring that the schools met certain minimum standards. (p. 89)

This system was proposed as part of Friedman's plan to transform schools to allow for greater "equity" and improve school quality. To shed light on this position I examine two pieces of writing by Friedman: the first is a chapter from his now-infamous book *Capitalism and Freedom*, and the second a short paper titled "Public Schools: Make Them Private."

In a chapter titled "The Role of Government in Education," Friedman lays out his argument for the privatization of schooling. First, Friedman elaborates what he calls "neighborhood effects," which are "circumstances under which the action of one individual imposes significant costs on other individuals for which it is not feasible to make him compensate them" (p. 83). Here Friedman is talking about shared societal goods. He wants us to consider how it is to society's benefit to have a literate and knowledgeable populace and whether or not we ought to be collectively paying for this good. Next, Friedman begins his case for a private system of education. For Friedman, "denationalizing" schooling will have the effect of creating far more choices for parents in terms of where they are able to send their children for the purposes of acquiring education. Friedman believes that this competition, in which schools function as for-profit institutions, will create a better schooling system based on the principles of other capitalistic markets.

Friedman then shifts to a discussion of some of the potential arguments against vouchers. He points out that if a person in a low socioeconomic area works hard enough, that person will be able to buy the same car as a person who lives in a more affluent neighborhood. Thus, if people work hard to make money, they can afford a better school experience for their children. The issue of transportation and rural towns that do not have the numbers of students to justify multiple schools is raised and dismissed just as quickly, as Friedman says, "[T]his argument . . . has been greatly weakened in recent decades by improvements in transportation and increasing concentration of the population in urban communities" (p. 93). The remainder of Friedman's section on K-12 schooling concludes with his defense of allowing teacher salaries to fluctuate along with the market and to do away with tax dollars being spent on elements of schools ("coaches and corridors" [p. 94], to use Friedman's words) that not all taxpayers deem necessary or appropriate.

In Friedman's more recent "Public Schools: Make Them Private" (1995), he reiterated his argument for vouchers in much the same way. In this work, Friedman advocates educational reform in the form of "enabling a private, for-profit industry to develop that will provide a wide variety of learning opportunities and offer effective competition to public schools" (p. 339). Friedman points out that in 1955 there were 55,000 school districts and that by 1992 there were only 15,000. He uses this statistic to showcase his point that schools are becoming more and more centralized. Friedman sees this process as counterproductive because he sees the shift in power away from the local community as an example of the lack of choices he is seeking to bring an end to. He next moves into a section on the changing political and economic conditions of the world, which, though he does not use either term directly, generally describes neoliberal globalization from a free-market perspective. Because of these changing economic realities abroad, Friedman believes the educational system holds the potential to stifle stratification in our own society and to maintain our elevated position economically on an international level. As he sees it, "We know from the experience of every other industry how imaginative competitive free enterprise can be, what new products and services can be introduced, how driven it is to satisfy the customers—that is what we need in education" (p. 343). Friedman concludes his article by stating that vouchers are not an end in and of themselves, but rather a means to reaching an end. The overtones of the above discussion dealing with instrumental and formal reason should be apparent here.

To summarize, Friedman wishes to see a fully privatized, for-profit, educational system replace the current public system, which is financed largely through taxation. He believes that by giving families vouchers funded by money that would have gone to public schools, parents will be incentivized to invest in schools of their choice, thus creating a demand for many different types of schools. Education as a commodity; schools as businesses; the purpose of education completely removed from its role in a democracy: these are extreme views, and make it quite clear that the Right wishes to privatize as much as possible of what we consider public or belonging to the public good. Vouchers are, for Friedman, the best way to create the conditions under which such a project might become reality. Yet while we do not (yet) have a national voucher system[4] we have nonetheless seen many of the effects Friedman longed for back in 1962 come to fruition. We need to examine more of these consequences of neoliberalism in education before we return to the movement to professionalize teaching.

Neoliberalism in Education: A Brief Summary

The practice of applying neoliberal logics to schooling and education more broadly has been well documented and critiqued in the research literature (see Apple, 2001; 2006; Casey, 2011; 2013; Casey, Lozenski, & McManimon, 2013; Davidson-Harden, Kuehn, Schugurensky, & Smaller, 2009; Hill, 2009; Hursh, 2007; Kliebard, 2002; Lipman, 2011; Robertson, 2008). While it is common in these works for authors to contend that teachers and students cannot be reduced to the status of commodities, that education is a right and not a product for consumption, rarely have they extended their critiques of neoliberal decision making in schools to the present realities and practices of teacher education. Some research does exist on teacher education's culpability in the maintenance of neoliberal schooling (see Apple, 2001; Kumashiro, 2010; Sleeter, 2008); however, these authors' critiques have not extended to calling for teacher education to move toward an explicitly anticapitalist stance (see Casey, 2013). We are presently experiencing domestically the very same policies that the U.S.-led World Bank has put in place in other countries around the world as a part of eliminating social welfare policies and procedures. To better understand this, we can look to critical scholarship in international education in order to identify similarities between the logics of the World Bank and the current educational reform movement at work in the United States.

Ball (1998) writes, about trends in international education, that "two complexly related policy agendas are discernible in all the heat and noise of [educational] reform. The first aims to tie education more closely to national economic interests, while the second involves a decoupling of education from direct state control" (p. 125). We can understand the impulse toward this first goal if we examine the ways in which national leaders talk about the needs of the capitalist economy as being synonymous with the individual human needs of students (Casey, 2011). To use what has become one my favorite quotes with which I like to demonstrate this point, from a speech delivered on August 9, 2010, at the University of Texas at Austin, President Barack Obama told those in attendance,

> We also know that in the coming decades, a high school diploma is not going to be enough. Folks *need* a college degree. They *need* workforce training. They *need* a higher education. And so today I want to talk about the higher education strategy that we're pursuing not only to lead the world once more in college graduation rates, but to make sure our graduates are ready for a career; ready to meet the challenges of a twenty-first century economy. (Obama, 2010; my emphasis)

From this example, we can easily imagine teachers who tell their students that they have to complete a particular task because failure to do so will result in their failing later on as workers and participants in the economic order. This view, or opinion, is not limited to the business elite and Friedmanites—that the primary purpose of education ought to be economic growth—it is a policy that is being lived out in classrooms across the country every day and is promulgated by the president of the United States.

Ball's analysis for his second aim in international educational policy is perhaps more central to our understanding of the current state of neoliberal education. "Decoupling education from state control" may at first be read as a move in favor of localized policy decisions, which we would then assume would allow for more opportunities for teachers to engage in making curricular and pedagogical choices based on the lived experiences of their students and the social contexts in which they live and learn. What we find instead is quite the reverse, as the loss of state control includes losing the state-certified actors in classrooms charged with educating their students: teachers.

This loss of state control can be seen in the creation and subsequent explosion of the number of charter schools since the 1980s. While some charter schools were established by critical educators with explicit aims of justice and liberation, charter schools, as such, remain as a product of neoliberal policy. Lipman (2011) addresses the origins of charter schools, saying that they "can be traced back to neoliberal and neoconservative agendas, particularly rollback of 'big government' and rollout of 'local control,' deregulation, and privatization" (p. 121). She goes on to address the disconnect between charter schools with critical missions and the neoliberal ideology imbedded in the creation of such alternatives to public schools. She writes,

> Whatever its progressive origins, the charter school strategy has been exploited and rearticulated to the interests of education entrepreneurs, venture philanthropists, investors, and corporate-style charter school chains. Charter schools have become the central vehicle to open up public education to the market, weaken teachers' unions, and eliminate whatever democratic control of public education there is. (pp. 121–122)

For Lipman, even those charter schools that advocate anti-oppressive and humanizing goals for their teachers and students are complicit in the perpetuation of neoliberal ideology and neoliberal educational policy.

The neoliberal turn to funneling public funds into private or pseudo-private educational institutions such as charter schools is occurring simultaneously with the rush toward nationalized "Common Core Standards" for P-12 education (Core Standards, 2010). These standards have been resisted by a few states,[5] with some arguing that their current state standards are more demanding than those proposed by the Common Core Standards advocates.

We should note, however, that on the Core Standards' webpage detailing state adoption of the standards, states that have refused to sign on are listed as "not yet adopted," signaling the presumed inevitability of nationalized curriculum in the United States.

The acceleration of nationalized standards can be seen as evidence for what Lipman (2011) has called "neoliberal accountability," in which teachers are forced to adapt their curricula and teaching practices to mirror national standards and have thus lost much of their agency in creating impactful lessons relevant to the lives of their students in favor of a mechanistic system of accountability for all teachers. Lipman writes of this point, "It is a shift from teacher professionalism[6] and relatively complex, socially situated notions of learning and teaching to postwelfarist [neoliberal] emphases on instrumental efficiency, effectiveness, productivity, and measurable performance" (p. 127). At the same time, given their role as employees of the state, the decoupling of educational policy from state authorities means that those who are seen as agents of the state (teachers) are excluded from decisions that immediately impact them and their students. As part of the larger neoliberal project to force education to justify its efficacy based on market-based conceptions of effectiveness, we are moving closer and closer to a nationalized, teacher-proofed curriculum.

In the name of local control, perversely, teachers have lost control over their own curriculums and school governance. What the neoliberal rhetoric omits in its move toward "local control" is acknowledgment that state employees, no matter how enmeshed in their own localities, are not the intended body to formalize and actualize local control over educational policy. This process, of limiting the amount of control teachers have over their own curriculums, has been critiqued as indicative of the World Bank's disregard for existing school structures and its lack of pedagogical knowledge. Heyneman (2003) writes, "Once the [World] Bank began to speak for all public educational expenditures, ipso facto, it acquired obligations over areas of education in which it was ill prepared to understand or accept responsibility" (p. 332). As the World Bank shifted to support neoliberalism to an ever greater extent, it moved from primarily only financing vocational education, as it had until the late 1970s, to determining the entirety of educational systems, something of which the World Bank leaders of the time admitted to having "little knowledge or experience" (p. 332). The neoliberal educational policies of the World Bank are now being put into place by policymakers in the United States, often under direct financing from philanthropic organizations tied to global capitalist conglomerates; most notably, the Bill and Melinda Gates Foundation. Teachers in the United States are being blamed for the failings of the neoliberal economy and are facing even more neoliberal reforms as a result.

Neoliberalism in Teacher Education

It is important, before proceeding, to make two points with regard to the arguments I shall develop in the remainder of this chapter. First, education for social mobility, for child-centered development, for social reconstruction, and for conformity to existing economic structures have all competed historically for space in the curriculum of U.S. schools (Kliebard, 2002; Labaree, 1997). An anticapitalist teacher education must acknowledge this historical struggle, and remember the absolute importance for students to engage with the economic realities of the society in which they live. This is especially true for students from historically (and presently) marginalized backgrounds: we must teach "the culture of power" and with it the present-day structures and personal skills necessary for full participation in society (Delpit, 2006). Which brings us to the second point I will ask readers to keep in mind: that teaching the culture of power, as such, will not transform the culture of power. Returning to Lisa Delpit's (2006) insights into the need to make the culture of power explicit and visible not only for students of color but for all students who show up at school without all the requisite experiences of academic discourse and white ways of being, we must not only teach the culture of power but also engage students in critically interrogating the oppressive and dehumanizing effects of our present political reality. Thus, we must teach traditional middle- and upper-class ways of being with regard to such life skills as banking, personal finance, and credit in order to support students who would otherwise never examine these practices and would thus be denied access and opportunity as a result. But this education must be accompanied by a critical interrogation of these practices and the ways in which capitalist exploitation has degraded and dehumanized individuals through these institutions. It is not enough to merely teach the culture of power and then assume that by doing so we have provided marginalized students with a "way out" of poverty. An anticapitalist teacher education is essential for this endeavor to be practiced in P-12 classrooms, and I now turn to the present-day realities of teacher education that prevent such a mobilization and radical transformation of pedagogical space.

Marx (1990) defined a commodity as an external object that satisfies human needs. In teacher education, we insist that all teachers hold to the notion that every child is capable of learning. The *purpose* of this learning, however, is rarely a focus of teacher education. While it is taken as common sense that the purpose of schooling should be the student's learning, when we examine what this learning is for we are left wanting. The recent push toward P-12 school systems preparing every student for college is a potential response to this question of purpose; all children must learn so that they can attend college. However, this answer in and of itself does not answer why every student must attend college. The justification for such an aspiration is almost always the demand of the capitalist economy for more highly skilled workers to sustain our national economic growth, a clear aim of capitalism. If we return to the above quote from President Obama we can see the ways in which teacher education is complicit in the neoliberal notion that the needs of the capitalist economy are synonymous with the needs of students. While it is certain that students must be able to obtain some kind of employment to support themselves as adults, we must take note that a slogan such as "Every Child College Ready"[7] is not in actuality a student-centered pronouncement, it is an economistic one.

This notion of education as preparation pervades not only P-12 schooling, but the education of future teachers as well. Yet it is in direct contrast to the work of progressive educators who for over a century have insisted that education and the purposes of learning must find their value in the lives of those presently engaged in the educative act (Dewey, 1897/2010; Freire, 2000). As Dewey (1897/2010) put it, "I believe that education, therefore, is a process of living and not a preparation for future living" (p. 22). Inherent in the name of teacher preparation is the notion that the educative aim of teacher education is preparation for future living, for future teaching. Further, when we examine P-12 schools' commitment to preparing students for future work as functionaries in the capitalist economic system, we see that such perspectives prevent the schools' seeing students as actual human beings engaged in their world. Instead, they see only their future use to the forces of production, as workers, and thus the schools must set about warping the students into ideal employees, well equipped to further their employers' pursuit of endless profits at the expense of the mass of humanity. Students are reduced to the status of instruments for satisfying external economic needs, rather than stewards of their own actual human needs (Casey, 2011).

Anyon (1981) found this to be the case in her study of working-class schools where teachers created assignments and classroom procedures designed to instill in students the ability to follow orders and complete repetitive tasks with little critical thinking. Students in this environment become objectified as commodities, as human resources to be used by others in their pursuit of profit. The abuse of workers, the creation of profit for employers based on the surplus labor of their workers, applies at all levels of the capitalist economy. Higher qualifications for more particular and specialized tasks (college degrees) change nothing about the use and abuse by employers of their workers. Higher wages, as Marx (1990) warned, can never overcome the exploitation of laborers in the capitalist economic system. Thus, teacher education's insistence on "high expectations" for all students does not challenge the existing structures of domination if those high expectations stop at the attainment of a postsecondary degree and successful employment.

Teacher education is also culpable in the perpetuation of neoliberal ideology in the ways it has increasingly come to position teachers as technicians. Christine Sleeter (2008) has documented the ways in which such pressures as high-stakes standardized testing (Hursh, 2008) and prescriptive curricula (Crocco & Costigan, 2007) have resulted in "districts serving low-income and/or culturally diverse students tend[ing] to adopt the most controlled and scripted curricula, in which not only content but also pedagogy is specified" (p. 1952). She notes in a footnote that "[s]cripted curricula specify exactly what teachers should say or do, in a step-by-step fashion. Teachers using them are literally expected to teach by following a published script" (p. 1952). Sleeter sees these pressures as leading to teacher education's being reduced to preparing "technicians who can implement curriculum packages" (p. 1952). It becomes necessary, however, to examine further what is carried in the term *technician* and what such a conception of teaching means in relation to neoliberalism as well as to pedagogy.

One result of the "teacher as technician" trope is the decline in teacher education of foundations of education courses and the increase of clinical practice (Kerr, Mandzek, & Raptis, 2011). While the work of Linda Darling-Hammond (2006) and others seeking to elaborate a direction for teacher education—one that would link together theory and practice through coursework and field experiences that support and build upon one another—clearly has the potential to work against neoliberalism, we must still ask what such a project is working toward, given teacher education's present commitments. It is not necessarily the turn to clinical practice as the central element of teacher education that has led to the construction of teachers as technicians, but rather what is represented in such a move. Teaching imagined as a complex, partial, and inherently unknowable act (Kumashiro, 2009) might well lead one to direct more energy into apprenticeship or co-teaching models in teacher education in the hopes that such experiences will better aid prospective teachers in developing the skills necessary to be successful in the classroom. But therein lies the neoliberal influence of such a position: imagining teaching as something one can be measurably good at, or, further, that there are particular ways of teaching that produce measurable results from which to generate decisions about "effectiveness."

Kevin Kumashiro (2009) warns us of the "need to problematize any effort to predetermine what it means to be a 'good' teacher. Commonsensical definitions of good teaching are often complicit with different forms of oppression" (p. 15). Imagining how teachers come to be seen as technicians becomes easier from this starting point. What the teacher as technician approach enables is to position teaching alongside other professions as a part of the professionalization of teachers, as we have been discussing. But such an approach reduces the complexity of teaching to a set of skills or best practices that one can employ simply in order to attain specific (already known) results. This is precisely the dehumanizing "banking" education that Freire (2000) cautions against, because the praxis of pedagogy is reduced to an ends-based conception of the value of such an education. In other words, the "effectiveness," and thus the worth of an educator, is discernable from what her students are able to produce, often reduced to standardized test scores (Hursh, 2008).

While the literal scripting of curricula has enabled the conception of the teacher as technician to further take hold, teacher education's need to justify its own efficacy by employing neoliberal logics of effectiveness and accountability reduces the pedagogical and political work of teaching to technique and teacher education itself to a form of technology: how best to educate future teachers for set, predetermined results. Despite the immensity of scholarship in the teacher education literature that argues against positioning teaching in such a way, teacher education, by imagining its work as part of the professionalization of the teaching profession, has participated in the neoliberalization of teaching by employing neoliberal logics and ideologies, both to justify as well as to understand itself. While Sleeter (2008) and others (Apple, 2001; Kumashiro, 2010) are right to point out that teacher education has been under attack by private corporate interests, this attack has been accelerated as teacher education programs have sought to appropriate the discourses of neoliberal capitalism into their own practices.

A further way in which teacher education is culpable in the maintenance of neoliberal ideology in education is by fetishizing productivity and student "achievement." Ladson-Billings (2006a) has written of her own use of the term *academic achievement* with regard to culturally relevant pedagogy, and that she has since come to regret using it in her framework for anti-oppressive teaching and learning with students. She writes of the term *academic achievement*, "What I had in mind has nothing to do with the oppressive atmosphere of standardized tests; the wholesale retention of groups of students; scripted curricula; and the intimidation of students, teachers, and parents" (p. 34). The use of academic achievement measures has resulted in, as Lipman (2011) has argued, "a moral and political crisis in teaching as democratic and humanistic purposes of education are superseded by corporate economic goals, and one-size-fits-all standards and high stakes tests reverse equity gains of the 1960s and 1970s" (p. 128). Achievement measures have done little to address the increasing wealth gap in the United States, and as Hursh (2007) has argued, have also done little to redress the academic disparities between white students and students of color. A focus on achievement as measured by standardized tests has come to replace what Ladson-Billings (2006a) has articulated as academic achievement, meaning student learning. The failure of standardized tests in this regard can be seen in Kumashiro's (2009) point that "[w]e can never know exactly what students are learning" (p. 37). Student learning as measured by high-stakes standardized tests can only measure what students produce on those particular tests, and thus there is no way that any such test could actually be a testament to everything students know. Teacher education's fetishization of productivity is a glaring reason why such a vulgar conception of student achievement has taken hold.

By "fetishizing productivity," I mean the ways in which teacher education strives to produce "expert teachers" who can maximize student achievement. How productive a teacher is rests on how quickly she is able to move through the standards for her grade level or subject area and how well her students perform on the subsequent test. While many teacher educators reject the idea that standardized test scores are synonymous with teacher effectiveness, we are still able to find ways in which teacher education furthers neoliberal aims of productivity for teachers. In Hammerness et al. (2005), for example, we learn from some of the most widely read and celebrated teacher researchers that "[e]xpert teachers are able to perform a variety of activities without having to stop and think about how to do them" (p. 361). The most generous reading of this theory I can give is that these authors are arguing that in teaching some things need to be routinized in order for thoughtful practices to go on elsewhere. Classrooms are complex spaces, and teachers' attention should be focused on those areas that are most deserving given the current situation and context. Thus, some things deserve careful consideration and others do not, and knowing the difference is part of the measure of an "expert teacher."

Yet, taken more critically, why would we, as teacher educators seeking to engage our future teachers in deep and critical reflection on their teaching practice—to in fact make such an act of praxis a part of what it means to teach—wish to encourage them to eventually stop engaging in such work? To say that an expert teacher is one who does not actively "stop and think" is to refute critical anti-oppressive educators' insistence that it is precisely those unintentional or hidden lessons, those moments when we are not thinking critically and carefully about what we are doing, that can carry the most oppressive messages in our classrooms (Apple, 2000; Kumashiro, 2009). Yet many of these authors have written powerfully about the need for teachers to be reflexive in their practice elsewhere (see Cochran-Smith & Lytle, 1993; Darling-Hammond, 2006; Zeichner & Liston, 1996). What is not entirely clear from the chapter is precisely which moments are worthy of deep and critical reflection and which are to be routinized. Further, there is no acknowledgment of the potential danger in not critically interrogating our routines for evidence of oppression. We should be leery of routinizing or proceeding in even the most innocuous task in a manner that does not call on us to interrogate what is being communicated, what hidden curriculum exists in any and everything in the classroom.[8] We must then ask what use such a practice, in this formulation, is working toward in terms of its aims for teaching and learning and how neoliberalism is able to manipulate even critical teacher educators into positioning their aims and work in neoliberal ways.

The less time teachers spend reflecting on the minute and complex details of their work in classrooms, the more time they will be able to give to their immediate task in a neoliberal education system: to maximize student achievement as measured by standardized tests. This is the fetishization of productivity in teacher education, where we encourage our future teachers to aspire to a time when they will be so skilled as teachers that they will no longer have to consider all the various ways in which their work in classrooms is working in contradiction to their goals (Kumashiro, 2009; Ladson-Billings, 2006a). To seek to minimize the amount of time teachers spend on matters that are not considered a part of the formal curriculum utilizes a neoliberal conception of surplus value wherein those who are able to accomplish more in less time are more valuable. This frame of thinking about schooling is what enables the notion that schooling in the United States is not "cost effective" when compared to other nations based on per-pupil spending (Guggenheim, 2010). The concept that we must maximize productivity, to make teachers able to move through content as speedily as their students' mastery of that content will allow (if not faster), pervades teacher education and neoliberal conceptions of the work of teaching.

To summarize, teacher education is complicit in the perpetuation of neoliberal ideology through its positioning of P-12 students as commodities, its conception of teachers as technicians, and its fetishization of productivity and student achievement. While these elements of teacher education could never be held collectively responsible for the onset and continual growth of the whole of neoliberalism, they are evidence of the ways in which teacher education has not lived out its commitments to positioning teaching as a part of a larger global project to usher forth a more just and equitable society for all people. As school administration becomes all the more akin to business administration (Kliebard, 2002), so does teacher education (and the act of teaching) become all the more akin to training workers for jobs on assembly lines. With demands for student achievement placed above demands for humanizing and impactful learning, teacher educators are able to put forth the aims of Hammerness et al. (2005), who conclude that expert teachers are deemed expert when they are "efficient" in their classrooms. This conception of expertise is again related to Freire's (2000) notion of the banking method of education wherein students are seen as receptacles, receiving knowledge passively and later asked to return on the investment in the form of performance, in this case, on standardized tests.

What about Professionalization?

There is a way all of the above can be placed in subordinate relationship to the movement to professionalize teachers. But here we have to stop, as the evidence presented above certainly paints a picture that is far too complex to lead to the conclusion that a group of educational researchers, no matter how prominent or accomplished, could have actually ushered in our present neoliberal reality in education. Arguments of blame are rarely very helpful, and when one is speaking of systemic realities it is rare that those who do not actually control the system are responsible for its operation. Rather, I conclude this chapter by restating a few of the above points, and finally coming back to some of what Labaree has raised in his critique of the professionalization movement.

Professionalizing the teaching force has led to teaching becoming positioned alongside the other professions in only negative ways. That is, in making teaching and coming to be a teacher more like becoming a doctor, we have actually exacerbated the distance, in terms of prestige, between teaching and other professions. Here is why. Insisting on a scientific knowledge base, similar to what they have in medicine, can never satisfy the fundamental purpose of schools in the first place. The scientific knowledge base for teaching takes schools, classrooms, and the vast majority of the arbitrary factory-like settings of schools and classrooms as inevitabilities and even as universals. In our quest to find "what works" we almost never stop to take seriously the notion that "no practice is always anti-oppressive" (Kumashiro, 2009) and that what works for one teacher or class almost never works in the same way for other teachers and other classes. This unknowability, the politically charged world that schools exist in, the needs and challenges of different peoples and groups; these are elements of teaching that make a scientific knowledge base an impossible aim if by it we hope to ever encapsulate the full complexity of work in classrooms.

Now, we should be clear here: medicine presents many of these same challenges. But we can quote one of the originators of the professionalization movement, Lee Shulman (2004), to define the difference between the work of a medical doctor and that of a teacher. Shulman writes, "The practice of teaching involves a far more complex task environment than does that of medicine. The teacher is confronted, not with a single patient, but with a classroom filled with 25 to 35 youngsters" (p. 258). He goes on, "[T]he teacher's goals are multiple; the schools obligations far from unitary" (p. 258). Thus, the comparison of medicine and teaching can only go so far, and as so many more doctors work in privately run, for-profit hospitals than teachers do in privately run, for-profit schools we should not be surprised that trying to make teaching more akin to being a medical doctor results in making teaching function more on the side of capitalism.

We do not need teachers to be seen as anything other than teachers, not as professionals or like medical doctors, because teaching is itself one of the last (potentially) anticapitalist endeavors we can aspire to in our present neoliberal order. Making teacher education a graduate program does nothing to change the importance and complexity of working with and learning with students in profound and humanizing ways. Offering teachers a stable body of scientific knowledge about teaching results in, as my student identified it at the beginning of this chapter, an approach that focuses on "what we have to know" rather than on what we can learn for ourselves, in powerful, affirming, self-appropriated ways. We need a new direction for teacher education, one that refuses to support the commodification of students, training teachers as technicians, and thinking of our work as maximizing efficiency. Fortunately, teacher education research has a wealth of knowledge and resources with which we can imagine new ways of orienting our work as teacher educators. That virtually none of it is seen as a part of the scientific knowledge base for teaching should fill us with hope and possibility to actualize our opposition to running schools as though they were businesses and treating students and parents as though they were customers. It is to this pedagogical vision for teacher education that I now turn.

EIGHT

Anticapitalist Antiracist Pedagogy in the Classroom

A Pedagogical Framework

It is not consciousness that determines life, but life that
determines consciousness.

—*The German Ideology*

They know that property, capital, money, wage-labour
and the like are no ideal figments of the brain but
very practical, very objective sources of their self-
estrangement and that they must be abolished in a
practical, objective way for man to become man not
only in *thinking*, in *consciousness*, but in massy *being*,
in life.

—*The Holy Family*

I almost dropped out. It was my first semester of graduate school
and I was fed up. I felt surrounded by people who were convinced
that schools could never function on the side of justice, because
that was never what schools were intended to do in the first place.
Schools were designed to eliminate cultural difference, to indoctrinate young people into civic participation in the United States,
and to provide them with the requisite experience necessary for
their eventual work roles in the capitalist economy. I am not sure
why this felt so personal to me, but I had a terrible time trying to

147

convince myself that schools were lost causes and that we needed to find a new way of combatting oppression because schools themselves were simply too far gone; too hierarchical, too racist, too sexist, and we could keep going. I resisted what I considered to be a pessimistic theory of schooling, until I realized I was making a mistake in how I was conceptualizing schools. Over time, I came to see schools as historically oppressive. But within schools are spaces in which transformation, justice, and change are enacted and lived out daily. I speak, of course, of classrooms. It was bell hooks (1994) who helped me realize my folly, who kept me in graduate school, and who inspired me to shift my focus in educational coursework from educational policy to curriculum and instruction. Classrooms are sites of imminent possibility, in which we can strive to live out versions of our best selves, our best ideas, and our deepest commitments. bell hooks sees classrooms as the space of learning, and the ending to her book *Teaching to Transgress* has been with me every day since I first found it. She writes,

> Learning is a place where paradise can be created. The classroom, with all of its limitations, remains a location of possibility. In that field of possibility we have the opportunity to labor for freedom, to demand of ourselves and our comrades, an openness of mind and heart that allows us to face reality even as we collectively imagine ways to move beyond boundaries, to transgress. (p. 207)

Teaching has been the most fulfilling and worthy part of my life these past ten years. Learning with students, supporting teachers as they explore new approaches to their work in classrooms, asking difficult questions of what it means to teach people who do not look or speak or act like their teachers; the complexities of being in the classroom are seemingly endless.

I always write two things on the board in the last few moments of the last night of class. The first is a quote from critical black feminist scholar Audre Lorde (1984): "The master's tools will never dismantle the master's house" (p. 110). Schools are the master's tools, a nineteenth-century invention modeled on industrial factories to turn young people from absolutely anywhere into Americans. Following Lorde's claim, it makes no sense to think that schools will ever dismantle what it was they were built for: teaching white middle- and upper-class norms and values to maintain the status quo across generations. But then I draw the following:

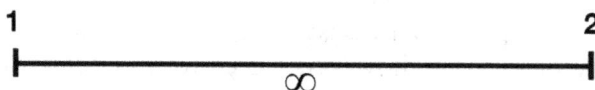

```
1                                              2
├────────────────────────────────────────────┤
              ∞
```

FIGURE 1. Bounded Infinity

Bounded infinity is the mathematical concept from chaos and complexity theory that between the points 1 and 2 on a number line there are in fact an infinite number of points. We could never actually list every possible number that exists just between the integers 1 and 2. This is my metaphor for classrooms. If we think of the point 1 as being all the human realities in a classroom, the students, their desires, and so on and think of the point 2 as all the restrictive controlling realities, standards, pressures from administration, from the state, and so on; the space in between is infinite. There is no way of knowing what is possible, even in a bounded space like the distance between 1 and 2. This is why classrooms, while they are in schools, are not the same thing as schools, and why I will never stop believing that worthy ways of being are inherently possible in classroom spaces.

This chapter is concerned with detailing what is meant by anticapitalist antiracist pedagogy at the level of the classroom. To accomplish this, I build on existent pedagogical theories of critical pedagogy (Freire, 2000), anti-oppressive education (Kumashiro, 2009), and culturally relevant pedagogy (Ladson-Billings, 2006a). Anticapitalist antiracist pedagogy constitutes a form of Freirean reinvention of these other critical approaches to teaching and learning. I expand on these pedagogical visions and work to detail how such commitments can be made into anticapitalist antiracist practice. These pedagogical theories cannot be neatly teased apart, but rather inform and react to one another. In other words, critical pedagogy overlaps with anti-oppressive education, and of course both speak to and overlap with culturally relevant pedagogy. My aim here is not to discuss the differences between these theories, but rather to bring them together so as to articulate a pedagogical vision of anticapitalist antiracism. I have organized the next sections of this chapter into three segments: learning, curriculum, and consciousness. While of course these concepts are impossible to separate from one another completely, they will allow us to focus in on particular facets of justice work in classrooms and what makes an anticapitalist antiracist stance so powerful.

Before proceeding, however, I need to make clear that what follows is not an account of what I do in the classroom. Nor is it a step-by-step guide, or a list of best practices. Instead, I offer a framework: a way of organizing conceptually the tasks of the anticapitalist antiracist teacher and the sociopolitical commitments necessary for such a practice. Thus, my orientation toward pedagogy, and to writing in advocating a pedagogical position, must be nuanced by the objective conditions of teaching and learning. Joe Kincheloe (2008) reminds us, "There are as many brilliant forms of practice as there are brilliant practitioners" (p. 116). There is no single way of practicing anticapitalist antiracism, in the classroom or outside of it. As pedagogues we must understand ourselves, as both people and as educators, as political actors capable of acting on and transforming our worlds. And the truism that there is no one best way to do this creates openings we may never have even sought out, were we convinced there was something that could always work best if we could only figure out exactly what it was and how to do it. Following this, the caution from Kumashiro (2009) that "[n]o practice is always anti-oppressive" means that even for educators committed to anticapitalist antiracism and the inherently political nature of their work in classrooms, there are no methods one can employ in every possible situation that will always function on the side of justice (p. 3). We must be willing to reject lessons and activities that we have used before if those lessons and activities are no longer grounded in the lived realities of our students and the wealth of experiences they bring with them into our classrooms (Freire, 2000). But this also opens up an endless number of possibilities: for if no practice is always-anti-oppressive the task of teaching in anticapitalist antiracist ways represents an endless array of possible lessons and topics that one can never disengage with, or reduce to an unthinking reaction.

This work can seem impossibly daunting at times, yet it is imperative that we see the inevitability of no practice always being anti-oppressive as an opening to newly imagined spaces, rather than disabling our abilities to make meaningful connections between our students and their/our world(s). Gloria Ladson-Billings (2006a) addresses this when asked by her teacher education students why she will not simply explain to them "how to do" culturally relevant pedagogy. She says,

> Even if we could tell you how to do it, I would not want us to tell you how to do it. . . . The reason I would not tell you what to do is that you would probably do it. . . . Without any deep thought or critical analysis. You would do what I said regardless of the students in the classroom, their ages, their abilities, and their need for whatever it is I proposed. (p. 39)

Ladson-Billings is demanding that her teacher education students see culturally relevant pedagogy (and for that matter critical pedagogy and anti-oppressive education) not as something one does, but rather as something one *is*. We do not *do* critical pedagogy; we *are* critical in our engagement with the word and the world. Ladson-Billings (2006a) is arguing "for why 'doing' is less important than 'being'. . . . Practicing culturally relevant pedagogy is one of the ways of 'being' that will inform ways of 'doing'" (p. 41). An emphasis on being, then, does not see questions of doing fall by the wayside. I am not arguing here for a directionless pedagogy, nor arguing that we should never consider what we are doing in the classroom. Rather, I am following other critical scholars to argue for a new hierarchy of pedagogical reflection in which the question of "being" comes before the question of "doing." Teachers are to consider first who they are being with and for their students, and then consider what they are doing in subordinate relation to whom they are being.

For an Anticapitalist Antiracist Theory of Learning

The famed American psychologist Carl Rogers (1989), while he makes for a rather odd way of beginning this section, offers us several crucial theories of learning and how particular kinds of learning become valued or practiced more than others. His conclusions form the basis of the theory of learning in anticapitalist antiracist pedagogy. First, he writes, "My experience has been that I cannot teach another person how to teach. To attempt it is for me, in the long run futile" (p. 301). The irony in a self-identified teacher educator subscribing to this notion may trouble the reader, but if we continue with Rogers's beliefs on learning, this point becomes more easily understood. Rogers's next two conclusions address the linkage of learning and behavior, in which he states he is "only interested in learnings which significantly influence behavior" (p. 302). From the perspective of anticapitalist antiracist pedagogy, this commitment can be read as an attention to learning in ways that lend themselves to action on lived reality, rather than mere passive participation. This is central to Freire's notions of the purpose of learning, that literacy for literacy's sake is empty: the purpose of learning to read words is so that one is better able to read the world in critical and humanizing ways. Thus, while at first we might consider Rogers to be too much of a behaviorist, we find much the same commitment in Freire's and other critical pedagogues' work.

Rogers goes on, writing that he has "come to feel that the only learning which significantly influences behavior is self-discovered, self-appropriated learning" (p. 302). For Rogers, this is the kind of learning that "cannot be directly communicated," the kind that if it were communicated would become a form of teaching that Rogers finds "absurd" (pp. 302–303)—absurd because the results are "inconsequential," and Rogers cites Kierkegaard here as someone else who found that merely communicating information to another is generally of little consequence to that other. This can be read, once again, in a Freirean way: so often, teaching represents the attempted transfer of knowledge the teacher possesses into the minds of learners. This, of course, is what Freire called the "banking method" of education, but Rogers's work helps us understand the Freirean critique more deeply. What Rogers is so troubled by is that his own knowledge that is of value to him is knowledge that he has self-appropriated, internalized, and personalized in such a way that it constitutes a part of who he is, what he does, his behavior, rather than a mere fact to be memorized. Thus, when Rogers says that teaching is inconsequential, he means that the communication of self-appropriated knowledge can only be impactful if it is seen as a knowledge-gathering process on the part of the learner. That is, if a young child asks an adult how to tie her shoes, and the adult then demonstrates and explains how he ties his own shoes, this is not an instance of banking education. Why? Because the agentic character of the learner is never undermined by the teacher: the learner wants to learn how to tie her shoes, thus making asking the question and watching the demonstration an active process of self-appropriated meaning making.

Rogers goes on to say that he feels the results of his teaching too often stifle learning, in the self-appropriated way he believes carries the most meaning for the learner. He goes so far as to say that he no longer wishes to teach, only to learn, and in groups if possible. Once again, the Freirean tones should be apparent. For Freire (2000), one of the primary tasks of the teacher is to trouble the traditional power differential between teachers and learners. This does not mean, as has sometimes been assumed by readers of Freire who have not done enough work to uncover his meaning that the teacher merely pretends as though she is not in a position of relative power vis-à-vis her students. Rather, the teacher is tasked with moving to being on the side of her students, to positioning herself as a learner in the act of teaching and, in radical solidarity with her students, working together to learn in ways that allow for humanization and transformation. Rogers wants us to go a step farther, to "do away with teaching. People would get together if they wanted to learn" (p. 303). But here, we can nuance Rogers somewhat to argue that what is most needed for teachers is that they stop thinking of themselves as the only teacher in a pedagogical site. Rather, teachers must see themselves as another learner, one who may well have read the particular course texts fifty times more than the other learners present, but still as someone who is fundamentally seeking to learn in humanizing ways with others.

Learning thus is the focus of any and all pedagogical activity, and as such we can concretize the common abstraction of being in solidarity with students into an active praxis: of a solidarity premised on the positionality of the learner. When a teacher has made up her mind that she has learned everything about a particular subject, that teacher can almost never be in solidarity with her students, who by definition carry with them the notion that they are incomplete, unfinished. This is not to say that teachers and students must be learning the same thing at the same time, only that the fundamental attitude of both be as learners, as human beings with questions and curiosities about their world(s).

Anticapitalist antiracist pedagogy entails a conception of learning that cannot be reduced to the status of a commodity: nothing one learns should derive its primary value based on its exchangeability. This means that learning cannot be primarily for job training, or preparation for future work. It means, further, that all information be subjected to critical scrutiny on the part of the learner based on their lived experiences. Anticapitalist antiracist pedagogy refuses abuses of teacher power, not only based on commitments to redistributing power, but because of the centrality of learning to the pedagogical act. In Freire's (1998) terms, "[T]here is no teaching without learning" (p. 29). Rather than privileging the teaching act, or making teaching into the mere delivery of information, teaching becomes fundamentally the process and practice of the facilitation of learning. If one stands and lectures and the students learn nothing, one is not teaching.

Thus, anticapitalist antiracist pedagogy places learning above all other aims and commitments, but learning defined as the self-appropriation of knowledge through a critical engagement with one's own lived experience. This means that authentic learning is never for an outside need, for economic participation, for credentializing, or for the will of others. We can test this rather humbly, if we just stop and think about something we know really well, and then ask ourselves how we came to know it really well. It is our own work to understand, to figure out, premised on genuine interest that produces knowledge we actually possess, what we have actually learned. Thus, the things we are most expert in are things we have largely learned ourselves or with others in a way that sought others' support as part of our process of knowledge creation and meaning making.

We all have favorite teachers, to be sure, but how often is it the case that someone tells of their favorite teacher by launching into a description of the best lesson they delivered? Virtually never. Rather, we most often describe our favorite teachers by the ways they made us feel. To put the former into more critical terms, we celebrate those teachers who created the conditions under which we were able to live out our curiosities and construct knowledge and meaning for ourselves. Not the teachers who taught us the most; the teachers who helped us learn the most.

For an Anticapitalist Antiracist Theory of Curriculum

On the first night of class, in the course Contemporary Approaches to Curriculum, I ask my students (practicing teachers) to come up with as many examples of what we mean by curriculum as they possibly can. The first few are usually the same every time: textbooks, teacher guides, workbooks, or the more abstract but no less accurate "what we teach." After a while, and with a short pause, someone usually opens up the floodgates with a concept such as "the hidden curriculum" or what we unintentionally teach—those hidden messages embedded in what we do in the classroom and in the texts we take up. In the end, the board is often filled up, to the point that I ask, "So, what *isn't* curriculum?" The ensuing conversation usually ends with someone making a definitional statement, something along the lines of, "Curriculum is anything you learn from." For anticapitalist antiracist pedagogy, this is precisely the case, and this opens up a number of possibilities for classroom praxis.

We often make the mistake of thinking that the best made plans and course materials are what matter most for teaching. When we think of the work a teacher does outside of class to get ready, we most often think of grading student work and designing course assignments and activities. Yet, how often have we experienced the teacher who cannot help but share a story or anecdote with her students? What if we took just as seriously the anecdotal, the extra, of classroom curricula and the more formal, state standard-esque form? The insight that curriculum is anything we can learn from truly means *anything*, and this is precisely what the anticapitalist antiracist pedagogue explodes in terms of course texts and activities. Students are able to bring in their own artifacts and experiences, to be discussed and examined. Students take up interesting and new problems, of their own invention, and work to solve challenges in cooperative solidarity. These tasks are enhanced exponentially when it is students' own desires and experiences that are privileged in this process. The "funds of knowledge" (Gonzalez

& Moll, 2002) that students bring with them to school every day must be understood as just as much a part of the curriculum as the formal textbook, scope and sequence, and standards. Why? Because students, as human beings, are always already learning from any number of curricular artifacts. Pretending that only that which is in the official curriculum is what is learned at school is ludicrous. The test is simple. Think of all the ways we learn how to carry ourselves, how to position our bodies, how to dress to achieve a certain affect, how we should wear our hair, and what kinds of foods we should be eating. There is no end to this list, because there is no limit to what we could possibly learn from the staggering array of curricula that we continually experience.

This conception of curricula has a special importance in anticapitalist antiracist pedagogy because it denies the privileged position of the formal curriculum its reified status as the "official knowledge" of a course (Apple, 2000). Curriculum in the formal sense is an exceptionally expensive commodity, and learning imagined as consumption is inevitable if we narrowly imagine all that people should (or will) learn as something that could be packaged, bought, and sold. There are, of course, challenges to such a commitment of making curriculum a means to rather than an end in itself, and we need to address these here. The first challenge is the role of standards and the academic disciplines as they have come to be practiced and protected in our current historical moment.

While it may be surprising, Freire and other critical educational theorists are most often supportive of standards or the academic disciplines as the basis for work in schools. It is not the curriculum itself that makes or breaks a critical classroom, but rather how curricular materials are taken up, and with what limits in place. For Ladson-Billings (2006a), "[T]eachers engaged in culturally relevant pedagogy must be able to deconstruct, construct, and reconstruct the curriculum" (p. 32). By deconstruction, she means examining particular curricula for those elements that may well be oppressive and placing them in context, making the learning of an event a form of critique, as we constantly compare our values and beliefs to practices and histories as they exist in formal curricula. Next, construction here means simply that teachers and students are both seen as able and capable of making curriculum, of naming the objects and subjects of their studies in powerful ways. Reconstruction, for Ladson-Billings, means putting things back together in new ways, taking both the "official knowledge" and the critical knowledge students have brought to bear on the curriculum to place it in context in ways that both enable students to have access to dominant theories and concepts while affirming their own lived experience.

Lisa Delpit's (2006) work around making the culture of power explicit to students from historically marginalized communities makes for a powerful example of Ladson-Billings's theories of curriculum in practice. Delpit is clear that not engaging dominant modes of discourse, white ways of being and speaking, and capitalist financial skills with students who do not experience these things at home is doing these students a profound disservice. Anticapitalist antiracist pedagogy places every person in the context of our present historical reality, which is profoundly oppressive and dehumanizing. No amount of socially just pedagogy in one isolated classroom is going to transform white supremacist capitalist patriarchy (hooks, 1994). This means that while we must place an emphasis on those curricular artifacts and funds of knowledge that students bring with them into our classrooms, we also must engage the official curriculum. Failure to do this is a failure to support students in their self-appropriation of learning. But this does not have to be an either/or dilemma, as Ladson-Billings has demonstrated above. We engage the official curriculum in ways that privilege our own experiences and knowledges. We work within disciplinary boundaries because they offer unique lenses to ask different kinds of questions and different ways to respond. The point is this: curriculum cannot be viewed as an end in itself. Rather, curriculum is a means *to*, through learning. It is a resource, which we can learn from in order to develop anticapitalist antiracist consciousness.

For an Anticapitalist Antiracist Theory of Consciousness

In the work of Paulo Freire the aim of pedagogy is humanization, through liberation. We can read Freire as offering a pedagogy of Marxism, and at the center of this pedagogy, as it was at the center for Marx, is a concern with developing the consciousness necessary for revolution, for transforming our oppressive reality. *Conscientização,* in Freire's terms, critical consciousness of consciousness must be the aim for our learning. Ladson-Billings (1995) makes a case for a form of critical consciousness, what she calls sociopolitical consciousness, as a part of culturally relevant pedagogy. She writes, "The first thing teachers must do is educate themselves about both the local sociopolitical issues of their school community (e.g., school board policy, community events) and the larger sociopolitical issues (e.g., unemployment, healthcare, housing) that impinge upon their students' lives" (p. 37). Consciousness thus has the function here of working to connect the local and the universal, both what is immediately at hand and the structures, systems, and frames that inform and act on both individuals and groups. The need is for teachers to come to position themselves as conscious political actors, in an inherently political reality, and to draw connections between what they experience in their local contexts and how those experiences inform the larger context in which those experiences take place.

For Marx, revolutionary consciousness is tied to an understanding of one's position in relation to the means of production. When workers understand that the owners of the means of production alienate and dehumanize in the pursuit of profits, that this is fundamentally what capitalism functions to do, they can then articulate their aims for liberation with the understanding that the present economic system denies them their capacity to be fully human. For anticapitalist antiracist pedagogy, this form of revolutionary consciousness is the product of learning and critical engagement with curricula, as outlined above. This consciousness is premised on the ability to see, in both local and global contexts, the present realities of white supremacy and the ways in which the logics of white supremacy function to legitimate capitalist exploitation. It is this ability to see that consciousness offers, not merely an abstract principle, but rather a self-appropriated ability to read both the word and the world in critical ways. Seeing the connection between local manifestations of white supremacy and global manifestations of capitalist abuse as a part of the same overarching system of signs and meaning is the principle aim of anticapitalist antiracist pedagogy. Importantly, however, this cannot be thought of as merely an intellectual skill, and, further, cannot be learned through banking methods. These last two points need to be explained in further detail.

Consciousness, and critical consciousness in particular, should be thought of less as an ability, and more of a way of being in the world. We can make rules for finding racism in practice, and we might learn those rules and then always be successful at identifying the racist connotations of a particular phrase or practice. But merely being able to name these processes offers us nothing. Rather, being able to name these processes while understanding their historical, social, and political dimension and the ways in which race and racism intersect in myriad other systems and forms of oppression offers us the ability to not only understand racism, but to orient our lives in opposition to it. This orientation, this way of being, carries with it the profound capacity to act on oppressive realities because it refuses to take any system or reality as an inevitability. That is, no creation by human beings is devoid of context, and if we understand capitalism, positivism, and instrumental reason as unnatural, as made by human beings, we can position ourselves in relation to these systems in ways that enable us to see cracks in the edifice. Consciousness of our oppressive order and the ways in which it has been created for particular aims is the precondition for radical solidarity.

There is a tendency, perhaps, to seek to accelerate the consciousness of others through banking methods. Anticapitalist antiracist pedagogy rejects the idea that one can acquire critical consciousness as if it were merely a technology, something to be used toward particular ends, rather than a practice. Freire (2000) warns us, "In the revolutionary process, the leaders cannot utilize the banking method as an interim measure, justified on grounds of expediency, with the intention of *later* behaving in a genuinely revolutionary fashion" (p. 86). Rather, the revolutionary process itself must be dialogical, in Freire's terms, from beginning to end. The process of coming to consciousness is one that must be self-appropriated for it to have any actual impact or bearing on individuals in their daily experience. This means that, rather than banking notions of white supremacy and capitalist exploitation, the learner must come to see these systems as they impact on their actual lives. We cannot treat oppression solely in abstract terms, as though the purpose of our work for justice was to elaborate a metaphysics of oppression. The purpose is, rather, to abolish the oppressive systems as such, to use the capacity for critical reflection and action to usher forth a new reality premised on justice rather than the accumulation of wealth and power.

Anticapitalist antiracist consciousness is thus a practice of living, a way of being in relation to others in the world. This consciousness is never finished; the end of capitalism will not create the end of the need for critical consciousness. Rather, it is only through the practice of critical consciousness that a more just reality is possible. This is the optimism inherent in the work of both Marx and Freire, though we should be clear that neither thinker should be thought of as utopian.[1] To claim that a more just reality is possible is not utopian; it represents the conscious desires of billions of men and women to live worthy lives. There will never be a time, even after capitalism is no more, when the need for critical scrutiny, for placing our immediate reality in context, is no longer necessary.

It is only through the cultivation of critical consciousness that a more just reality can ever come about, but this does not mean that there will not be disagreements on how we ought to organize our lives. Marx is famously ambiguous about what he thinks the postcapitalist world will look like, because it will be up to the women and men of the world to dictate what their lives are to be and how best to organize society for achieving justice. These are not future people, but rather existing human beings, in the world now. Thus, anticapitalist antiracist pedagogy holds out no vision for the contents of daily life in a world where white supremacy and capitalism have ceased to be the dominant ideological formations of the globe. Rather, what is necessary is the capacity for creating such a society—a way of being that will enable both the revolution and postrevolutionary existence to be premised on the same aims of humanization and critical interrogation of the ways in which power and wealth function in human groups.

Consciousness is not a preparation for revolutionary action; it is the lifeblood of revolutionary action. Anticapitalist antiracist pedagogy resists any claims for learning premised on future needs because those needs are not those elaborated by learners themselves, but rather by the oppressive system learners find themselves in. Education as preparation for later employment can only function on the side of capitalism and the existing global order. Dewey (1897/2010) was critical of the idea of education as preparation, and, rather, sought to make democracy a way of being in much the same way as I am describing anticapitalist antiracist consciousness as a way of being. For Dewey, education is always already happening, human beings are always making meaning from their experiences, we are always learning. To behave as though learning was something that only happened in school, and then only at certain times, and with only certain predetermined subjects or facts, is to deny what it means fundamentally to be human.

Thus, anticapitalist antiracist pedagogy as a practice of being must transcend the space of the classroom in order to fully realize itself in consciousness. Anticapitalist antiracist pedagogy is not a technology, a tool to be used, but rather a way of being and living. And while this may seem overly daunting, we already have practices embedded in our present capitalist order that make this more easily imaginable. In the United States, we commonly define ourselves based on our occupations. "What do you do?"—to return to the example raised in earlier chapters—is perhaps the most common question asked when two adults meet for the first time. When we answer, "I'm a teacher," we often mean that that is what we do for employment. What is called for here, in an anticapitalist antiracist consciousness, is that we never stop acting as though "what we do" is not "what we are doing" and thus, "who we are." The call then, is to live our pedagogies, not merely in the classroom, but in any and all social spaces where human beings are creating meaning for themselves. This process never stops, and thus consciousness never stops, but rather leads to more consciousness, to consciousness of consciousness, and thus to revolutionary action.

Anti-Oppressive Education:
Anticapitalist Antiracism in/with the Postmodern

Up to this point, I have been primarily concerned in this chapter with detailing the central precepts of anticapitalist antiracist pedagogy in direct relation to the work of Marx and Freire. Yet I have insisted in this work that no one practice of anticapitalist antiracism exists, that there are in fact any number of possible ways to engage anticapitalist antiracist consciousness in the classroom. Kevin Kumashiro does not locate himself in the Marxist tradition, and thus exploring his work offers us more insight into possibilities for anticapitalist antiracist work in classrooms.

Perhaps most central to Kumashiro's (2009) pedagogy is his notion of "crises" as powerful learning opportunities. He writes, "By 'crisis,' I mean a state of emotional discomfort and disorientation that calls on students to make some change. When in crisis, students feel that they have just learned something that requires some response" (p. 30). An example of this process will help make Kumashiro's point more impactful; at least it has for me.

In my first semester of graduate school, I was in a course titled "Critical Theory in Education." I was the only person in my twenties, let alone the only master's-level student in the course, and I was intimidated mightily by the other students and the instructor, who all seemed to possess a depth of understanding of the course texts we were taking up that I did not. I rarely spoke up, but one day I found the courage and the moment to share a personal story to demonstrate a point we were discussing. I cannot remember what my story responded to, but that will prove to be in support of Kumashiro's theory of learning in crisis. I told a story of when I was a resident assistant in a freshmen dorm, and I used the terms *girls* and *guys* to refer to the young men and women I was talking about, because those were the terms we had used in residence life to describe them. I used the term *girls* probably four times in my story, and by the end the woman sitting across from me was on her feet staring right at me. She addressed me, saying, "How dare you degrade those young women by calling them girls. They are adults who make decisions about their sexuality, reproductive rights, and lifestyles and you reinforce your own male privilege and patriarchy every time you reduce them to girls." I was stunned. I mumbled some kind of apology, and spent the duration of class thinking about what she had said. I knew she was right, and that I was doing exactly what she said I was. The moment called on me to make a change in how I was not only talking about the young women who had lived on my floor, but also how I understood them as human beings. It is possible that such a crisis could have happened for me without what, at the time, felt like an attack. However, the educative impact of the exchange has been a profound one in my own development of pro-feminist consciousness.[2] Since that class, I have used the term *girls* only in the rarest of instances, and opt for the more inclusive *women* or *young women* when referring to those groups.

This story illuminates Kumashiro's theory in profound ways because it points to the ways in which something we often avoid in classrooms, conflict, often offers the most powerful learning opportunities. While then as now I located myself in solidarity with the feminist movement, reading about male privilege and patriarchy was not enough for me to see it in my own discourse and way of thinking. I experienced a powerful reaction to the woman who stood up and critiqued me, but I learned in humanizing self-appropriated ways. In an anticapitalist antiracist pedagogy, we cannot avoid moments of conflict and crisis out of our fear of hurt feelings or a sense that the classroom will no longer be deemed "safe." Learning—conscious, self-appropriated learning—must always be our aim in the classroom, and denying that moments of crisis offer powerful learning opportunities functions on the side of maintaining our existing oppressive order.

Kumashiro also believes that uncertainty should be a central feature in anti-oppressive education. He writes, "We can never know exactly what students are learning" (p. 37). He goes on, "Yes, teaching is impossible, but only if we believe that teaching is successful when students learn exactly what we said beforehand that they were supposed to learn" (p. 41). The first notion, that we can never hope to know everything our students are learning, can at first make it seem as though it makes teaching "impossible," because if we cannot tell what our students are learning how can we know if we are teaching? Of course, this impossibility is unnecessary in anticapitalist antiracist pedagogy because the only learning privileged is that which is self-appropriated. The teacher herself is never at the center of student learning, and could never hope to record everything her students know, nor everything they have learned in her class. For Kumashiro, our aim must be student learning, not a perfect transference of information from the textbook, to the teacher, to the student. This is banking education, and in our refusal of banking we must accept the inherent unknowability of learning in humanizing ways.

Kumashiro's use of postmodern concepts such as uncertainty and unknowability can be appreciated better when read alongside his theory, which was mentioned earlier in the chapter, that "no practice is always anti-oppressive." For Kumashiro, "[A]ny way of making sense of the world is necessarily partial: Only certain people with certain values and experiences have made certain choices to create these perspectives" (p. 27). In other words, we can never be pure in our teaching, perfect anticapitalist antiracist pedagogues. Kumashiro demands that we understand that any choice of materials represents a choice of not only what to include, but what to exclude as well. We are always excluding certain perspectives when we advance our own or another's perspective. But this inevitability again presents powerful learning opportunities in the context of anticapitalist antiracist pedagogy. By addressing explicitly the partiality of our own beliefs and experiences, we invite students not only to critique us but to also critique their limited and partial understandings. This is a form of consciousness that is complementary to anticapitalist antiracism because it calls out our inherent unfinishedness and the need to practice consciousness as we test and amend our existing theories, beliefs, and knowledges.

So positioned, Kumashiro's anti-oppressive education offers what can be thought of as the postmodern wing of anticapitalist antiracism. Yet we should not be derailed by believing that with unknowability and uncertainty no definite course of action is possible. While we will never be able to know all of what there is to know, this does not give us permission to stop asking questions or to stop struggling for justice. Kumashiro does not fall into the trap of making systemic change an impossibility; he merely wants to remind us that any such transformation will have intentional and unintentional consequences that, depending on our context, we will feel or not feel, and this uncertainty must be something we work through rather than against. In this spirit, it bears repeating that anticapitalism and antiracism are not, on their own, wholly inclusive of every justice struggle. By centering capitalism and white supremacy we leave other forms of oppression aside. But this is not a critique of anticapitalist antiracism; it is, rather, an inevitability. We must make choices, and struggle for change in those areas that bear directly on our lives as human actors. Thus, anticapitalist antiracism is a partial project, but it should be stated plainly that, despite its partial nature, even if we were to abolish capitalism and white supremacy there is no way of knowing what impact this would have on other oppressions, what new oppressions this could create, and what the future will hold. We cannot let this derail us, or sway us from our aims and commitments. Rather, Kumashiro's work enables us yet another vantage point through which we can critique ourselves as we continue to elaborate, expand, and refine our anticapitalist antiracist consciousness.

While some critical readers may well find these poststructural insights drawn from Kumashiro as counterintuitive, if not completely at odds with the more Marxist arguments presented throughout this text, I include them here because of the complexity they bring to bear on the praxis of teaching and learning in classrooms in anticapitalist antiracist pedagogy. I am reading Kumashiro through my own lens of critical pedagogy and Marxism (detailed in chapter 3), and thus I am making particular choices about how such insights can be mobilized for transformative work toward redistributory justice. Thus, my reading of Kumashiro's conceptions of "unknowability" become paradoxically bounded: while we can never know everything about our students and what they are learning, this does not then inevitably leave us without recourse, without possibilities for action. Further, it does not mean that we cannot know the oppressive conditions faced by so many inside and outside of schools. That our understandings are always already partial does not mean they cannot be acted upon. Such a reading of Kumashiro makes available more possibilities for generating anticapitalist antiracist consciousness. While Cole (2008) and others have critiqued the ways in which poststructuralism sits far too comfortably within neoliberal capitalism, Kumashiro's work can and, I argue, should be read with a critical eye toward what it makes possible in terms of better understanding the inherent complexity in teaching and learning for justice.

On Resistant Students

I conclude this chapter with a brief comment on a question that might have been looming in the reader's mind throughout this chapter. Namely, what to do with students who do not position themselves as oppressed, who see no problem with capitalism, or who hold bigoted beliefs about those whom they deem as "other" from themselves. We make a mistake, in antiracist education in particular, of assuming that social justice is a commonsense principle that one either possesses or does not. The only way justice commitments can become actualized is for human actors to self-appropriate knowledge of oppression in ways that enable them to understand oppression in context, in relation to both local and larger systemic forces. Importantly, there are many ways to self-appropriate knowledge, and many ways to express commitments to justice. When we encounter students who do not share our commitment to humanization, we still have the moral and pedagogical responsibility to take them seriously, as experts of their own lives, with funds of knowledge that can and should be brought to bear on the classroom. Perhaps another member of the class will create a moment for crisis that will lead the resistant student to question a deep-seated belief. Perhaps not. To say that all of our students will advocate for anticapitalist antiracism is nonsense, if our vision of anticapitalist antiracism means only behaving in certain ways, for certain ends. Whether or not a student shares our commitments, we can support their own self-appropriation of knowledge and scaffold in ways that help make oppressive systems more clearly visible. We can help students question what they do not see as evidence that other perspectives exist, and appreciate the historical context in which they have come to exist as they do in the world and how their existence is different from others'.

But perhaps most importantly, we must take consciousness as always ongoing to mean that what happens over the course of a school year, a semester, or a workshop is never what is at stake in teaching and learning. Our responsibility as teachers is to offer ways of interrogating the self, our community, our society, and our world in ways that can (not will) lead to critical consciousness. We cannot bank critical consciousness. We cannot make antiracism merely the right answer or what is politically correct. Thus, we must learn to love our resistant students as much as we love those who critically throw themselves into their learning in authentically humanizing ways. Above all, we must be with others in pedagogical ways that support the self-appropriation of knowledge. When we are questioned, we must answer honestly, and in the spirit of Freire, we must always remain humble.

Anticapitalist antiracist pedagogy is a vision of political teaching and learning. It is one among countless others, with countless variations that make naming every possible concrete practice an impossibility. Yet we must be content with this impossibility, because we can never know everything our students are learning. But we can position ourselves in solidarity with our students as fellow learners. We can support students in their self-appropriation of knowledge and meaning creation. We can demystify curriculum and make every object from which we might learn a part of the purview of our courses. And we can continue to actualize, practice, and refine our consciousness of ourselves and our world(s). Much remains to be done, but we are capable of doing it. While no classroom on its own will transform our oppressive global order, we can never transform our global order without working to do so in classrooms.

NINE

Anticapitalist Antiracist Pedagogy as a Programmatic Vision for Teacher Education

> The capitalist's profit would come not from over-charging the worker for this fractional part, but from the fact that in the whole of the product he sells a fractional part which he has not paid for, and which represents, precisely, *surplus labour time*.
>
> —*Grundrisse*

> Value which insists on itself as value preserves itself through increase; and it preserves itself precisely only by constantly driving beyond its quantitative barrier, which contradicts its character as form, its inner generality. Thus, growing wealth is an end in itself. The goal-determining activity of capital can only be that of growing wealthier.
>
> —*Grundrisse*

While I was working on the first draft of this text, I received a phone call from an undergraduate elementary education major at my alma mater, Arizona State University. She was calling both to tell me about the new teacher education program that she was entering, and asking if I could support the college of education financially with a contribution. She also had a few survey questions for me, about where I was now, and what I was doing with my teaching degree. After I told her about my work at the University of Minnesota, and that I did not have the funds to make a contribution, our conversation shifted. She told me that the new program would see her and other teacher candidates student teach for an entire school year, rather than the traditional semester of student teaching that I completed when I was in the program. She asked me if I had any advice for her, since I am now a teacher educator. I asked her a couple questions in reply: "Why do you want to be a teacher" and "Why elementary?" She told me that she wanted to be a teacher because she loved to see "growth," that students who liked their teachers will work harder in class and "grow" more and that she wanted to work with young students because she thought this process of "growth" was more easily visible and attainable at the elementary school level.[1] I gave her two pieces of advice. First, I cautioned her that we must be careful as teachers to remember that student learning must be for the students themselves. The point is not for us as teachers to feel good about our work in the classroom, but rather for our students to self-appropriate knowledge and learn in powerful ways in which they can utilize their funds of knowledge and existing experiences. The second piece of advice I gave her was to remember that schools are not businesses, and she is not a manager, that thus we must reject economistic logics (such as classroom management; see Casey, Lozenski, & McManimon, 2013) for our work in schools and classrooms. She thanked me, saying that this was the best phone call of this kind that she had made to an alumnus. Her story makes for an interesting case study of the effects of professionalization in teaching.

The shift to a full year of student teaching can be seen as an increase in the "clinical practice" of teaching. More time in the classroom, especially seeing the early days of the school year, will help young teachers develop their own classroom practice. But she also told me that she would be expected to take a full load of courses while she was student teaching, expecting a seventy hour work week when student teaching and coursework are taken all together. This need for more clinical practice, and for courses that are immediately contingent upon teacher candidates being in classrooms full time, is a response by many in the current wave of educational reform who are seeking to remove or diminish courses in educational theory and foundations of education from teacher education programs in favor of more "practical" course work and clinical experience in the classroom. Education Secretary Arne Duncan makes for a great example of the reform rhetoric in action.

In a speech on February 28, 2013, to the National Association of Secondary School Principals, Duncan told those in attendance, "Independent research has portrayed [teacher and principal education programs] as having low admission standards, undemanding coursework, and inadequate clinical training" (Department of Education). He went on in that speech to commend work in Kentucky and Tennessee for their "scaled-up clinical pre-service programs." While Duncan has dropped some of his least popular proposals for educational reform from recent speeches, such as tying principal and teacher pay to the standardized tests scores of the students they work with, we see here once again a critique of the lack of "clinical" experience as what is wrong with teacher and principal education. Further, we see the argument that more "clinical" experience, assumedly replacing "undemanding coursework" such as educational foundations, is responsible for higher achievement scores.

Critical pedagogy scholar Henry Giroux (2010) writes of Duncan on these points, saying:

> Within the last year, Duncan has delivered a number of speeches in which he has both attacked colleges of education and called for alternative routes to teacher certification. According to Duncan, the great sin these colleges have committed . . . is that they have focused too much on theory and not enough on clinical practice. . . . Duncan wants such colleges to focus on practical methods in order to prepare teachers for an outcome-based education system, which is code for pedagogical methods that are as anti-intellectual as they are politically conservative. This is a pedagogy useful for creating armies of number crunchers, reduced to supervising the administration of standardized tests, but not much more. (p. 2)

For Giroux, Duncan's policies are in line with neoliberal aims for education more broadly, including his fervent support for charter schools, high-stakes testing, alternative (non-university) teacher certification, merit pay linked to student test scores, abolishing tenure, and weakening teachers' unions, just to name a few. As "A Nation at Risk" continues to reverberate thirty years after its release, its influence expressed in the cultural logic that schools in the United States are "failing," the reformers have shifted their gaze to teacher education.

Under direct assault are those courses and programs in colleges of education that are seen as standing in the way of the realization of neoliberal aims for schools and education more broadly. Courses such as School and Society, courses on multicultural approaches to teaching and learning, on culturally relevant pedagogy, and the many others we could list here that are deemed by Duncan and others as "too much theory" are disappearing from teacher education and from colleges of education more generally (Kerr, Mandzek, & Raptis, 2011).[2] For the neoliberal reformers, colleges of education are failing to train teachers for the practical skills they need in a data-driven school environment. Reading educational theory, it is argued, is time that would be better spent learning the scientifically generated best practices from empirical research in classroom settings on how to maximize student gains on standardized tests. With teacher-proofed curricula on the rise (Crocco & Costigan, 2007),[3] the need for teachers to be exposed to sophisticated theorizations regarding their and their students' lives and work in the classrooms is seen as superfluous at best. Giroux calls these reform efforts and their neoliberal ideology an "instrumental view of teacher education" (p. 5). Recalling the earlier discussion of instrumental reason, we should remember here that instrumental reason in this context refers to conceptualizing reason, or theory, as a technology, always to be used for something else, for particular ends. Thus, in the case of Duncan, education is seen as only useful based on the ends it produces: schools are reduced to training future laborers to take their place in the existing economic order. Any commitment to serious study or to the self-appropriation of knowledge is deemed unworthy, as just more theory, because the instrumentalist view sees value in schools only for their function as job training centers.

We have thus reached a moment in teacher education when we are confronted with essentially only two options: we can either acquiesce to the neoliberal imperative, or we can resist. We should note that for virtually the whole of the neoliberal educational reform movement, colleges of education and the universities that house them are seen as inherently "liberal"[4] spaces, training "liberal" graduates, in "liberal" ways. The shift to neoliberal policies has not seen this conception dissipate; it is as though the university, no matter how many economistic and corporate logics it employs, will never be seen as anything but a "liberal" bastion for radical professors to indoctrinate their students with "liberal" biases. My proposal in this chapter is rather simple: if we are doomed to always being seen as radical, progressive, or at the very least "liberal," then we should *act* like it. That is, if teacher education's efforts at remaking itself in the neoliberal image have not shifted the perception that teacher education is a progressive space, we should stop trying to change this perspective and, rather, embrace it.

In this chapter, I lay out a programmatic vision for teacher education premised on the theory developed thus far in this work as anticapitalist antiracist pedagogy. I take as my starting point the pedagogical framework developed in the previous chapter and rearticulate the elements of the framework as aims for an anticapitalist antiracist teacher education. Then, I turn to Ira Shor's (1987) work to elaborate "Freirean themes for teacher education." After describing what Shor includes under each theme, I expand on each to elaborate ways to further the aims of anticapitalist antiracism in our work with teacher candidates. I conclude this chapter with a brief discussion of the role of the teacher educator in anticapitalist antiracist pedagogy to address both the limitations of such work as well as the possibilities.

Anticapitalist Antiracist Aims for Teacher Education

In the previous chapter, I worked to develop a theory of anticapitalist antiracist pedagogy premised on three sub-theorizations. The first, on learning, argued that self-appropriated learning must be the focus of any and all pedagogical activity and that anticapitalist antiracist pedagogues position themselves in solidarity with their students through their shared positionality as learners. The second, on curriculum, argued that we should view curriculum in the most expansive way possible, as anything we can derive meaning from, and thus learn from. With formal curriculum, our task is to work with students to understand the standards, critique the standards, and reposition the standards vis-à-vis our critical understanding of the connections and intersections of ideas, practices, and politics. The third, on consciousness, argued that anticapitalist antiracism is a way of being with and for others that is always ongoing and cannot be limited solely to the classroom, but rather serves as the basis for transformational justice.

Taken together, these three theories represent the aims for anticapitalist antiracist teacher education. This entails not only a commitment to engaging in anticapitalist antiracist pedagogy in teacher education courses, but also to supporting teacher candidates in developing their own expressions of anticapitalist antiracist pedagogy, in ways that are meaningful for them and will enable them to support their own students in their self-appropriation of knowledge and cultivation of their own critical consciousness. While these proposals are truly radical, we should think seriously about the ways that we already require teacher candidates to believe certain things (at least, to say they believe certain things). "Every child can learn" is a rule, not a theory to be tested in teacher education. It is the line that teacher candidates are coached on early and often; it is expected to be repeated at their subsequent job interviews; and as teacher educators we seem perfectly content to protect and defend this humanistic principle. The point is this: If we already have required dispositions, commitments on the part of teacher candidates, embedded in teacher education, why not make those more explicitly anticapitalist and antiracist?

In order to realize such a program in teacher education we must first be willing to reexamine our criteria for admittance to teacher education. It is, quite simply, not enough to have a love of young people and learning to become a teacher. Rather, we must work to bring into teacher education those who refuse to understand schools and classrooms in neoliberal ways. We should require aspiring teacher candidates to articulate their understanding of oppression as it manifests in daily experience and in systemic reality. This point cannot be overstated: it is only from a position that acknowledges the realities of oppression that anticapitalist antiracist teacher education can be fully realized. We must shift from requiring teacher candidates to believe that every student is capable of learning, to an articulation of why such a stance is necessary and what the political and social commitments entailed in such a position are in light of an understanding of systemic oppression. Thus, in order to be accepted into teacher education, teacher candidates must believe that every child can learn in humanizing ways that work against oppression.

While this may seem unrealistic to mandate as policy, I have found that the vast majority of the more than one thousand teachers and teacher candidates I have worked with in teacher education courses possess at least some understanding of oppression in our society and world. This understanding of oppression is often undermined in education courses that focus on educational psychology, development theories, and banking methodologies. Rather than seeing teacher candidates who possess an understanding of oppression as merely an added bonus, as the "good" students in a particular cohort of teacher candidates, we could center the understanding of systemic oppression throughout teacher education coursework and field experiences. This would function to engage teachers in deep reflection into how their own work operates alongside or against oppression and to imagine ways to work against oppression both in their classrooms and in their lives more broadly. Thus, what I am proposing here is not imagined for some abstract population of critical teacher candidates, but rather for those who are already engaged in teacher education programs, the vast majority of whom have political commitments to work with young people that are rarely examined or expanded in teacher education courses. Critical people are everywhere, resisting and taking action in more ways than we will ever know. Anticapitalist antiracist teacher education simply entails making these radical commitments a visible and central part of the curriculum, rather than only being whispered behind closed doors where those in power cannot see.

Freirean Themes for Teacher Education: Toward an Anticapitalist Antiracist Teacher Education

Among the first scholars in the United States to take up and extend the work of Paulo Freire was Ira Shor. His work with Freire and others in the 1980s in particular established him as one of the foremost experts on critical pedagogy, especially in relation to university teaching. Shor (1987) presents seven "Freirean themes for teacher education," which he positions as a "Freirean agenda for the learning process" in teacher education (p. 23). These themes are *Dialogue Teaching, Critical Literacy, Situated Pedagogy, Ethnography and Cross-Cultural Communications, Change-Agency, Inequality in School and Society,* and *Performing Skills.* In what follows I detail what Shor includes under each heading before expanding on what these practices, topics, and commitments mean for anticapitalist antiracist pedagogy and for teacher education. While I rely on Shor's initial work to define these aims, my explication of his theories is coupled with my own insights and interpretations building from both my engagement with Freire and his work as well as the theory of anticapitalist antiracist pedagogy as I have developed it thus far. To put this more concretely, despite their generative potential, Shor's descriptions of these themes are incomplete and requires further critical elaboration and, in the Freirean spirit, additional reinvention.

Dialogue Teaching

Shor positions dialogue teaching, or dialogic teaching, primarily as a means of problem-posing discussion that works to "reduce student withdrawal and teacher-talk in the classroom" (p. 23). This will require making "the teacher education curriculum itself dialogic," meaning that teacher candidates will experience a form of education in which they are not positioned as unknowledgeable fledgling teachers but rather as sophisticated women and men who possess a wealth of experience that must be a central part of their learning experience. Dialogue here functions in the Freirean sense of countering banking models to allow learners themselves to articulate their own problems or problematics that they wish to uncover and explore in more detail. To accomplish this, Shor believes we need to focus the work of teacher education on "group dynamics, the social relations of discourse, and the linguistic habits of students in their communities in relation to their sex, class, race, region, age, and ethnic origin" (p. 23). Such courses, discussions, and experiences could explore theories of discourse; how power works in, with, and through discourse; and practices that enable teacher candidates to develop not only the attitude of dialogue, but also the capacity to actualize dialogue in any number of social spaces.

Often, in classroom spaces, efficiency is the aim, wherein we fetishize the end result of learning rather than celebrate the process of learning itself. Learning to ask questions that allow others to examine their beliefs and knowledges will be crucial in such a program of teacher education—in fact, an entire series on questioning and pedagogy could replace traditional methodology courses as they are currently practiced. The capacity for dialogue is something that all people possess. However, it is often buried under the realities of banking education and the need to maximize student output, and thus minimize depth of coverage on a particular topic. Teacher candidates would thus be able to explore the ways in which we so often stifle authentic dialogue for the sake of moving quickly through all the required material. They could further work, perhaps as an end of the course project, to elaborate their own strategies for maintaining dialogue in the classroom and minimizing the amount of direct instruction necessitated by standards and banking curricula.

This would further aid the teacher educator in critical self-reflection on their own process, because the teacher candidates would be actively working on their own ability to participate in dialogue and in active reflection on the context of the teaching moment. Teacher educators, practicing a dialogic pedagogy, would ask students to theorize what is presently happening in a classroom, how power is operating, and how we can work to democratize our practice through problem-posing education that is student-centered and student-authored. For anticapitalist antiracist pedagogues, this process would enable the examination of the ways in which white supremacist and capitalist logics permeate our daily experience and the discourses we use to make sense of that experience. Engaging in dialogue in this way offers up both powerful pedagogical strategies as well as a means for critical self-reflection that function in opposition to dominant norms of teacher-focused banking education.

Critical Literacy

For Shor, critical literacy entails a form of "literacy that provokes critical awareness and desocialization" that is more than "basic competency" (p. 23). Rather, critical literacy is needed across the teacher education curriculum, "asking all courses to develop reading, writing, thinking, speaking, and listening habits, to provoke conceptual inquiry into self and society and into the very discipline under study" (pp. 23–24). This form of critical literacy requires that we problematize all subjects of study, which for Shor means, "understand[ing] existing knowledge as a historical product deeply invested with the values of those who developed such knowledge" (p. 24). Shor asks us to think of critical literacy as an approach to teaching and learning as a form of "research and experimentation, testing hypotheses, examining items, questioning what we know" (ibid.). Critical literacy is then what Freire (1987) called "reading the word and the world," as detailed in chapter 2.

Literacy in this context thus means much more than the ability to read and write, but rather requires us to understand reading and writing as an intervention in our world and to understand the ways in which contexts shape our experiences, both of texts and of events. As critical literacy ought to be practiced across all teacher education experiences, Shor does not detail what kinds of courses are necessary for realizing critical literacy throughout a teacher education program. What is important here, for anticapitalist antiracist pedagogy, is that we take very seriously the need for teachers to be able to read, write, speak, and listen in critical humanizing ways. This means teacher candidates should study writing and prose, should work at their reading of both text and context to develop critical habits of questioning, and should work at their abilities to speak and listen with others in pedagogical ways. Critical literacy thus offers a means into living out our critical consciousness; a way of practicing in our study, our speech, and our interactions with others the very same processes with which we engage our students in classrooms. We read, write, speak, and listen pedagogically, paying special attention to the ways in which oppression functions in these activities and the ways in which we can work against oppression in humanizing ways.

Situated Pedagogy

We can think of situated pedagogy as a form of teaching and learning that stems directly from the contextual nature of those engaged in the learning task. Shor writes, "[T]his goal asks teachers to situate their learning in the students' culture—their literacy, their themes, their present cognitive and affective levels, their aspirations, their daily lives" (p. 24). The aim of such an approach is to "integrate experiential materials with conceptual methods and academic subjects" (p. 24). This works to make course materials a part of the "subjectivity" of the learners. Shor writes of this point, "Material that is of subjective concern is by definition important to those studying it" (p. 24). Shor is imploring us to position all learning activities as in connection to the learners' lives and experiences. These connections, importantly, are a part of what the anticapitalist antiracist pedagogue works to make in her classroom and in her interactions with learners. The ability to connect what at first appear to be disparate things, or subjects of study that feel removed from the lived experience of the learner, is a critical capacity of the anticapitalist antiracist pedagogue.

To make such connections, one must have orienting principles for how disciplines and bodies of knowledge operate as part of a collective whole. In many ways, a dialectical conception of reality is necessary for such work, in order to provide a basis for such connections as part-whole, oppressor-oppressed, and so on. Beginning from a standpoint of questioning what a particular discipline or body of knowledge can offer us in terms of our work for justice invites learners to interrogate their own lives at the same time as they are exploring what we have traditionally imagined as "official knowledge." The point, in situated pedagogy, is that everything derives meaning from the experience of the learners themselves, rather than from an abstracted expert or group of experts who believe that everyone should simply know, uncritically, a series of particular facts.[5] So positioned, learners engage with bodies of knowledge that can be understood as a series of facts, but their own agency in the learning process is privileged as they are beckoned to use traditional disciplines and subjects as a means for their own self-appropriation of knowledge. Situated pedagogy thus does not mean that standards and disciplines are no longer a focus of study, but rather that the standards be seen as a means to an end, rather than an end in themselves. Mastery of subject matter is meaningless if it does not support one's own aspirations for living and being in critical humanizing ways.

This is a way of responding to Lowenstein's (2009) critiques of teacher education literature on white teacher candidates as promoting a deficit-lens of these white people as "deficient learners about diversity" (p. 164). Such a stance, while it is based on research, is incommensurate with a situated pedagogy framework, because such a pedagogical stance necessitates understanding students as capable, resilient, and as possessing knowledge and expertise on their own experiences. Following Lowenstein, we need ways of positioning our white teacher candidates that do not conform to the dominant and damaging trope that sees white people as always lacking in relation to multicultural education. Situated pedagogy as a part of anticapitalist antiracist pedagogy in teacher education is one such way of answering these calls that does not discount the important work of challenging oppressive ideologies. This is not to say that there are no white teacher candidates who harbor oppressive ideologies, but rather to understand these white people as unfinished, as searching for meaning, and as capable of cultivating the critical capacity for consciousness and transformation.

The vision of situated pedagogy, further, offers us a way of reconceptualizing course work and related experiences in child development and educational psychology. Rather than learning abstract theories of developmentalism and stages, in a situated pedagogy learners would explore their own questions of the psyche, of cognition, and of growing up through the vehicle of psychology. Teacher candidates would explore the work of Piaget, Vygotsky, and others not from the perspective of a rigidly banking "this is how learning works," but rather as a means of testing their own experiences as learners and the lives of those with whom they live and work. In this way, many of the current teacher education courses and experiences could be maintained with regard to their subject matter. What is needed is a reorientation of the purpose of said subject matter and a move away from the capitalistic logics of mastery and efficiency to the anticapitalist antiracist logics of critical examination, questioning, and reconstructing.

Ethnography and Cross-Cultural Communication

Shor sees ethnographic work on the part of the teacher candidate as a necessary component in the practice of dialogue, critical literacy, and situated pedagogy. As teachers we can never support students in their self-appropriation of knowledge based on their lived experiences if we have no sense of what those experiences are. Shor writes of this point, "To situate critical literacy and dialogue inside the language, themes, and cognitive levels of the students, a teacher needs to study the population he or she is teaching for" (p. 24). The work of Gonzalez and Moll (2002) on accessing funds of knowledge through ethnographic home visits is an example of such work. Visiting students in the spaces where they live, being with their parents and siblings, seeing their neighborhoods, the things that decorate or enhance the space in personalizing ways; all of these "data" represent important ways that teachers can draw on their students' funds of knowledge in a situated pedagogy. Approaching this work from the perspective of an ethnographer is especially powerful because it calls on the teacher-researcher to ask questions of context and the specificity of unique cases and circumstances.

Further, such work can be essential when the teacher and learners do not possess the same cultural codes, ways of speaking and being, and past experiences. Ethnographic work on the part of the teacher in this case can be a way of collapsing those false barriers between teachers and students that persist so often as a means of maintaining systemic oppression. Rejecting stereotypes and misinformation about cultural communities can be exceptionally challenging work, yet entering those communities in loving and humanizing ways offers us the ability to recast our past assumptions and test out new theories and approaches to working across cultural differences. It is important here, from the perspective of anticapitalist antiracism, that the work of cross-cultural communication be dialogical. We must trust our students as experts on their own lives, but we must further work to understand everything and everyone in context. Too often it falls squarely on the shoulders of students of color to explain themselves or their culture to their teachers. These tokenizing moments, when students are asked to stand in as representatives for an entire race or country or region of people, function to reproduce white supremacy. Ethnographic work on the part of the teacher works in opposition to these all too common tendencies by placing the burden on the teacher as learner to investigate and seek to understand in more complex detail her students' lives and experiences.

Change-Agency

Here, Shor moves back into the realm of imagining new courses and new course content for teacher education. In order for teachers to be agents of change, he writes, "teachers need to study community analysis and models of community change. How do communities structure themselves? How do they change?" (p. 25). If we claim that the purpose of work in schools is societal transformation, making our communities more fully human, just, and loving, we need to understand how communities have shifted and changed historically. While we almost always hear from first-year teacher candidates that they want to be teachers to "make the world better," we almost never study societal change in teacher education. Why? The critical answer would argue that engaging in such practices would negate the intended function of schools, which is not social change but rather social cohesion and maintenance of the existing social order. Yet, virtually every teacher candidate enters teacher education with at least some inkling that work in schools can function on the side of justice. Shor believes that we should study these processes in teacher education.

The study of social and community change, however, must be coupled with study of "school organization, school-based curriculum design, the legislative environment for education, and professional politics" (p. 25). Again, we spend virtually no time in teacher education on analyzing how schools and school districts are organized, how they are funded, who makes the decisions that impact classroom practice, and how these policies and procedures are evidence of larger ideological forces. In this, we deny teachers access to uncovering the ways in which schools are governed, which can function to maintain the existing power relations that see teachers barred from decision making that immediately impacts both them and their students. In a teacher education program designed around anticapitalist antiracism, then, there would be serious study that focused explicitly on examining both community change and school organization. We would explore the ways schools are funded, the legislative and juridical procedures in place that most impact work in schools, and the history of societal change in relation to work in classrooms.

Anticapitalist antiracist pedagogy would go even farther in such work to examine the ways in which white supremacy and capitalism function in both the history of social movements and how schools are structured. One result of such a study could involve teacher candidates elaborating, based on their historical and sociological work, a theory or course of action to affect the change they desire and how this process could come about both inside and outside the school. Teacher candidates would explore the deeply political nature of schooling, and not in the narrow way in which the "right answer" is that all education is political, but devoid of any meaning for concrete practice. Rather, the actual politics of schools, communities, legislation, and society are all taken as sites for critical inquiry into how the relations of power and access impact learning and practice in classrooms. If we believe teachers are capable of creating change, we ought to be studying such change in teacher education.

Inequality in School and Society

Given the above discussion, and the explicit commitments in anticapitalist antiracist pedagogy to examine the ways in which inequity, white supremacy, and capitalist exploitation function to dehumanize, the study of the ways in which schools have functioned in support of oppression should be present in every aspect of teacher education. In particular, we should follow Kumashiro's (2009) notion that we often perpetuate oppression, or other forms of oppression, even as we seek to combat it. Thus, this work cannot be seen merely as historical, but rather we must explore educational inequity in ways that ask how people both consciously and unconsciously perpetuate oppression in and through schools.

One can easily imagine a history of education course in which the central theme is the history of oppression in schools. We often do not think of schools' culpability in maintaining oppression, or of the ways in which those in power have used schools and schooling to protect their own material interests. William Watkins's (2001) *The White Architects of Black Education* is an excellent example of such work, as he details both the larger ideological aims of the post–Civil War era (white supremacy, scientific rationalism, social Darwinism, capitalism, and Christianity, to cite the most impactful) and the ways in which these ideologies manifested in the work of particular powerful actors who worked to use schools as a part of "accommodationism." That is, eliminating slavery while maintaining black peoples' position on the bottom of the economic order to protect the material interests of the elite. The history of Native American boarding schools, wherein schools were used to "kill the Indian and save the man," represent another important story of the ways in which schools were used to protect the interests of white supremacy and capitalism in the United States (see Wallace-Adams, 1995).

But such inquiry would also need to explore current practices in schools that serve to perpetuate capitalist exploitation and white supremacy. The school to prison pipeline, for instance, wherein young people (particularly people of color) are being criminalized at earlier and earlier ages coupled with the increased number of police officers present in schools must be examined in anticapitalist antiracist teacher education. In Minneapolis, Minnesota, black students are suspended from school at a ratio of 11:1 in comparison to white students. While they make up only 37 percent of the district population, they experience 80 percent of the district's out of school suspensions.[6] By examining not only historical but present manifestations of systemic white supremacy and capitalist exploitation, teacher candidates will be able to live out their commitments to justice not as responding to historical phenomena, but as combatting present and daily oppressions as they manifest in their lives.

Performing Skills

Shor's last Freirean theme for teacher education concerns the need for teacher candidates to develop "their skills of presentation and discussion leading. To be a creative problem poser in the classroom, drama and voice skills are helpful" (p. 25). Shor sees the development of these skills as aiding new teachers in particular, as "performing skills can habituate new teachers to the intimidating challenge of standing up each hour in front of a large group . . . a dramatic teacher models the aesthetic joy of dialogue, the pleasure of thinking out loud with others" (p. 25). While we often regard teachers who are passionate and excited about their courses as the best classroom practitioners, we spend virtually no time in teacher education on honing the performative aspects of such engagement. Too often, we leave these abilities to be developed in student teaching or practicum experience wherein little or no theoretical work is done to help teacher candidates articulate their own version of dynamic pedagogy. An emphasis on classroom performance, drawing on the rich literatures of theatre work and other performance-based mediums should be an essential element in teacher education.

For anticapitalist antiracist pedagogy, these abilities of performance should not be imagined as a kind of song-and-dance approach to learning with others. Rather, learning to act in social spaces in ways that model the kinds of engagement we hope for in our learners represents a crucial element in the humanizing work of learning in critical ways. If we are not excited, as teachers, about what we are asking students to explore, how can we ever expect students to be excited? And further, as teachers are human beings with complex lives, the ability to act in ways that place the needs of students first can be especially important on days when teachers find their struggles unbearable. Being in the classroom in humanizing ways is not only a disposition, it is a practice of being. Developing the ability to act, to perform, should thus not be seen as a mystification but rather as a student-centered vocation to *be* in particular ways for and with others. Teacher education experiences of this nature would allow for teacher candidates to role-play, engage in creative activities in which they can hone their ability to critique and to problematize, and to develop habits of practice that will aid them in supporting their students in their self-appropriation of knowledge.

On Anticapitalist Antiracist Teacher Educators

As teacher educators, we often fail to live out our own commitments in our teacher education courses. Returning to Lowenstein

(2009) and her review of multicultural teacher education with white teacher candidates in which she found that too often we approach our students in deficit-oriented ways, as learners who bring little or no experience with them into multicultural education coursework, makes for an important entry point into conceptualizing the role of anticapitalist antiracist teacher educators. This move, of positioning our students as "deficient learners about diversity," is in complete contradiction with culturally relevant pedagogy and critical pedagogies that work to center the lived experiences of students in order to call upon their funds of knowledge in the learning act. We have a responsibility, as teacher educators, to live out our commitments to justice. We must model the practices we hope our students will take up with their learners, and harboring notions of "all white people as racist" or other deficit models prevents us from realizing our aims. Teacher educators, in anticapitalist antiracist teacher education programs, are thus called upon to be critically reflexive in their practice, and to discuss and describe their practice with their students.

We have to humble ourselves, and work against so much of what we have learned in the past about what it means to be the teacher. Traditionally, teachers are imagined as experts, and too often we hide behind a façade of expertise rather than engaging in the humanizing work of revealing our fears and failures. Sharing with teacher candidates the moments when we fail to live out our commitments, when we do unnecessary violence that works in opposition to our aims, functions both to humanize the teacher educator and to model the powerful practice of positioning one's self as fallible, as human, and thus as flawed. This work is counterhegemonic, and anticapitalist, because it refuses to allow dominant notions of who teachers are supposed to be and the kinds of interactions that teachers and students are able to have. We inhabit classroom spaces as members of any number of identity groups, and in the relation of teacher and student, much work must be done in the anticapitalist antiracist classroom to collapse the false chasm between teachers and learners. This is not merely a theoretical or mental exercise, but rather something we should be explicit about with students in our classrooms. We can never move away from a top-down model of education if we refuse to problematize our own work with our students, in front of our students, and in dialogue with them.

Further, anticapitalist antiracist teacher educators must refuse the all-too-common trope of student bashing. Steeped in deficit rhetoric, it is far too common across the university to hear instructors bemoaning their students' lack of critical engagement, their abilities as writers and thinkers, and their apathy toward the subject under study. The anticapitalist antiracist teacher sees such phenomena as evidence not of a lack on the part of their students, but rather as a failure of their own pedagogy and approach to working with their students. We have a responsibility to support all of our students in humanizing ways, whether they possess the skills we wish they had or not. Refusing the capitalistic notions of efficiency and expediency, we must approach struggling learners as opportunities for us to engage in the critical humanizing work of supporting the self-appropriation of learning in powerful ways. Just because a student arrives to class without having developed her own ability to write in powerful ways does not mean that student is doomed to a life of being unable to communicate in writing. Anticapitalist antiracist educators reject a developmentalist approach that believes that students are fixed in their abilities at any time in their lives. It is never too late to learn to write powerfully, or to learn any other number of things. Thus, we must shift away from a focus on ensuring that students are all at the same starting point so as to make the end goal more easily systematized and managed. Instead, we position all learners, including ourselves, as unfinished, as continually evolving, and as inherently capable of acting on and transforming our worlds and our selves.

On Hope

Above all, anticapitalist antiracist teacher educators must remain hopeful in the face of overwhelming oppression. This hope is not naive, but is, rather, grounded in their belief that justice is imminently possible and that living in worthy humanizing ways is the only way we will ever realize our aims for a socially just reality. Hope entails what Freire (2006) called "armed love," a form of love that compels us to be more for one another even as we face terrible odds. For anticapitalist antiracist teacher educators to sustain themselves in this work, we must have a sense of imminent possibility. Hope is the wellspring of this possibility; it is the source of the belief in change, justice, and humanization for all peoples. Hope is not utopian, because there is no finality to the concept of hope. Hope is not something that we can use as a tool or technology and later cast aside once desired results have been achieved. Hope is thus eternal, compelling us ever onward to strive to live out our deepest commitments. Anticapitalist antiracist pedagogy is imbued with hope, and can be seen functioning on at least three levels.

First is the need for a personal hope, the belief that one is never finished learning, never finished questioning, and thus never content with only living out what is expected. We all have desires and aspirations, but it is only through a sense of hope that these dreams become reimagined as possibilities. Hope is sustaining, because it keeps our attention ever focused on what can be, rather than merely on what is.

Second is the need for hope in our daily experiences. To greet each day as a series of definite absolutes is wildly dehumanizing, and this is precisely the effect of capitalist exploitation. Over time, we begin to lose our faith in others, in those around us, and can easily collapse into cynicism. Hope in our daily lives compels us out of this malaise and again beckons us to question, "What more could be?" It also allows us to approach others from a position of imminent possibility and ceaseless curiosity. The hope that change is always possible, not just for ourselves but for everyone around us, creates new openings and opportunities, new ways of being with and for one another that may well have been altogether impossible in the past but now appear in reality as doable. We must have hope for those around us, and approach others in generous ways that actualize our belief in hope.

Third is the need for hope for the human species, for all peoples throughout the world. This is by far the most difficult kind of hope to maintain because we are constantly confronted with evidence that things cannot get better, or if they did some other evil would spring up to take a past oppression's place. Yet it is precisely hope at the level of humanity that makes anticapitalist antiracism possible. Despite the overwhelming obstacles, hope for humanity offers us ways of imagining heretofore unimaginable possibilities. This is the hope at the center of the work of Paulo Freire, the hope that has moved thousands if not millions to reject banking methods of education and to act in classrooms as best they can to combat oppression in all of its forms. This is the hope that Marx had, that has led billions of people to demand justice, to overthrow regimes, and to seek to create new ways of being with one another that function on the side of humanity. We can think of this as revolutionary hope: the belief that the world is what we make of it, and thus can be remade and refashioned in ways that enable the whole of humanity to realize their full potential as conscious human actors.

This is what anticapitalist antiracist pedagogy seeks to accomplish: an end to oppression, the shift from white supremacy to radical solidarity, and the universalization of revolutionary hope.

Notes

Prologue

1. In the Althusserian (1971/2008) sense of interpellation in ideology.
2. Patricia Hill Collins (2000) defines ideology as "the body of ideas reflecting the interests of a group of people" (p. 7). Important in this definition is the stance that ideology, as such, should not be understood solely in negative terms, as though we ought to be avoiding issues and ideas that feel "ideological." Rather, ideology is essential to socially just transformation—as Gramsci (1978/2008) put it, ideology is central to project of articulating a "hegemony of the proletariat."
3. Edited by Dave Hill, Peter McLaren, Mike Cole, and Glenn Rikowski and first appearing in 2002.
4. Edited by Mas'ud Zavarzadeh, Teresa L. Ebert, and Donald Morton in 1995.

Chapter 1. How My Family and I Became White

Each subsequent chapter begins with quotes from the work of Karl Marx, whose theories form the basis of this project and are treated in detail in chapter 3. Chapter 3 provides a synopsis of Marxism that is intended both for those who have spent little to no time engaged with Marx as well as for those who have taken up his work in serious detail. Writing with both populations in mind, my hope is that readers will find new insights regardless of their present stance on anticapitalism and Marxism more broadly.

1. In reference to the famous general strike in France, often thought of as the last gasp of communist success in a global-capitalist superpower country.
2. The shift in the social sciences to making culture the primary focus of scholarship, perhaps exemplified most with the emergence in the humanities of Cultural Studies in the tradition of the Birmingham School.
3. In reference to the shift in philosophy and theory more generally to being concerned most with the connections between philosophy and language, perhaps exemplified best in the work of Derrida and the French poststructuralists (see Cusset, 2008).
4. Neoliberalism is defined by David Harvey (2005) as "a theory of political economic practices that proposes that human well-being can best be advanced by liberating individual entrepreneurial freedoms and skills within an institutional framework characterized by strong private property rights, free markets, and free trade" (p. 2).
5. On my mother's side I was never able to find a text of this magnitude, one that felt like I was being punched in the gut every time I read it, about the whiteness of my matrilineal ancestors. My research into the Swenson family revealed, however, that many in their/our family, after first immigrating to the United States from Sweden, were the beneficiaries of homestead legislation that would grant 160 acres of land to any free white person intent on settling the land and farming it for a set number of years (Lee, 1979). In Kansas, much like Montana, the process of westward expansion by white people, of "Manifest Destiny," saw the U.S. government sanction the redistribution of land from Native American tribes to white people. My mother's family was poor as she was growing up, and they shuffled back and forth from home to home across Kansas and Wyoming following the demands of the oil industry and the needs of the family. Despite this, her ancestors benefited materially from their relative white privilege that saw them given land formerly held by Native peoples by the federal government.

It is worth noting; a major part of the impetus for homestead legislation and much of what was occurring in Kansas from the 1840s to the beginning of the Civil War was in opposition to Southern slave plantations. But homesteads, with almost no exceptions, were never given to Native Americans or African Americans in the nineteenth century.

6. I use the term *teacher candidates* to refer to students in teacher education programs. Rather than "pre-service," which signals that the actual work of teaching is not yet happening, or that the purpose of work in teacher education is only for later work in classrooms, rather than positioning learning as an engaged practice of being.

7. These authors represent the most important insights I mobilize in these chapters, however this work is also motivated by many other whiteness scholars including Ruth Frankenberg, George Lipsitz, Toni Morrison, Timothy Lensmire, and Shannon Sullivan, among others.

Chapter 2. Freirean Critical Study

1. To use a more critical-psychoanalytical term, I would argue we "fetishize" methods in education (Žižek, 2009). Fetishism is addressed in more detail in relation to commodity fetishism in the next chapter.

2. See Sandra Harding's (1987) *Feminism and Methodology* for a discussion of methodology from various feminist lenses.

3. See Cynthia Brown's (1978) "Literacy in 30 hours: Paulo Freire's process in North East Brazil" for more on Freire's history and the specifics of his literacy program.

4. Freire builds on past Marxist scholarship in his discussion of praxis in his most famous work *Pedagogy of the oppressed*. I read Freire's work on praxis alongside that of both Marx (in *Grundrisse* and *Capital* Volume 1 in particular) and Gramsci's (1978/2008) *Prison Notebooks*, the *latter* of which argues for a "philosophy of praxis." Freire's conception of praxis then represents a pedagogical philosophy of praxis—and the influence of Gramsci on Freire can also be seen in the similarity between Gramsci's "organic intellectuals" and the ways in which Freire calls on us to approach our work with students and with "the

oppressed" in particular. Praxis represents, perhaps more than any other Freirean concept, the Marxist character of Freire's philosophy and pedagogy.

5. Despite the numerous critiques of Hardt and Negri's work, largely arguing that the latter remains both far too much inside of capitalism (Ebert & Zavarzadeh, 2008) and teeters on the edge of becoming merely anarchism (see Bates, 2011 for an extensive discussion of this latter criticism), this insight is especially useful for the project of Freirean Critical Study.

6. I am using *postmodern* here as elaborated by Frederick Jameson (1991) in his work *Postmodernism, or, The Cultural Logic of Late Capitalism*. Jameson argues that in late capitalism, with the rejection of metanarratives, all truth claims are relativized, becoming not the truth, but merely a truth.

7. The Foucauldian (Foucault, 1990; 2004) maxim that power is always already comes to mind here, and importantly is not incommensurate with Gramsci's notion of replacing our present capitalist hegemony with a "hegemony of the proletariat." If power is unavoidable, much the same hegemony is unavoidable. What remains possible is power wielded on the side of justice, of hegemonic love in the Freirean sense becoming the dominant form. This hopeful gesture will be returned to in greater detail later in subsequent chapters.

8. Chapter 3 returns to ideology to detail additional insights from Marx's own work and writings. I will ask the reader to keep this current discussion in mind through the next section, as the more orthodox Marxist conception of ideology is not incommensurate with what I have worked through here, but should rather be seen as an enhancement and refinement of what ideology means in the context both of my method of Freirean Critical Study and in the larger project at hand.

9. Horkeimer and Adorno's most famous work together is *Dialectic of Enlightenment*, first published in 1944.

Chapter 3. Marx, Marxism, and Me

1. I will note here that this overview is intended both for those who are new to Marx's work as well as for those who have spent considerable time studying Marxism and critical theory.

For this latter group, gaining a sense of my own positionality on foundational Marxist concepts will allow for closer and more critical readings of later chapters.

2. For Marx and others, the French Revolution stands as the greatest historical example of this shift. In the context of the United States, we could even position the War of Independence (the Revolutionary War) as a fundamentally bourgeois revolution as the leaders of the independence movement were drawn almost solely from the propertied (largely slave holding) colonial elite.

3. Japanese economist Nobuo Okishio (1961) makes for an interesting example of this criticism, as he argued that if one capitalist introduces a technique that cuts costs and if workers' wages do not rise, the capitalist will in turn see more profits. Contemporary Marxist economist Andrew Kliman (2005) has argued against Okishio's theorem that produced these critiques of Marxian economics. Kliman argues that Okishio's theorem has never actually been proven and that the labor theory of value still accounts for profit, arguing further that the misinterpretation of Okishio's work has resulted in Marxian economists being falsely labeled as "dogmatic apologists." It should go without saying that pro-capitalist economists often reject Marx out of hand, or believe that with the abolition of the gold standard his work is no longer relevant. For an example of these pro-capitalist criticisms see Solow (1988).

4. This is to say that virtually the whole of human existence, in capitalism, is either directly a part of or is informed by the economy. Examples of this would include the notions of "wasting time" or "time is money" as we commodify time; notions of land as property, "what something is worth"; even to the level of vernacular expressions: "I buy it," "I'm sold," and so on. While we are not always actively thinking in strictly economic terms as social actors, we can look around any social space and see things both for what they are (use value) and for what they represent in terms of capital and money (exchange value). The concept of "human resources" is here perhaps the most fundamental example of Marx's point: if we can see people as tools of capitalism, we must include this conception of humans in our own work and theories.

5. A general definition of fetish would be an inanimate object that has within it special powers—these powers might include the object's supposed ability to create pleasure, produce meaning, achieve status, and so on. Here, we should think of a fetish as an irrational attachment to an object based on properties the object does not in fact possess, but that the person interacting with the object believes it does. The inverse also works as an example of fetishism, wherein a person fails to recognize the properties of an object for what they actually are (e.g., who made them).

6. Marx spends significant time detailing the unique role of gold as commodity and as capital in his work. With the shift away from the Gold Standard in the United States under Nixon, much of this work only applies in certain circumstances, as all the money in circulation is no longer tied directly to a supply of gold that said money stands in for.

7. The work of Naomi Klein (2008) in *The Shock Doctrine* comes to mind here as well, in which she explicates how disasters such as the Iraq War and Hurricane Katrina actually represent lucrative opportunities for the accumulation of capital. Her term for this is "disaster capitalism."

8. Fiat money, for example the U.S. Dollar and the Euro, is money whose value stems from governmental regulation or law, rather than a direct convertibility into a fixed standard, such as gold. See this chapter's note 3 for more.

9. This is in reference to the "cultural turn" in critical social theory, wherein more and more energy has been devoted to detailing how culture functions as the most salient concept for explaining identity construction and political struggle. We can think of this, in educational terms, as a part of the theoretical underpinnings for multiculturalism: the valuing of all cultures and the stance that different cultural peoples experience reality differently.

10. Ebert and Zavarzadeh include a number of thinkers under this group, including Jacques Derrida, Judith Butler, Jean Baudrillard, Gilles Deleuze, and Michel Foucault. They are careful, however, to say that much of the "blame" for the confusion of "cultural logic" with materialist logic rests on the many

theorists and scholars who have built on and expanded the aforementioned theorists' concepts.

Chapter 4. White Racial Identity in the United States

1. I will return to this field of whiteness studies in detail in chapter 5.
2. Applebaum and others whom I characterize as advocating a white privilege pedagogy are also addressed in detail in chapter 5.
3. While these categories of whiteness scholarship exist to some extent already, part of the conceptual work of this and the following chapter will be to unpack and explain the various underpinnings and conceptions of white racial identity inherent in each. As both will include other scholars who did not first use these terms, I have capitalized them here.
4. While I will attempt for clarity's sake to move through this section chronologically, my focus on individual scholars and their works will see me move back and forth across spans of time to connect particular ideas and theorists. This will prove useful in the following chapter when I employ specific authors, rather than time periods, in my critique of White Privilege and Race Traitor conceptions of white racial identity.
5. For more on the comparison of racialization and nationalization processes in the histories of Brazil, South Africa, and the United States see A. W. Marx (1998). As an example of the point I make here, Brazil abolished slavery in 1888, one year before establishing its independence from Portugal. The abolitionist movement and independence movement coincided into almost the same popular will; clearly, this was not the case in the United States where slavery was not abolished until 1865, some eighty-nine years after declaring independence.
6. It should be noted that laws that allowed for segregation were applied in every state in the union, and that many continue to restrict access to schools, housing, and employment opportunities, just to name a few of the impacted areas. It is a widely cited statistic, for example, that many states now have more

racially segregated schools than they did before *Brown v. Board of Education* (Garland, 2012).

7. Inscribed here in reference to the Foucauldian (2004) notion of juridical and discoursal "regimes of power"—I use it here to call attention to the ways in which it is the very body of black peoples that comes to be read as a text in the white imaginary and is meant to insight fear and mistrust. The stereotypic visions of abnormally large reproductive organs, the slow strut-walk associated presently with looking "tough" or "hard," and the many other examples we could list here are all quite literally written onto black people, and become what (mostly white) others "read" in them or read them as. For these purposes, inscribed in this sense is an especially powerful theoretical concept.

8. There is a certain way in which one can read these arguments in Morrison and construct a conception of a "dialectics of race" in which white and black both negate and call each other into being. As this is not a concept that Morrison details at all in her work, I call attention to it here only to point out the recurring presence of dialectics in both the racial analyses presented here as well as the critiques of neoliberal capitalism presented in later chapters.

9. Morrison makes explicitly clear, and gives much needed explanation to, why so much of race scholarship, particularly on whiteness, has taken up the ways in which whiteness was literally invented in opposition to blackness. This is not to say, however, that additional practices of white supremacy and white identity formation have been primarily imagined in opposition to other peoples of color. For further discussion on this point see Cole (2015).

10. See Lensmire and Snaza (2010) for a detailed analysis of the ways in which blackface minstrelsy impacted, and continues to impact, white racial identity formation. This work is especially helpful as it locates teacher educators as the audience for this reconceptualizing work and juxtaposes whiteness scholarship on minstrelsy with whiteness scholarship in teacher education.

11. A personal story comes to mind here. Six years ago, in my first semester teaching at the University of Minnesota, I was alarmed at the racial demographic question on the end of year

teacher evaluation forms. Across the university, every form had the "ethnicity" of *Caucasian* on them, rather than the far more inclusive and less white supremacist term *white*. I wrote to the university director for assessment, who assured me that while the forms are printed en masse, that once the current forms were used up, the term *Caucasian* would be replaced with *white*. As of my departure from the University of Minnesota in 2013, no such change had been made.

12. *The Bell Curve* was a best-seller when it was first released. See Leman (1997) for a discussion of the ways in which the book itself was shielded from initial scrutiny by book critics and others before its publication.

13. Latin@s here stands for Latinos and Latinas.

14. Unfortunately, there are no available data containing the number of those who possessed valid documentation at the time of their deportation.

15. A process whereby banks are able to design differential lending procedures and rates given their own beliefs about the relative "value" of a given community: redlining often results in working-class people of color paying higher mortgage rates with higher interest than their white counterparts in other parts of town.

Chapter 5. The Impossibility of Whiteness

1. The full title of the text is actually *Being White, Being Good: White Complicity, White Moral Responsibility, and Social Justice Pedagogy*. The latter of which, theorized as "white complicity pedagogy," will be returned to later in this chapter.

2. This is in reference to Mary Kennedy's (1999) notion of the struggle for future teachers to not only understand teaching concepts and methods, but to be able to put these ideas into practice.

3. I will simply use the italicized *Race Traitor* henceforth to refer to this journal.

4. The biblical tone here is made explicit in the text. The next line reads, "We want to be ready, walking in Jerusalem just like John." While there is, of course, a problematic irony in a

Marxist theory of class-based solidarity using Christian symbology, truly waiting for a kind of "second coming" in this example, this will not be a focus of the critique that follows.

5. Privileges for McIntosh constitute "daily conditions of unearned over-advantage" (McIntosh, 1988).

6. Meaning that the interpolation of whiteness always proceeds in one direction, from one place.

7. In the example of South Africa, whiteness is invested with a symbolic meaning of power and dominance, however it is not marked as normal. Rather, whiteness' prestige rests in its visibility rather than its invisibility, unlike the United States where whiteness is often theorized as a norm against which people of color are judged and found wanting.

8. Specifically, the demand to approach students as able learners who bring with them a wealth of experience and knowledge to their learning. Gonzalez and Moll (2002) have theorized this as a "funds of knowledge" approach, wherein all students bring their own "funds" with them into the learning act, and it is the task of the pedagogue to validate and scaffold this previous knowledge in the context of whatever the particular learning aim might be. See Lowenstein (2009) for this argument in relation to teacher education and white future teachers.

Chapter 6. Whiteness, Nationalism, and Neoliberal Capitalism

Portions of this chapter are also explicated in my book chapter "Whiteness, Nationalism, and Neoliberalism: What Pat Buchanan and the Right Can Teach Us about Resisting Neoliberalism in Schools" (Casey, in press).

1. Obama's neoliberal conception of the purposes of education will be addressed later in chapter 7.

2. The full title of this text is *Suicide of a Superpower: Will America Survive to 2025?*

3. As an example, currently in the United States same-sex partners do not qualify for the same partner benefits or naturalization processes that heterosexual couples receive when one partner is a U.S. citizen and the other is not.

4. Again, the example of Brazil comes to mind. See A. W. Marx (1998) for a discussion of the shifts over time in the racial categories available on the census and how these shifts have corresponded to various political projects of both othering and including.

5. To avoid any confusion, this is in reference to Anthony W. Marx, the U.S. political scientist, and not to Karl Marx. I reference A. W. Marx when referring to Anthony W. Marx and simply Marx when referring to Karl Marx.

6. We can think here of "black nationalism" and the various black nationalist movements from Malcolm X and the black Muslims, to the Black Panthers, and the myriad other groups we could list here.

7. The lone GOP candidate of color for the 2012 election was Herman Cain, the former Godfather's Pizza CEO who was leading in the polls for several weeks in 2011 before allegations of sexual impropriety resulted in his withdrawing his candidacy.

8. Measured by subtracting all debts owed to reach a figure for household net worth. It should be further noted that this is not a result of their still being more white people than any other racial group; rather, these are per capita data.

9. The North American Free Trade Agreement, signed by Mexico, Canada, and the United States and becoming law in 1994 saw restrictions on exports and imports between these countries virtually disappear, resulting in little or no protection for smaller-scale producers and privileging large companies to export not only their commodities but their labor force as well. For more on NAFTA see Harvey (2005).

Chapter 7. Professionalizing the Teaching Force

Portions of this chapter are adapted from my article "Toward an Anticapitalist Teacher Education" (Casey, 2013).

1. Later, we will examine how this movement stretches farther back in time than the 1980s, but for the purposes of orienting the reader it is easiest for now to think of 1986 as the year the movement to professionalize teaching fully came into being.

2. The full title of Berliner and Biddle's text is *The Manufactured Crisis: Myths, Fraud, And the Attack on America's Public Schools*.

3. Of course, in neoliberalism we are experiencing a complete assault on teacher autonomy, and as such I address this failing of the teacher professionalization movement later in this chapter.

4. John McCain included a national voucher plan as a part of his 2008 campaign for the presidency. While Mitt Romney was not as explicit in his vision for education, we should note that vouchers remain as one of if not the primary way the Right imagines we can abolish public schools. See Kumashiro (2008) for further discussion of this point.

5. At the time of this writing there are forty-six states who have signed on to the Common Core Standards.

6. It should be noted that Lipman's use of the term *professionalism* here is evidence for just how much neoliberal rhetoric produces slippages, even in the most critical among us. It does not take away from the point she is making. However, we will return later to how much of neoliberal education can be understood as a part of the professionalization of teaching.

7. A slogan of the Minneapolis, Minnesota, Public School District.

8. In my own teaching I am perpetually haunted by a fight that broke out in my classroom that I have described and theorized elsewhere (see Casey, 2011). The fight occurred at a moment when I was preoccupied with sorting and organizing my desk, when the students were watching a film and taking notes, and everyone seemed to be on task. I did not have to stop and think, until I had to respond to the fight, the blood on the desk and floor, and the bloody tooth that had been knocked out of one student's mouth. While this is an extreme example, the memory of this incident has followed me into every classroom I've been in since. I am not constantly on guard to prevent physical violence, but I continually question and consider how I am interacting with students and what behaviors I am modeling, because a joke I made at one of these students' expense resulted in the verbal exchange that led to the fight. Had I been paying more attention, and had a less routinized system been

in place for how I was interacting in that space, the fight might not have happened.

Chapter 8. Anticapitalist Antiracist Pedagogy in the Classroom

1. Žižek (2009) has argued that the most utopian position in our current society is actually that which argues that capitalism will simply go on indefinitely.
2. The notion of pro-feminist here is taken from the work of bell hooks (2003) in which she argues that those who position themselves in opposition to patriarchy adopt a stance of pro-feminism, or that they "advocate" feminism. I have worked to cultivate such a stance largely in relation both to this particular story and to my engagement with the field of critical black feminism (see also Collins, 2000).

Chapter 9. Anticapitalist Antiracist Pedagogy as a Programmatic Vision for Teacher Education

1. I interpreted her conception of growth as skill-oriented, as the kinds of "growth" one hopes to detect on standardized tests that show improvement in measurable skills. Her examples and discourse gave me this impression, though perhaps she had a more sophisticated or nuanced sense of "growth" that she did not elaborate and that I did not hear evidence of.
2. The basis for Kerr et al.'s (2011) argument stems from their analysis of the Standards for Academic and Professional Instruction in Foundations of Education, Educational Studies, and Educational Policy Studies, which was endorsed by the American Education Research Association. These standards stated, "16% of teachers' professional studies should be within the realm of the humanistic and social foundational studies" (p. 120). Focusing in particular on education history, the authors find that despite these standards there has been a 45 percent decline in education faculty members whose primary

appointment is in foundations of education across the ten Canadian universities featured in their study.

3. Often these forms of curricula require teachers to read from a prepared script, following this script exactly, and work to reduce or even eliminate the experiences and pedagogical beliefs of teachers. These practices are especially common in schools that serve primarily students of color and students living at or around the poverty level (Sleeter, 2008). We can think of these curricula as "teacher-proofed" because the teacher is denied any agency or autonomy; she is reduced to the status of a machine.

4. Think of "liberal" here in the vernacular sense employed by rightist thinkers such as Buchanan (2011) as a catchall term for those positions seen as being in opposition to "traditional conservative values," including especially religion.

5. See E. D. Hirsch's (1988) *Cultural Literacy* for a list of more than four thousand such facts that constitute "What every American needs to know."

6. These stats are from the work of Lozenski (2013) as a part of the Minnesota Minority Education Partnership's work to redress what they call the "discipline gap."

Bibliography

ABC News. (2008, August 16). Howard Dean accidentally calls the Republican Party the "white" party. *ABC News*. Retrieved from http://abcnews.go.com/blogs/politics/2008/08/howard-dean-acc/.

Alexander, M. (2010). *The new Jim Crow: Mass incarceration in the age of colorblindness*. New York, NY: New Press.

Althusser, L. (2008). *On ideology*. London, UK: Verso.

Aminzade, R. R. (2013). *Nationalism and the politics of exclusion: An historical sociology of Tanzanian nationalism*. Manuscript in preparation, University of Minnesota, Minneapolis, MN.

Anyon, J. (1981). Social class and the hidden curriculum of work. *Journal of Education, 162*(1), 67–92.

Apple, M. W. (2000). *Official knowledge: Democratic education in a conservative age*. New York, NY: Routledge.

Apple, M. W. (2001). Markets, standards, teaching, and teacher education. *Journal of Teacher Education, 52*(3), 182–196.

Apple, M. W. (2006). *Educating the "right" way: Markets, standards, God, and inequality*. New York, NY: Routledge.

Applebaum, B. (2011). *Being white, being good: White complicity, white moral responsibility, and social justice pedagogy*. Lanham, MD: Lexington Books.

Arendt, H. (1987). *Amor mundi: Explorations in the faith and thought of Hannah Arendt* (J. W. Bernauer, Ed.). Boston, MA: M. Nijhoff.

Ball, S. J. (1998). Big policies/small world: An introduction to international perspectives in education policy. *Comparative Education, 34*(2), 119–130.

Bates, D. (2011) *Immaterial labour and the retreat from class: Some reflections on Hardt and Negri.* Studies in Marxism, 12. pp. 51–78.

Baudrillard, J. (1994). *Simulacra and simulation.* Ann Arbor, MI: University of Michigan Press.

Berliner, D. C., & Biddle, B. J. (1995). *The manufactured crisis: Myths, fraud, and the attack on America's public schools.* Reading, MA: Addison-Wesley.

Blow, C. M. (2010, April 17). A mighty pale tea. *The New York Times,* p. A17.

Buchanan, P. J. (2011). *Suicide of a superpower: Will America survive to 2025?* New York, NY: Thomas Dunne Books.

Burke, L. V. (2013, January). Black unemployment rate shoots up from 12.9% to 14%. *Politic365.* Retrieved from http://politic365. com/black-unemployment-rate-shoots-up-from-12-9-to-14/.

Butler, J. (1990). *Gender trouble: Feminism and the subversion of identity.* New York, NY: Routledge.

Brown, C. (1987). Literacy in 30 hours: Paulo Freire's process in Northeast Brazil. In I. Shor & P. Freire (Authors), *Freire for the classroom: A sourcebook for liberatory teaching.* Portsmouth, NH: Boynton/Cook.

Calhoun, C. J. (2004). *Nationalism.* Minneapolis, MN: University of Minnesota Press.

Case, K. A. (2005). Distancing strategies: White women preservice teachers and antiracist curriculum. *Urban Education, 40*(6), 606–626.

Casey, Z. A. (2011). Toward a reconceptualization of needs in classrooms: Baudrillard, critical pedagogy, and schooling in the United States. *The Journal for Critical Education Policy Studies, 9*(2), 77–90.

Casey, Z. A. (2011). The fight in my classroom: A story of intersectionality in practitioner research. *i.e.: inquiry in education:* Vol. 2: Iss. 1, Article 3.

Casey, Z. (2013). Toward an anticapitalist teacher education. *Journal Of Educational Thought, 46*(2), 123–143.

Casey, Z. A. (in press). Whiteness, nationalism, and neoliberalism: What Pat Buchanan and the Right can teach us about resisting neoliberalism in schools. In M. Abendroth & B. J. Porfilio (Eds.), *School against Neoliberal Rule*. Charlotte, NC: Information Age Publishing.

Casey, Z. A., Lozenski, B. D., & McManimon, S. K. (2013). From neoliberal policy to neoliberal pedagogy: Racializing and historicizing classroom management. *Journal of Pedagogy, 4*(1), 36–58.

Cochran-Smith, M., & Lytle, S. L. (1993). *Inside/outside: Teacher research and knowledge*. New York, NY: Teachers College Press.

Cole, M. (2008). *Marxism and educational theory: Origins and issues*. Milton Park, Abingdon, Oxon: Routledge.

Cole, M. (2015) *Racism: A critical analysis*, London, UK, and Chicago, IL: Pluto Press.

Collins, P. H. (2000). *Black feminist thought: Knowledge, consciousness, and the politics of empowerment*. New York, NY: Routledge.

Core Standards. (2010). In the states. *Common Core State Standards Initiative*. Retrieved from http://www.corestandards.org/in-the-states.

Counts, G. S. (1978). *Dare the school build a new social order?* Carbondale, IL: Southern Illinois University Press.

Crenshaw, K. (1992). Race, gender, and sexual harassment. *Southern California Law Review, 65*, 1467–1476.

Crocco, M. S., & Costigan, A. T. (2007). The narrowing of curriculum and pedagogy in the age of accountability: Urban educators speak out. *Urban Education, 42*(6), 512–535.

Cusset, F. (2008). *French theory: How Foucault, Derrida, Deleuze, & Co. transformed the intellectual life of the United States*. Minneapolis, MN: University of Minnesota Press.

Darling-Hammond, L. (2006). Constructing 21st-century teacher education. *Journal of Teacher Education, 57*(3), 300–314.

Davidson-Harden, A., Kuehn, L., Schugurensky, D., & Smaller, H. (2009). Neoliberalism and education in Canada (D. Hill, Ed.). In *The rich world and the impoverishment of education: Diminishing democracy, equity and workers' rights* (pp. 21–50). New York, NY: Routledge.

Deliovsky, K. (2010). *White femininity: Race, gender, & power*. Black Point, N.S.: Fernwood.

Delpit, L. (2006). *Other people's children: Cultural conflict in the classroom*. New York, NY: New Press.

Dewey, J. (1897/2010). My pedagogic creed. *School Journal, 54*, 77–80. Retrieved March 10, 2010, from http://dewey.pragmatism.org/creed.htm.

Dewey, J. (2007). *Democracy and education*. Middlesex, UK: Echo Library.

DuBois, W. E. B. (2005). *The souls of black folk*. Stilwell, KS.: Digireads.com Publishing.

Duncan, A. (2013, February 28). *Supporting and strengthening school leadership*. Speech presented at National Association of Secondary School Principals National Conference in National Harbor, MD.

Eagleton, T. (2011). *Why Marx was right*. New Haven, CT: Yale University Press.

Ebert, T. L., & Zavarzadeh, M. (2007). *Class in culture*. Boulder, CO: Paradigm.

Edison Research. (2012). President exit polls. *The New York Times*. Retrieved December 12, 2012, from http://elections.nytimes.com/2012/results/president/exit-polls.

Ellison, R. (1953). *Shadow and act*. New York, NY: Vintage International.

Foucault, M. (1990). *The history of sexuality: An introduction*. (R. Hurley, Trans.). New York, NY: Vintage Books.

Foucault, M. (2004). *Society must be defended*. London, UK: Penguin Books.

Frankenberg, R. (1993). *White women, race matters the social construction of whiteness*. Minneapolis, MN: University of Minnesota Press.

Freire, P. (1998). *Pedagogy of freedom: Ethics, democracy, and civic courage*. New York, NY: Rowman & Littlefield.

Freire, P. (2000). *Pedagogy of the oppressed*. New York, NY: Continuum.

Freire, P. (2006). *Teachers as cultural workers: Letters to those who dare teach*. New York, NY: Westview.

Freire, P., & Macedo, D. P. (1987). *Literacy: Reading the word & the world*. South Hadley, MA: Bergin & Garvey.

Frey, W. H. (2012, May). Why minorities will decide the 2012

U.S. election. *The Brookings Institution.* Retrieved December 12, 2012, from http://www.brookings.edu/research/opinions/2012/05/01-race-elections-frey.

Friedman, M. (1962). *Capitalism and freedom.* Chicago, IL: University of Chicago Press.

Friedman, M. (1995). Public schools: Make them private. *Cato Institute Briefing Papers*, (23).

Garland, S. (2012, December 5). Was "Brown v. Board" a failure? *The Atlantic.* Retrieved February 12, 2013, from http://www.theatlantic.com/national/archive/2012/12/was-brown-v-board-a-failure/265939/.

Gay, G., & Howard, T. C. (2000). Multicultural teacher education for the 21st century. *The Teacher Educator, 36*(1), 1–16.

Giroux, H. (2010, June 1). Dumbing down teachers: Attacking colleges of education in the name of reform. *Truthout.* Retrieved from http://archive.truthout.org/dumbing-down-teachers-attacking-colleges-education-name-reform59820.

Gonzalez, N., & Moll, L. C. (2002). Cruzando el puente: Building bridges to funds of knowledge. *Educational Policy, 16*(4), 623–641.

Gramsci, A. (2008). *Selections from the prison notebooks of Antonio Gramsci* (Q. Hoare, Trans.). New York, NY: International.

Guggenheim, D. (Director). (2010). *Waiting for superman* [Motion picture on DVD]. USA: Paramount Vantage.

Hall, S. (1997). The centrality of culture: Notes on the cultural revolutions of our time. (K. Thompson, Ed.). In *Media and cultural regulation* (pp. 207–238). London, UK: Sage.

Hammerness, K., Darling-Hammond, L., Bransford, J., Berliner, D., Cochran-Smith, M., McDonald, M., & Zeichner, K. (2005). How teachers learn and develop (L. Darling-Hammond & J. Bransford, Eds.). In *Preparing teachers for a changing world: What teachers should learn and be able to do* (pp. 358–389). San Francisco, CA: Jossey-Bass.

Haney-Lopez, I. (1996). White by law: The legal construction of race. New York, NY: New York University Press.

Hardt, M., & Negri, A. (2000). *Empire.* Cambridge, MA: Harvard University Press.

Hartlep, N., & Porfilio, B. J. (in press). Revitalizing the field of educational foundations and PK-20 educators' commitment to social justice and issues of equity in an age of neoliberalism. *Educational Studies*.

Harding, S. G. (1987). *Feminism and methodology: Social science issues*. Bloomington, IN: Indiana University Press.

Harvey, D. (2005). *A brief history of neoliberalism*. Oxford, UK: Oxford University Press.

Herrnstein, R. J., & Murray, C. A. (1994). *The bell curve: Intelligence and class structure in American life*. New York, NY: Free Press.

Heyneman, S. (2003). The history and problems in the making of education policy at the World Bank 1960–2000. *International Journal of Educational Development, 23*(3), 315–337.

Hill, D. (2002). *Marxism against postmodernism in educational theory*. Lanham, MD: Lexington Books.

Hill, D. (2009). *The rich world and the impoverishment of education: Diminishing democracy, equity and workers' rights*. New York, NY: Routledge.

Hirsch, E. D. (1988). *Cultural literacy: What every American needs to know*. New York, NY: Vintage Books.

hooks, b. (1994). *Teaching to transgress: Education as the practice of freedom*. New York, NY: Routledge.

hooks, b. (2003). *Teaching community A pedagogy of hope*. New York, NY: Routledge.

Horkheimer, M. (2004). *Eclipse of reason*. London, UK: Continuum.

Horkheimer, M., & Adorno, T. W. (2002). *Dialectic of enlightenment: Philosophical fragments* (N. G. Schmid, Trans.). Stanford, CA: Stanford University Press.

Hursh, D. (2007). Assessing No Child Left Behind and the rise of neoliberal education policies. *American Educational Research Journal, 44*(3), 493–518.

Hursh, D. (2008). *High-stakes testing and the decline of teaching and learning: The real crisis in education*. Lanham, MD: Rowman & Littlefield.

Ignatiev, N. (1999). *How the Irish became white*. New York, NY: Routledge.

Ignatiev, N., & Garvey, J. (1997). *Race traitor*. New York, NY: Routledge.

Jackson, K. T. (1987). *Crabgrass frontier: The suburbanization of the United States.* New York, NY, and Oxford, UK: Oxford University Press.

Jacobson, M. F. (1999). *Whiteness of a different color: European immigrants and the alchemy of race.* Cambridge, MA: Harvard University Press.

Jameson, F. (1991). *Postmodernism, or, the cultural logic of late capitalism.* Durham, NC: Duke University Press.

Jansen, J. D. (2008). Bearing whiteness: a pedagogy of compassion in a time of troubles. *Education as Change, 12*(2), 59–84.

Jansen, J. D. (2009). *Knowledge in the blood: Confronting race and the apartheid past.* Stanford, CA: Stanford UP.

Kennedy, M. (1999). The role of preservice teacher education. In L. Darling-Hammond and G. Sykes (Eds.), *Teaching as the learning profession: Handbook of policy and practice* (pp. 54–85). San Francisco, CA: Jossey-Bass.

Kerr, D., Mandzuk, D., & Raptis, H. (2011). The role of the social foundations of education in programs of teacher preparation in Canada. *Canadian Journal of Education, 34*(4), 118–134.

Kincheloe, J. L. (2008). *Critical pedagogy primer.* New York, NY: P. Lang.

Klein, N. (2008). *The shock doctrine.* New York, NY: Picador.

Kliebard, H. M. (2002). *Changing course: American curriculum reform in the twentieth century.* New York, NY: Teachers College Press.

Kliman, A. (2005). The Okishio theorem: An obituary. *Libcom.* Retrieved from http://libcom.org/library/okisho-theorem-obituary-marxist-humanism.

Kumashiro, K. K. (2000). Toward a theory of anti-oppressive education. *Review of Educational Research, 70*(1), 25–53.

Kumashiro, K. K. (2008). *The seduction of common sense: How the Right has framed the debate on America's schools.* New York, NY: Teachers College Press.

Kumashiro, K. K. (2009). *Against common sense: Teaching and learning toward social justice.* New York, NY: Routledge.

Kumashiro, K. K. (2010). Seeing the bigger picture: Troubling movements to end teacher education. *Journal of Teacher Education, 61*(1-2), 56–65.

Kumashiro, K. K. (2012). *Bad teacher!: How blaming teachers distorts the bigger picture.* New York, NY: Teachers College Press, Columbia University.

Labaree, D. F. (1997). *How to succeed in school without really learning: The credentials race in American education.* New Haven, CT: Yale University Press.

Ladson-Billings, G. (1995). Toward a theory of culturally relevant pedagogy. *American Educational Research Journal, 32*(3), 465–491.

Ladson-Billings, G. (2006a). "Yes but how do we do it?" Practicing culturally relevant pedagogy (J. Landsman & C. W. Lewis, Eds.). In *White teachers, diverse classrooms: A guide to building inclusive schools, promoting high expectations, and eliminating racism* (pp. 29–42). Sterling, VA: Stylus.

Ladson-Billings, G. (2006b). From the achievement gap to the education debt: Understanding achievement in U.S. schools. *Educational Researcher, 35*(7), 3–12.

Lakoff, G. (2002). *Moral politics: How liberals and conservatives think.* Chicago, IL: University of Chicago Press.

Lakoff, G. (2004). *Don't think of an elephant!: Know your values and frame the debate : The essential guide for progressives.* White River Junction, VT: Chelsea Green Publishing.

Larrain, J. (1995). Identity, the other, and postmodernism. In M. Zavarzadeh, T. L. Ebert, & D. E. Morton (Eds.), *Post-ality: Marxism and postmodernism* (pp. 271–289). Washington, DC: Maisonneuve Press.

Lawrence, S. M. (1997). Beyond race awareness: White racial identity and multicultural teaching. *Journal of Teacher Education, 48*(2), 108–117.

Lee, L. B. (1979). *Kansas and the Homestead Act, 1862–1905.* New York, NY: Arno Press.

Lemann, N. (1997, January 18). The bell curve flattened. *Slate.* Retrieved February 10, 2013, from http://www.slate.com/articles/briefing/articles/1997/01/the_bell_curve_flattened.single.html.

Lenin, V. I. (1960). What is to be done?: Dogmatism and "freedom of criticism." Retrieved from http://www.marxists.org/archive/lenin/works/1901/witbd/i.htm.

Lensmire, T. J. (2011). Laughing white men. *Journal of Curriculum Theorizing, 27*(3), 102–116.

Lensmire, T. J., & Snaza, N. (2010). What teacher education can learn from blackface minstrelsy. *Educational Researcher, 39*(5), 413–422.

Leonardo, Z. (2004). The color of supremacy: Beyond the discourse of "white privilege." *Educational Philosophy and Theory, 36*(2), 137–152.

Lewis, A. E. (2003). *Race in the schoolyard: Negotiating the color line in classrooms and communities.* New Brunswick, NJ: Rutgers University Press.

Lipman, P. (2011). *The new political economy of urban education: Neoliberalism, race, and the right to the city.* New York, NY: Routledge.

Lipsitz, G. (1995). The possessive investment in whiteness: Racialized social democracy and the "white" problem in American studies. *American Quarterly, 47*(3), 369–387.

Lipsitz, G. (2006). *The possessive investment in whiteness: How white people profit from identity politics.* New York, NY: Temple University Press.

Lorde, A. (1984). *Sister outsider: Essays and speeches.* Trumansburg, NY: Crossing Press.

Lowenstein, K. L. (2009). The work of multicultural teacher education: Reconceptualizing white teacher candidates as learners. *Review of Educational Research, 79*(1), 163–196.

Lozenski, B. D. (2013, January 12). *Cultural workers & perspectives: Developing a cultural understanding of teaching & learning.* Lecture, Minneapolis, MN.

Luhby, T. (2012, June 21). Recession widens the wealth gap by race. *CNNMoney.* Retrieved from http://money.cnn.com/2012/06/21/news/economy/wealth-gap-race/index.htm.

Macedo, D., & Freire, M. A. (2006). Foreword. In P. Freire (Author) & D. Macedo & D. Koike (Trans.), *Teachers as cultural workers: Letters to those who dare teach.* New York, NY: Westview.

Mamdani, M. (2001). *When victims become killers: Colonialism, nativism, and the genocide in Rwanda.* Princeton, NJ: Princeton University Press.

Manzo, K. A. (1998). *Creating boundaries the politics of race and nation.* Boulder, CO: Lynne Rienner.

Marx, A. W. (1998). *Making race and nation: A comparison of the United States, South Africa, and Brazil.* Cambridge, UK: Cambridge University Press.

Marx, K. (1981). *Capital: A critique of political economy* (B. Fowkes & D. Fernbach, Trans.). London, UK: Penguin Books in association with New Left Review.

Marx, K. (1992). *Grundrisse: Foundations of the critique of political economy (rough draft)* (M. Nicolaus, Trans.). Harmondsworth, Middlesex, UK: Penguin Books.

Marx, K., & Engels, F. (1956). *The holy family.* Moscow, Russia: Foreign Languages Publishing House.

Marx, K., & Engels, F. (1998). *The German ideology: Including Theses on Feuerbach and introduction to The critique of political economy.* Amherst, NY: Prometheus Books.

McIntosh, P. (1988). White privilege: Unpacking the invisible knapsack. *Independent School,* Winter, 31–36.

McWhorter, L. (2005). Where do white people come from? A Foucaultian critique of whiteness studies. *Philosophy & Social Criticism, 31*(5–6), 533–556.

Moon, D., & Flores, L. A. (2000). Antiracism and the abolition of whiteness: Rhetorical strategies of domination among "race traitors." *Communication Studies, 51*(2), 97–115.

Moore, M. (2011, March 5). *400 Americans have more wealth than half of all Americans combined.* Speech, Madison, WI. Retrieved March 15, 2011, from http://www.youtube.com/watch?v=wgNuSEZ8CDw&feature=player_embedded.

Morrison, T. (1993). *Playing in the dark: Whiteness and the literary imagination.* New York, NY: Vintage Books.

National Committee on Pay Equity. (2011, September). Pay equity information. *National Committee on Pay Equity NCPE.* Retrieved April 24, 2012, from http://www.pay-equity.org/info-time.html.

Obama, B. (2010, August 09). *Remarks by the president on higher education and the economy at the University of Texas at Austin.* Speech. Retrieved September 25, 2010, from http://www.whitehouse.gov/the-press-office/2010/08/09/remarks-president-higher-education-and-economy-university-texas-austin.

Okishio, N. (1961). Technical changes and the rate of profit. *Kobe University Economic Review, 7.*

Puri, J. (2004). *Encountering nationalism.* Malden, MA: Blackwell.

Roediger, D. R. (1998). *Black on white: Black writers on what it means to be white.* New York, NY: Schocken Books.

Roediger, D. R. (2007). *The wages of whiteness race and the making of the American working class.* New York, NY: Verso.

Rogers, C. R. (1989). Personal thoughts on teaching and learning. In H. Kirschenbaum & V. L. Henderson (Eds.), *The Carl Rogers reader.* Boston, MA: Houghton Mifflin.

Romney, M. (2012, August 14). *Speech in Chillicothe, Ohio.* Speech. Retrieved from http://mittromneycentral.com/speeches/2012-speeches/081412-mitt-romneys-speech-in-chillicothe-ohio/.

Shor, I., & Freire, P. (1987). *Freire for the classroom : A Sourcebook for liberatory teaching.* Portsmouth, NH: Boynton/Cook.

Shulman, L. S. (2004). *The wisdom of practice: Essays on teaching, learning, and learning to teach* (S. M. Wilson, Ed.). San Francisco, CA: Jossey-Bass.

Silverleib, A. (2011, October 19). Obama's deportation record: Inside the numbers. *CNN.* Retrieved from http://articles.cnn.com/2011-10-19/politics/politics_deportation-record_1_ice-director-john-morton-undocumented-immigrants-criminal-alien-program?_s=PM:POLITICS.

Sleeter, C. E. (1995). Reflections on my use of multicultural and critical pedagogy when students are white. In *Multicultural education, critical pedagogy, and the politics of difference.* Albany, NY: State University of New York Press.

Sleeter, C. E. (2005). How white teachers construct race. In *Race, identity, and representation in education.* New York, NY: Routledge.

Sleeter, C. (2008). Equity, democracy, and neoliberal assaults on teacher education. *Teaching and Teacher Education, 24*(8), 1947–1957.

Smith, R. M. (1997). *Civic ideals: conflicting visions of citizenship in U.S. history.* New Haven, CT: Yale University Press.

Solow, R. M. (1988, March 28). The wide, wide world of wealth. *New York Times.*

Sullivan, S. (2006). *Revealing whiteness: The unconscious habits of racial privilege.* Bloomington, IN: Indiana University Press.

Thandeka. (1999, June 25). *Why anti-racism will fail.* Lecture presented at UUA General Assembly, Salt Lake City, UT.

Thandeka. (2006). *Learning to be white money, race, and God in America.* New York, NY: Continuum.

Wallace Adams, D. (1995). *Education for extinction: American*

Indians and the boarding school experience, 1875–1928. Lawrence, KS: University Press of Kansas.

Watkins, W. H. (2001). *The white architects of black education: Ideology and power in America, 1865–1954.* New York, NY: Teachers College Press.

Watkins, W. H. (2012). *The assault on public education: Confronting the politics of corporate school reform.* New York, NY: Teachers College Press.

White Privilege Conference: What is the WPC? (2013). *White Privilege Conference -.* Retrieved from http://www.whiteprivilegeconference.com/wpc.html.

Williams, R. (1977). *Marxism and literature.* Oxford, UK: Oxford University Press.

Wilson, W. J. (1978). *The declining significance of race Blacks and changing American institutions.* Chicago, IL: University of Chicago Press.

Winant, H. (2001). *The world is a ghetto: race and democracy since World War II.* New York, NY: Basic Books.

Wise, T. J. (2008). *White like me: Reflections on race from a privileged son.* Brooklyn, NY: Soft Skull Press.

Wise, T. J. (2009). *Between Barack and a hard place: Racism and white denial in the age of Obama.* San Francisco, CA: City Lights Books.

Zavarzadeh, M., Ebert, T. L., & Morton, D. E. (1995). *Post-ality: Marxism and postmodernism.* Washington, DC: Maisonneuve Press.

Zeichner, K. M., & Liston, D. P. (1996). *Reflective teaching: An introduction.* Mahwah, NJ: L. Erlbaum.

Zernike, K., & Thee-Brenan, M. (2010, April 15). Poll finds Tea Party backers wealthier and more educated. *The New York Times,* p. A17.

Žižek, S. (1989). *The sublime object of ideology.* London, UK: Verso.

Žižek, S. (2009). *First as tragedy, then as farce.* London, UK: Verso.

Index

217